A QUEER HISTORY OF THE UNITED STATES

OTHER BOOKS BY MICHAEL BRONSKI

Pulp Friction: Uncovering the Golden Age of Gay Male Pulps, 2003

The Pleasure Principle: Sex, Backlash, and the Struggle for Gay Freedom, 1998

Taking Liberties: Gay Men's Essays on Politics, Culture & Sex (editor), 1996

Flashpoint: Gay Male Sexual Writing (editor), 1996

Culture Clash: The Making of Gay Sensibility, 1984

OTHER SERIES PUBLISHED BY BEACON PRESS

QUEER ACTION SERIES

Come Out and Win: Organizing Yourself, Your Community, and Your World,
by Sue Hyde

Out Law: What LGBT Youth Should Know about Their Legal Rights,
by Lisa Keen

QUEER IDEAS SERIES

Beyond (Straight and Gay) Marriage: Valuing All Families under the Law,
by Nancy D. Polikoff

From the Closet to the Courtroom: Five LGBT Rights Lawsuits That Have Changed Our Nation,
by Carlos A. Ball

Queer (In)Justice: The Criminalization of LGBT People in the United States,
by Joey L. Mogul, Andrea J. Ritchie, and Kay Whitlock

A
QUEER HISTORY
OF THE
UNITED STATES

MICHAEL BRONSKI

ReVisioning American History

BEACON PRESS BOSTON

BEACON PRESS
25 Beacon Street
Boston, Massachusetts 02108-2892
www.beacon.org

Beacon Press books
are published under the auspices of
the Unitarian Universalist Association of Congregations.

15 14 13 12 11   8 7 6 5 4 3 2 1

*Beacon Press's ReVisioning American History series
consists of accessibly written books by notable scholars
that reconstruct and reinterpret U.S. history from diverse perspectives.*

This book is printed on acid-free paper that meets the uncoated paper
ANSI/NISO specifications for permanence as revised in 1992.

Text design by Jody Hanson, Wilsted and Taylor Publishing Services

Library of Congress Cataloging-in-Publication Data
Bronski, Michael.
A queer history of the United States / by Michael Bronski.
p. cm. — (ReVisioning American history)
Includes bibliographical references and index.
ISBN 978-0-8070-4439-1 (hardback)
1. Homosexuality—United States—History. 2. Gays—United States—History.
3. Homosexuality—United States—Miscellanea. I. Title.
HQ76.3.U5B696 2011
306.76'60973—dc22   2010050225v

DEDICATED TO

Carl Wittman (1943–1986)

John Mitzel

Charley Shively

comrades, all

and

John Bronski

my father

CONTENTS

AUTHOR'S NOTE

A Queer History of the United States is the first book in Beacon Press's ReVisioning American History series. This series is committed to offering fresh perspectives and examining our history through the lens of those groups whose stories have been excluded from the canon.

I am a cultural critic, independent scholar, progressive activist, and college professor who has written for four decades on a broad range of topics concerning lesbian, gay, bisexual, and transgender culture. This book makes a series of observations and arguments concerning how to think about the place of LGBT people in U.S. history. It looks at how American culture has shaped the LGBT, or queer, experience, while also arguing that queer people not only shaped but were pivotal in creating our country.

Readers may not find names and events they expected and may be surprised to find little-known names and historical connections. This is not a comprehensive history, so I have been judicious about what I have chosen to include. It is foolish to think that there can be an objective view of history. Every writer approaches the "facts" with her or his own experiences, views, and biases. Like Howard Zinn's *A People's History of the United States*—a book that inspired me, but was not the inspiration for this book—*A Queer History of the United States* has a political point of view. I hope that point of view serves as a guide to help the reader make sense of the materials presented, but also makes my own biases clear enough so that my interpretations can be resisted.

My earliest involvement in the gay community was in the gay liberation movement of the early 1970s. We had very strong opinions then. I have come to realize that in life and politics, there is always more to take into consideration. If there is one clear, unambiguous argument here, it is that the LGBT history of America is, and has always been, U.S. history.

Michael Bronski

INTRODUCTION

A decade ago, when I first began teaching lesbian, gay, bisexual, and transgender studies at Dartmouth College, I was invited to a fraternity house to moderate a group discussion titled "Don't Yell Fag from the Porch." The frat was renowned for its rowdiness, and indeed, someone had recently yelled "faggot" at a student passing by—undoubtedly not for the first time. After being publicly challenged on this behavior, the frat brothers decided to host a public forum on homophobia in the Greek system. The discussion went well and became an annual event. "Faggot" was yelled with less frequency, and in a few years the fraternity even had a few "out" gay members. But that evening, and over the years, what bothered me was that the entire discussion was predicated on the idea that Dartmouth College was essentially a straight place that had to be open to "gay people." But that makes no sense. We all know that life—and history—is far more complex than that. Or do we?

All too often most of us think in terms of simple dichotomies, including gay and straight; but who might answer to the call of "fag" when its history has been shown to be more than a simple either/or question? Here are a few lines from a letter Daniel Webster, a Dartmouth alumnus and hero to the college, wrote in 1804 at the age of twenty-two to the twenty-three-year-old James Hervey Bingham, his intimate from their college days: "I don't see how I can live any longer without having a friend near me, I mean a male friend. Yes, James, I must come; we will yoke together again; your little bed is just wide enough." Was Daniel Webster gay? Did he love James? Did they have a sexual relationship? If so, what did this mean for his two marriages later in life? Is this queer history?

The last ten years of teaching LGBT studies has for me been a continual process of trying to figure out what is LGBT history. How do we understand it? How do we use it to think about the past? How do we use it to think about the present and the future? I certainly would have liked to quote Webster's words while moderating "Don't Yell Fag from the Porch." What would the students have thought about Webster's obsessive desire to lie in bed with his friend James once again and hold him fast to his body? Or what if I had told them that poet Richard Hovey, who wrote the lyrics to the school's "Alma Mater," was also a lover of men, and although married and an ardent feminist, socialized in gay male circles in America and Europe? (Oscar Wilde once famously hit on him at a party.) Would it have been another reason for their not shouting "faggot" as frequently? Would this have "queered" Dartmouth for them? One of the reasons for titling this book *A Queer History of the United States* is an attempt to "queer" how we think about American history.

The questions of this book are much larger than who might have been "gay" in the past or had sexual relations with their own sex. Over the past forty years a great deal of incredible scholarship on LGBT history has been written, and I have drawn extensively upon it, rethought it, and synthesized it here. What follows is a long meditation on not only LGBT history but, because it is inseparable, all of American history. After two years of thinking and writing, I want to start by suggesting that there are two crucial concepts to consider when examining LGBT history in the United States.

The first is that the contributions of people whom we may now identify as lesbian, gay, bisexual, or transgender are integral and central to how we conceptualize our national history. Without the work of social activists, thinkers, writers, and artists such as We'Wha, Walt Whitman, Emily Dickinson, Martha "Calamity" Jane Cannary Burke, Edith Guerrier, Countee Cullen, Ethel Waters, Bayard Rustin, Roy Cohn, Robert Mapplethorpe, Cherrie Moraga, and Lily Tomlin, we would not have the country that we have today. Women and men who experienced and expressed sexual desires for their own sex and those who did not conform to conventional gender expectations have always been present, in both the everyday and the imaginative life of our country. They have profoundly helped shape it, and it is inconceivable, and ahistorical, to conceptualize our traditions and history without them.

The second, and slightly counterintuitive, key concept is that LGBT history does not exist. By singling out LGBT people and their lives, we are depriving them of their centrality in the broader sweep and breadth of American history. The impulse to focus on lives that have been shunned, marginalized, censored, ignored, and hidden in the past—and in previous histories of the United States—has been revolutionary in the growth of a vibrant LGBT community. This impulse is part of a larger social and political movement of Native American, African American, Latino/Latina, and other marginalized identities and cultures to reclaim and celebrate our "lost" histories. (Although as an identity, LGBT has, as we will see, a much newer history than other identities.) But it is equally important to understand that this is a transitional moment in history that has emerged in the past forty years precisely because those marginalized groups were so deeply dismissed.

If LGBT history resides in the queer space of being both enormously vital and nonexistent, can we even write and speak about it? How do we uncover and explicate the past so that it brings new understandings to popular culture and scholarly pursuits alike? How will this history resonate with our understanding of our own contemporary and historic lives?

We have been taught, in our nation's fairly unimaginative educational system, that history is a stable linear narrative with a fixed set of facts—names, dates, political actions, political ideas, laws passed and repealed. In *The Dialectic of Sex,* a groundbreaking book of radical feminist theory, Shulamith Firestone writes that this conventional way of understanding the historical process as a series of snapshots—here is the American Revolution, here is the Declaration of Independence, here is the Emancipation Proclamation—is limiting and ultimately unhelpful. History, she states (drawing loosely on Marxist theory), is "the world as process, a natural flux of action and reaction, of opposites yet inseparable and interpenetrating . . . history as movie rather than as snapshot."

Much of the popular LGBT history that has been published in our newspapers, magazines, and blogs falls into the category that Firestone criticizes. It is essentially a list of famous lesbian or gay people and events used to justify contemporary understandings—

here is Oscar Wilde, here are the Stonewall Riots, here are queer couples being married in Boston. This family album approach is appealing, because it provides a sense of identity and history, but it is ultimately misleading. In past decades women's and gender studies scholars called this method of analysis "add one woman and stir." The "important" women were added to the mix to create a gender balance, but there were no new layers of complexity or nuance as to what these women's lives, thoughts, desires, and actions might actually mean for a shared historical past.

More serious writing on LGBT history has avoided this approach. Historians such as Jonathan Ned Katz, Lillian Faderman, Allan Bérubé, George Chauncey, and Esther Newton, among many others, have examined how LGBT history complicates and enriches the American imagination and the national story we already know. I have drawn extensively on these writers, and many other sources, to present a daringly complex vision of the past, one that forces a fundamental rethinking of what we thought we knew, as well as of the present and even the future. Its broad use of facts, historic personalities, and events is an invitation to join in a larger intellectual project of reinterpretation. As Firestone argues, history is a movie— not a Hollywood film with a traditional narrative, but rather an experimental film that presents a reality that makes sense only when we appreciate its intrinsic narrative complexity. History is an ongoing process through which we understand and define ourselves and our lives.

LANGUAGE AND IDENTITY

We cannot understand history or know what it means to us today without first understanding the process by which it is written. The writing and reading of history is always, consciously or not, a political act of interpretation. The political, intellectual, and social conditions of a particular time period affect who is writing, what they are writing, and why they are writing. The writer must construct a narrative that makes sense for her or his present social and cultural context, as well as contextualize that narrative in a broader historical framework. This process depends on the availability of both historical facts and language that can convey a clear, precise understanding of the facts and their context.

While the contemporary project of writing LGBT history began in earnest during the gay liberation movement of the early 1970s, previous writers penned what might be seen as early attempts to construct histories of people with same-sex desires. Plato's mythical analysis, in his *Symposium*, of why some people were sexually attracted to their own sex had an enormous effect on how other writers in the Western tradition conceptualized same-sex desire. Some historians of the classical period—Plutarch in his *Lives* and Suetonius in *The Twelve Caesars*, for example—were interested in chronicling the same-sex desires of notable men. Vasari, in his 1550 *Lives of the Painters*, hints at the same-sex desires of Michelangelo and other Renaissance artists. While these works did not focus strictly on homosexual activity, they did not avoid or hide it. In the mid to late nineteenth century, two social and legal reformers—Karl-Maria Kertbeny, an Austrian-born Hungarian, and Karl Ulrichs of Germany—separately wrote articles, pamphlets, and books about same-sex behavior, as did John Addington Symonds, an English art historian. All three drew upon notable figures of antiquity and the Italian Renaissance to prove that there was a centuries-old tradition of same-sex behaviors. Their works sought to make a case for both the naturalness of same-sex desire and the reformation of laws that criminalized homosexual behavior.

These works are clearly contextualized by their times. Plutarch and Suetonius present the little data they have—some of it gossip—nonjudgmentally. While not particularly naming same-sex activity, they describe it as a facet of human activity. This is also true of Vasari, but he is more coded, since by the Renaissance homosexual activity was branded a grave sin and a serious crime by the Roman Catholic Church. These writers were also limited by writing about people and events very close to their own times. This type of historical project—like writing about a recent presidential administration—has clear boundaries for access to materials. Kertbeny, Ulrichs, and Symonds took a different approach. They cautiously, but quite consciously, drew upon a far wider range of materials, including recent historical research, advances in archaeology, and scholarly reconstructions of past literatures. Their class and educational backgrounds gave them the necessary social and political access to write and disseminate their ideas.

Each of these historical works is as much a portrait of the time in which it was written as it is a narrative of the past. Each was written to make emotional and psychological sense to its contemporary readers. Plutarch and Suetonius were interested in exposing the political and psychological foibles of their subjects. Varsari was trying to "explain" as best he could the social and emotional relationship of Renaissance artists to their audience and to a hierarchy of patronage that funded and controlled their work. While these three writers had definite points of view—we could fairly call them political and social "agendas"—Kertbeny, Ulrichs, and Symonds were making a clear, unequivocal case for the cultural and legal acceptance of same-sex desire and activity. Post-Enlightenment German and British cultures were progressive enough to allow such ideas to circulate, albeit in a limited sphere.

Existing terminology, like the larger cultural context, limits the scope of what writers are able to say. Religious terms that described same-sex activity as sinful, such as "sodomite," were in common use in Europe and England from the late thirteenth century. Sexual offenses, especially homosexual behavior, were often referred to in canon law and civil codes with the elliptical terms "crimes against nature" or "the unmentionable vice," thus emphasizing that such actions were so aberrant as to be literally unspeakable. Beginning in the late sixteenth century, the term "catamite"—a corruption of Ganymead, the boy lover and cup bearer for Zeus in Greek mythology—was used, usually negatively, to describe men who had sex with men. In eighteenth-century Great Britain, "molly" was used so frequently to describe men, often gender deviant, who desired other men that the private homes or tavern rooms in which they congregated were called Molly Houses.

The rise of capitalism in Europe and the strong influence of individuality within post-Reformation Protestantism gave rise to a new cultural notion: self-identity that was specific to an individual but associated with a larger group. Ulrichs began using "urning," a term he borrowed from Plato's *Symposium,* as well as "invert," which connoted a person who possessed the soul of the other sex, to refer to people who experienced same-sex attraction in a nonjudgmental way. Kertbeny invented the word "homosexual" in 1869 to help him construct a narrative around a person defined by his or her same-sex sexual desires and actions. Beginning in the late nineteenth century in Europe and Great Britain, "sapphist," from the Greek poet Sappho, was used occasionally to describe women who loved women, and the practice was referred to as "sapphism." The word "lesbian," referring to the Isle of Lesbos, the home of Sappho, was first used by sexologist Havelock Ellis in 1897. Until fifty years ago, it was common for lay people, journalists, and social scientists to use "invert" along with "homosexual."

In the twentieth century, we have become accustomed to a far wider range of words for an ever-growing number of public and private identities. "Queer," originally meaning "odd" or "quaint," acquired the meaning of "bad" and "worthless" in the early eighteenth century. Since the 1920s, mainstream British and U.S. vernacular has used "queer" negatively to describe homosexuals, although within the homosexual community it was always a purely descriptive term. "Faggot," "dyke," and "gay" came into usage in the United States in the 1930s. The two former words had negative mainstream connotations, and the latter was used only within the homosexual community until the 1970s, when it gained more mainstream acceptance. In a process of taking community control of language, "fag" and "dyke" eventually became acceptable terms used by LGBT people. The naming of the first national post–gay liberation gay male publication, Boston-based *Fag Rag,* started in 1970, was a political move to expressly challenge linguistic suppositions. The same was true of *Dyke,* a short-lived New York–based lesbian publication from the mid-1970s. In the late 1990s, the grassroots political action group Queer Nation popularized the reclaimed "queer" so successfully that within a few years, national television shows such as *Queer Eye for the Straight Guy* used the word without offense. Today we routinely use LGBT, a fairly recent, and accepted, amalgamation of identities, each of which has a specific history that often had little to do with the others.

WHAT HISTORY TEACHES

While language informs identity, the elaborate emotional, psychological, and political intricacies of lives exceed identity, and even language itself. There is never a perfect word or set of words to fully understand oneself. Suetonious writes that Emperor Tiberius would bathe in a deep pool and have young boys, whom he called his "minnows," swim between his legs and nip at his genitals. Plato may have considered himself a pederast, that is, a teacher and lover of boys and young men. Michelangelo may have thought himself a sodomite. Joan of Arc certainly saw herself as a divinely inspired savior of France who needed to wear soldier's garments and gear in order to defeat the British. Emily Dickinson may have thought of herself as just a woman who had affectionate and sexual feelings for other women. Virginia Woolf, who never actually named her own sexuality, did use the word "sapphist" in her writing; it is reasonable to think that this may have been a label she entertained for herself. I have been as linguistically accurate as possible when writing this book, but language is both an entryway and a dead end.

The same is true of the word "sexuality," the main topic of this book. I use this word as expansively as possible, like the words "queer" and "gay." Here "sexuality" connotes the never-ending constellation of factors that inform how people understand their sexual desires and actions. My use of the term is meant to connect the present with the past so that we can better understand both. Whatever sexuality means today and did not mean before, the word, like others before it, has always attempted to describe something we know is not reducible to a word, an identity, or even a set of behaviors.

Interpretations are best made with the long view in mind. They allow us to recognize the significance of what on the surface might have nothing to do with being LGBT. Of the many trends, similarities, and repeated occurrences throughout this book, I have found three that struck me as crucial in understanding the most important historical developments for LGBT people in the past five hundred years. Some of these surprised me; others reconfirmed what I already suspected.

Perhaps the most startling revelation, which did not occur to me until I had finished writing, was that many of the most important changes for LGBT people in the past five hundred years have been a result of war. From the American Revolution to the war in Vietnam, wars have radically affected LGBT people and lives. These wars have had an enormous impact on all Americans, but their effects on LGBT people have been particularly pronounced, in part because the social violence of war affects sexuality and gender.

The second realization was that entertainment in its broadest sense—popular ballads, vaudeville, films, sculptures, plays, paintings, pornography, pulp novels—has not only been a primary mode of expression of LGBT identity, but one of the most effective means of social change. Ironically, the enormous political power of these forms was often understood by the people who wanted to ban them, not by the people who were simply enjoying them.

One of the most salient themes here is the battle between the social purity movements (which began in the nineteenth century and have numerous descendants) and the right of LGBT people, and all Americans, to decide how to use their imaginations and bodies. This has always been a tension in American life, but the circumstances of the nineteenth century institutionalized it. This tension remains with us today.

This history is told chronologically, beginning just before Columbus in 1492. I end the main narrative with the AIDS activism of ACT UP in the late 1980s. The story I tell covers five hundred years, and obviously much is left out, although some surprising details are included. My intention is to tell the story of this country through the lens of the multitudes of LGBT individuals and experiences. I hope to give a secure and realistic sense of how the lives, thoughts, and actions of LGBT people have made this nation into the country it is today, and show all non-LGBT people how this history has affected them as well. I believe it is the only way to honor both LGBT people and the nation to which they have contributed so mightily, even as that political entity often treats them with grave disrespect and harm. The heritage of LGBT people is the heritage of Americans.

This book is titled *A Queer History of the United States*. But by beginning the story in 1492, I am really writing about America, an entity that existed centuries before the political entity of the United States was conceived and that continues today independent of the Republic. "America" is a mythical entity that has no boundaries. "America" is what people imagine it to be, as well as what people have made it.

Gertrude Stein, the mother of all queer wit, begins her novel *The Making of Americans* with the epigram, "Let me recite what history teaches. History teaches." Stein's recitation speaks to the intrinsic nature of my project. History teaches something new every time it is rewritten or interpreted. Pedagogy, like history, will never be able to contain all of America—a great country, an evil country, a place of tremendous generosity and welcome as well as pronounced disdain for foreigners and outsiders. America is not one thing or another. America is queer. *A Queer History of the United States* is one explanation of how it got that way. To become American, to benefit from the contributions of LGBT people to this fabulous, horrible, scary, and wonderful country we call America, is to be a little queer. As history teaches, America only gets queerer.

ONE

THE PERSECUTING SOCIETY

If you were to ask average Americans when lesbian, gay, bisexual, and transgender history started in this nation, some would cite the Stonewall "riots" that took place in New York's Greenwich Village in 1969. Others might go back to 1950, when Harry Hay founded the Mattachine Society, the first public gay group in the United States. Some may reach back even further in the previous century to Walt Whitman's *Leaves of Grass*, his homoerotic poetry of male love—what he called "male adhesiveness"—or Emily Dickinson's love poems to her sister-in-law, Sue Gilbert. The well-informed might mention Deborah Sampson, an impoverished indentured servant who, as Robert Shurtliff, fought for the colonists during the Revolutionary War.

These examples highlight some of the problems that arise in writing a queer history of the United States. What do we consider to be gay history? How is it defined? In order to grapple with these issues in all their complexity, I begin this history in the late fifteenth century. The United States as a political entity will not exist for another 270 years. The word, and social identity, "homosexual" will not come into being for 350 years. Yet we know there were women and men who engaged in sexual activity with their own sex, as well those who resisted following the accepted, enforced gender roles of their time.

Understanding these people's lives requires understanding basic social, political, intellectual, and psychological frameworks. To understand North America in the sixteenth century, we need to look at the lives and cultures of the people who were here before the European colonists arrived and how the clash between indigenous cultures and European cultures set the stage for the next five hundred years of United States history.

Europeans came to the Americas with an extraordinarily rigorous sense of how gender and sexuality should be organized. These strict ideas were bulwarked by rigid civil and religious statutes. The Europeans attempted to eradicate many non-European gender-normative customs, traditions, and behaviors. They often did this through accepted practices of violence, such as capturing and enslaving non-Christians and forced conversion. This legal and religious repression and violence provided a template for how mainstream European culture would treat LGBT people throughout much of U.S. history.

STRANGERS IN A STRANGE LAND

Numerous Europeans who journeyed to the "new" continent of America did so for the political and economic advantage of newly emerging and quickly growing European nation-states . Beginning with Columbus in 1492 and continuing for over a century, Italian, Spanish, Dutch, and British soldiers, sailors, merchants, and adventurers sailed to the New World on business ventures. While this century-long project was entrepreneurial, what continues to influence our culture today is the religious and sexual attitudes of the Europeans. They saw the gender norms and behaviors of indigenous peoples as markedly different from their own, even as the cultures of individual tribes were completely different from one another. These startling gender differences took many forms. The presence of female divinities who were responsible for creation, or the fact that in many nations, women were the house builders, was antithetical to European theology and practice. Europeans found the native peoples alarmingly innocent and dangerously sexual. They were shocked that some tribes lived naked or wore few clothes, that they engaged in a wide variety of "immoral" sexual practices—not predicated on reproduction—and that marriage laws and traditional European mating conventions were unknown. Particularly disturbing was that some cultures allowed women various degrees of sexual equality. For the Europeans, the most extreme examples were the women and men who dressed and behaved as, in their eyes, the other sex.[1]

Often referred to by French explorers as *berdache*—an incorrect name, implying a catamite or young male sodomite—these women and men took on the dress and the tribal duties of the other sex. Their roles in each culture differed. Sometimes they were placed in socially elevated positions as religious figures, shamans, or artisans. Among the Crows, "men who dressed as women and specialized in women's work were accepted and sometimes honored; a woman who led men into battle and had four wives was a respected chief."[2] In some cases, these "third sex" figures were integral to traditions of tribal violence and warfare. In some cultures young boys became berdache through enforced, institutionalized concubinage. For example, the Yuma, who resided in what is now Colorado, "appointed an infant to fill the post of fourth tribal berdache. Presumably upon growing up, this boy became a sexual resource or passive . . . for the nubile boys in the tribe."[3]

Contemporary LGBT writing on gender roles in indigenous cultures has often oversimplified, even sentimentalized, this history. The systems of berdache that existed before and after the European invasions were complicated and served different purposes for each tribe. More fluid than European gender arrangements, the creation of nonbinary genders was a different model and not necessarily more liberatory. Some contemporary writers, including LGBT Native Americans, interpret the berdache as equivalent to our contemporary understanding of "gay." While superficial similarities exist between behaviors in some berdache cultures and present-day gay male, lesbian, or transgender cultures, the circumstances separating the two are radically dissimilar.

Military men, clergy, and explorers repeatedly made connections between indigenous people's (real and imagined) sexual practices and their lower place in a European moral and economic hierarchy. In his journals of 1673–77, Jacques Marquette, the French Jesuit missionary, describes berdache practices among the native peoples he met on his first voyage down the Mississippi:

I know not through what superstition some Ilinois [*sic*], as well as some Nadouessi, while still young, assume the garb of women, and retain it throughout their lives. There is some mystery in this, for they never marry and glory in demeaning themselves to do everything that the women do. They go to war, however, but can use only clubs, and not bows and arrows, which are the weapons proper to men. They are present at all the juggleries, and at the solemn dances in honor of the Calumet; at these they sing, but must not dance. They are summoned to the Councils, and nothing can be decided without their advice. Finally, through their profession of leading an Extraordinary life, they pass for Manitous,—That is to say, for Spirits,—or persons of Consequence.[4]

The 1702 "Memoir of Pierre Liette on the Illinois Country" notes that "the sin of sodomy prevails more among [the Miami] than in any other nation, although there are four women to one man. It is true that the women, although debauched, retain some moderation, which prevents the young men from satisfying their passions as much as they would like."[5] In a diary from his 1775 trip to what is now California, Franciscan Pedro Font provides a lens to the way in which many Christian Europeans viewed indigenous cross-dressing figures, as well as his religious duty to them:

Among the women I saw some men dressed like women, with whom they go about regularly, never joining the men. . . . From this I inferred they must be hermaphrodites, but from what I learned later I understood that they were sodomites, dedicated to nefarious practices. From all the foregoing I conclude that in this matter of incontinence there will be much to do when the Holy Faith and the Christian religion are established among them.[6]

In *Original Journals of the Lewis and Clark Expeditions* (written between 1804 and 1810), Nicholas Biddle notes that "Among Mamitarees if a boy shows any symptoms of effeminacy or girlish inclinations he is put among the girls, dressed in their way, brought up with them, & sometimes married to men."[7] Such reports, which continued to be written into the early years of the twentieth century, were mixtures of journalism and crude anthropology that emphasized the sexual and gender "foreignness" of native people.

Violence against all native peoples, not just those that violated European gender norms, was widespread. Columbus, in his second expedition in 1495 after his search for gold faltered, invaded the interior of Haiti and abducted fifteen hundred Arawak children, women, and men to be shipped to Europe as slaves. Of the five hundred slaves shipped to Spain, only three hundred arrived alive and were put up for sale by an archbishop "who reported that, although the slaves were 'naked as the day they were born,' they showed 'no more embarrassment than animals.'"[8]

European religious and social thought held that people who did not adhere to Christian concepts of sexual behavior, gender affect, or modesty were less than human; they were like animals. This qualified them to be deprived of individuality, liberty, and life itself. Pietro Martire d'Anghiera, an Italian historian who documented the military campaigns of Spanish explorers, notes in his 1516 *De Orbe Novo* that Vasco Núñez de Balboa had vicious mastiffs rip apart forty Panamanian men dressed as women who were engaging in sodomy with other men. This account was the first mention of berdache in European literature.

PURITANISM: THE INDIVIDUAL AND THE COMMUNITY

France, Spain, the Netherlands, and Great Britain viewed the Americas as potential financial and political windfalls, and they embarked on myriad destructive colonization projects. The British, however, had the most influence on what was to become the United States. French and Spanish cultural legacies—especially a tradition of Roman Catholicism—are integral to American identity, but English common law and British Protestantism overwhelmingly shaped American thinking and culture, particularly in relationship to sexual behavior and gender.

British colonies grew rapidly: Jamestown, founded in 1607,

quickly began to ship raw materials back to England. In 1620 just over one hundred British "Pilgrims," members of a radical religious separatist group, landed in what is now Massachusetts and signed the Mayflower Compact, the template for self-governance in the newly forming colonies. Ten years later, nearly a thousand Puritans fled religious persecution in England and, under the leadership of John Winthrop, formed a self-ruling community and established the city of Boston. The growth of the colonies was the beginning of a distinctly new colonist culture that was intent on defining itself.

The Puritans' view of the world and sexuality—which would have a tremendous effect on America—was shaped by their experiences in Great Britain before arriving in the New World. The Reformation and the founding of the Anglican church by Henry VIII in 1534 brought about the collapse of a cohesive Roman Catholic polity in Europe. From 1558 to 1649 Elizabeth I, James I, and Charles I ruled England and the colonies. During that time English culture accepted and promoted a wide range of diverse, sometimes conflicting, views about sexuality and gender. These ideas were intimately connected with how Elizabethan and post-Elizabethan culture thought about religion and religious practice. Cross-dressing—which had been condemned by Catholic theologians such as Augustine and Tertullian since the second century—was a mandated theatrical convention, since women were not allowed to perform on the stage. There was an enormous public fascination with female cross-dressing, as witnessed by several plays. For instance, Thomas Middleton and Thomas Dekker's popular 1607 play *The Roaring Girl* dramatized the life and celebrated cross-dressing criminal career of Mary Frith, who was also known as Moll Cutpurse. Ben Johnson's 1609 play *Epicoene* revolved around cross-dressing and included numerous allusions to same-sex sexual behavior.

Social and legal prohibitions against same-sex activity in Elizabethan England were applied haphazardly. Same-sex relationships were illegal, but the culture was accepting enough to allow for public representation and discussion of same-sex attraction and sexual behavior. Christopher Marlow was widely rumored to have sex with men and was accused, during a trial for heresy, of stating that "all they that love not tobacco and boys are fools." More shocking, he is alleged to have proclaimed that "St. John the Evangelist was bed-fellow to Christ and leaned always in his bosom, that he used him as the sinners of Sodom." Marlow's 1592 play *Edward II* detailed the death of an English monarch murdered, in part, because of his relationship with Piers Gaveston. Shakespeare's sonnets are filled with gender and sexuality ambiguity that give us a sense of the wide range of what was culturally permissible during the Elizabethan era. Furthermore, James I, who reigned from 1603 to 1625, was widely understood to have had erotic relationships with court "favorites" such as George Villiers, First Duke of Buckingham—even as his treatise *Basilikon Doron* lists sodomy among crimes "ye are bound in conscience never to forgive."

In response to this sexually permissive behavior—as well as the economic and class dissatisfaction that eventually led to the English Civil War and the beheading of Charles I in 1649—highly politicized, radical religious groups dissented from the Church of England. The theological and political range of these groups, which included the Levelers, Ranters, Muggletonians, Quakers, and Puritans, was broad, but they all sought radical reorganization of British society. Ranters and Levelers were utopian and anarchistic, seeking to eliminate class and economic privilege and rejecting norms around sexual behavior. They rejected so much traditional Christian doctrine that mainstream social and religious leaders accused them of licentiousness and were suspicious of their views about gender behavior. Quakers were considered particularly dangerous, since they rejected established government, forbade men to carry arms or fight, and encouraged women to speak at religious meetings.

The Puritans not only rejected the Church of England, but also rejected what they saw as the political and social excesses of the other dissenting groups. They critiqued the Church of England for veering toward Rome and wanted to return it to a "pure" state. All of the Protestant sects in England and throughout Europe viewed the Roman Catholic Church as emblematic of the decadent sensibility, including sexual profligacy, that they witnessed in England. They commonly referred to the Papacy as "the painted whore of Babylon" and viewed Italian culture itself as promoting sexually deviant, same-sex acts. Daniel Defoe, in his 1703 poem "A True Born

Englishman," opined "Lust chose the Torrid Zone of Italy / Where Blood ferments Rapes and Sodomy."

Not accepted by others, and not accepting of them back, the Puritans fled England. They explicitly understood their emigration as an exodus, a direct analogy to the Jews leaving Egypt for Israel, seeking a promised land and freedom. John Winthrop, in his famous 1630 sermon "A Model of Christian Charity," likened the new colony to old Jerusalem: a "city upon a hill."

When the Puritans established a religious society in the colonies, they were determined to ensure that its members did not fall prey to the temptations and errors they had left behind in England. Therefore they enacted strict legal sanctions against deviance from sexual and gender norms. Many of these norms directly impacted people who sexually desired members of their own sex or who challenged traditional gender roles. Sodomy laws in Europe and America were not specifically aimed at same-sex activity; they were intended to punish all nonreproductive sexual activity. Laws passed in the colonies to instill personal and social sexual morality were most often an amalgam of preexisting British law, such as Henry VIII's Buggery Act of 1533, and biblical injunctions, in particular Leviticus 20:13. Dozens of these laws existed in the new colonies. They varied widely in specifics—some laws targeted public masturbation rather than anal sex—but they all had two commonalities: they used phrases such as "abomination" and "the unspeakable crime against nature," and they considered such crimes capital offenses.[9]

Whatever the law, Puritans were having sex. Historian Richard Godbeer notes that more than one hundred women were convicted of having children out of wedlock in Essex County (in the Bay Colony) between 1640 and 1685, and that the Suffolk County Court adjudicated over two hundred of cases of illicit sex during the 1670s.[10] Clearly, as indicated by the ever-increasing birthrate in the second half of the seventeenth century, husbands and wives were actively procreating.[11] And other forms of sexual activity were not unknown. *The Problems of Aristotle,* a late seventeenth-century sex manual read in the colonies, discussed oral sex in the question of whether "carnal copulation [can] be done by the mouth." Although such nonreproductive sexual information may have met with some disapproval, it was nevertheless available and part of public discourse.[12]

There were, without a doubt, women and men who desired and interacted sexually with members of their own sex. Over time, sodomy laws were used more often against same-sex coupling than opposite-sex coupling, and some men, and occasionally women, were punished for their sexual actions. Because most sexual behavior is private, much of the information we have about same-sex activity is from court cases or other public records, which provide a vivid but incomplete sense of the time.

Historian Jonathan Ned Katz charts numerous incidents of men being punished, sometimes by death, for sodomy. In 1624 the Virginia colony hanged Richard Cornish, a ship's master, for sexually assaulting a younger shipmate.[13] In 1629 Rev. Francis Higginson noted in his diary that during his trip to the Massachusetts colony, five "beastly Sodomiticall boyes" were caught engaging in sexual activity and sent to be punished, potentially by death, in England.[14] In his midcentury journals, John Winthrop wrote of Plaine of Guilford "being discovered to have used some unclean practices. . . . He had committed sodomy with two persons in England. And had corrupted a great part of the youth of Guilford by masturbations, which he had committed, and provoked others to the like above a hundred times."[15] We can assume that there was public concern about sex between women, or that it was occurring, since Rhode Island's 1647 law and New Haven's 1655 law both explicitly prohibit sexual activity between women.

It is misleading, however, to think that Puritan legal culture vigilantly sought out and punished all sexual transgressions immediately and with the same ferocity. The case of Nicholas Sension of Windsor, Connecticut, is a good example. Sension was married and childless. From the 1640s to 1677, when Sension was brought before the colony's General Court for sodomy charges, he had a long and fairly well-known history of propositioning men for sex, offering to pay for sex, and sexually assaulting male servants. Although town elders had admonished Sension in the late 1640s and again in the late 1660s, he was not formally charged for another decade. While some of his neighbors disapproved of his behavior, there was a general consensus not to bring formal legal charges. Historians speculate that some of Sension's activity was with willing partners and was viewed, by enough people, as moderately acceptable. Perhaps Sension's status in the community protected him, or the fact that many of his partners were men of lesser social rank may have lent his crimes a lower profile. Sension's trial in 1677 resulted in his being convicted of attempted sodomy. He was whipped, publicly shamed on a gallows with a rope around his neck, and "his entire estate was placed in bond for his good behavior."[16]

Windsor's laxness in prosecuting Sension may have been because his sexual activity took place in private. While his actions were certainly considered grievously illegal and immoral, as private acts they had less impact on the community than, say, an act of adultery, which might result in pregnancy or the dissolution of a marriage. Puritans in the colonies viewed marriage as a civil contract, not a sacrament, and were concerned about the impact of divorce on the community, generally permitting it only for abandonment. Nonmarital sexuality was immoral because it did not contribute to the family on which society organized.

The Puritans had fled Great Britain to secure religious freedom for themselves, not others; they never intended to found a democracy. John Winthrop was clear: "If we should change from a mixed aristocracy to mere democracy, first we should have no warrant in scripture for it: for there was no such government in Israel. . . . A democracy is, amongst civil nations, accounted the meanest and worst of all forms of government. [To allow it would be] a manifest breach of the 5th Commandment" (honor your father and mother).[17] For the Puritans, the family was central to religious and civil society; immoral and illegal acts that, by taking place in private, did not directly threaten it may have been viewed with some leniency.

We have a few clues about how men like Sension related (likely in private) to others who engaged in similar behavior, or what kind of nonfamilial community they formed. The Boston Gay History Project examined court records between 1636 and 1641 of men accused of sodomy, "lude behaviour and unclean carriage" and charted what appears to be a series of relationships among a number of men, including Thomas Roberts, John Alexander, Abraham Pottle, and

George Morrey. In 1640, when the court ordered Thomas Roberts to no longer live with George Morrey, it is possible to infer that what was worrisome to the judiciary was not a personal and possibly sexual relationship, but the publicness of men with such reputations living together.[18] Did these men, who may all have been involved in sexual relationships with one another, see themselves as part of a minority community? Did their sexual activity give them a specific personal or social identity, or sense of a sexual self, even if the concept of "gay" did not exist?

Personal diaries and letters must be interpreted in historical context. When a letter writer uses elaborately passionate language, as Susanna Anthony did when writing to Sarah Osborn in the early eighteenth century—"my bosom friend, I feel my love to you to be without dissimulation, therefore wish you the same strength and consolation, with my own soul"—can we presume an erotic intent?[19] Conversely, there is a long history of interpreters of historical material who refuse to see *any* same-sex desire in letters and diaries. If we acknowledge that some personal writings attest to the presence of same-sex desire, we then must discern what these erotic feelings meant to the writer.

The diaries of Michael Wigglesworth exemplify this point. As a tutor at Harvard College in 1653, the distraught, twenty-three-year-old Wigglesworth wrote in his diary, "Such filthy lust flowing from my fond affection to my pupils whiles in their presence on the third day after noon that I confess myself an object of God's loathing as my sin is my own; and pray God make it no more to me." Is this passage proof that Wigglesworth experienced same-sex desires, and given Puritan culture, he felt guilt? Historian Alan Bray notes that a close reading of the diary also indicates that while Wigglesworth may have understood his sexual thoughts as incongruent with his morality, they were, because they were involuntary, less of a problem than the intense emotion that accompanied them. These intense feelings were a sin, because they were dangerously discordant with the Puritan concept of individualism that demanded, especially for men, emotional control. According to Bray, Wigglesworth's "sin" was feeling emotions too strongly, not necessarily the content of the feelings.[20]

After considering the place of privacy, family, and community in understanding same-sex activity in early colonial culture, it is also important to examine this culture's relationship to the body. The Puritans in the colonies were on a distinct social and religious mission. While they were reacting against what they perceived as the sexual excesses of Elizabethan culture—they would have disapproved of Shakespeare's overt sexual puns as being immodest—this was not because they thought pleasure inherently bad. Rather, Puritan theology promoted the intrinsic worth and holiness of the body. This is one of the central reasons the Puritans called for the individual to have a personal, direct relationship with God. As authority in England was being deeply questioned, Puritans were attempting to "find a new master in themselves, a rigid self-control shaping a new personality. Conversion, sainthood, repression, collective discipline, were the answer to the unsettled conditions of society, the way to creating a new order through creating new men."[21] The Puritans readily acknowledged sexual desire and pleasure but insisted that it needed to be expressed within the sanctity of marriage, for the sake of the family, community, and individual.

"Society," claims Alan Bray, "is a process," and nowhere is this more evident than in Puritan life in the American colonies.[22] The "process" of Puritan society was found in the need to constantly refocus on theological "purity"—the essence of holiness and social order. However, the exigencies of surviving in this new land presented situations that led even the strictest Puritans to compromise some principles. Also, as exemplified by Wigglesworth, strictly articulated sexual mores were often not followed in the letter or even the spirit of the law.

Puritanism was an experiment of a particular form of social and religious organization, not an arbitrarily repressive system. Puritanism was not, as twentieth-century social critic and wit H. L. Mencken famously defined it, "the haunting fear that someone, somewhere may be happy." Puritan children were permitted simple toys and games when they were not doing chores or studying the Bible. Puritans allowed moderate drinking. While not sartorially extravagant, they did not adopt the plain dress of Quakers, but allowed color and some ornamentation. (All the colonies had laws regulating dress, usually with the intent of maintaining class distinctions, but in 1696 Massachusetts passed a law that explicitly forbade cross-dressing. Some historians argue that this law was intended to curb the possibility of same-sex sexual encounters.)[23] While procreative sex between a husband and wife was the only officially acceptable mode of sexual activity, some statistics show that at least 10 percent of Puritan marriage occurred after a pregnancy, and premarital sex generally went unpunished if it resulted in a stable marriage.

The individual soul was the life of the Puritan community and, conversely, the community was an embodiment of the soul. The concept of the individual was inseparable from the concept of community. It was vital, then, that the structures of this community be stable.

As a theologically based society, Puritans acted harshly toward religious diversity. In 1634, when Salem, Massachusetts, pastor Roger Williams was accused of spreading "diverse, new, and dangerous opinions"—advocating more religious freedom and toleration of native peoples—he was exiled. (The commonwealth law under which Williams was exiled was not repealed until 1936.) Upon leaving the Bay Colony, he founded Providence Plantations, now Rhode Island. Three years later Anne Hutchinson was imprisoned, then exiled from Massachusetts Bay Colony, for dissenting from Puritan doctrine, freely interpreting the Bible, preaching as a woman, and running Bible study groups for women. She and her followers settled in Providence Plantations. Massachusetts Bay Colony ministers labeled Hutchinson a "Jezebel"—the implication being that she, like the figure from the Book of Judges, was a sexually dangerous woman. Hutchinson's theological boldness caused others to view her behavior as gender deviance. "You have stepped out of your place," noted one minister. "You have rather been a husband than a wife, a preacher than a hearer, and a magistrate than a subject." Over the decades, Providence Plantations became, for its time, a progressive colony. Capital punishment was rare, and debtors' prisons and trials for witchcraft were abolished. In 1652 it was the first colony to ban all slavery, regardless of color.

In 1624 Thomas Morton and others, including thirty male indentured servants, founded a decidedly non-Puritan colony in Wollaston, now the township of Quincy outside of Boston. They named the colony Merrymount, punning on Mare-Mount and Mary-Mount, direct references to bestial sodomy and Roman Catholicism. Morton befriended the local Algonquian tribe, whose culture he admired, and urged intermarriage between native women and male colonists. He also released the indentured servants and made them equal "consociates." In 1627 he erected an eighty-foot-tall maypole with buck's horns attached to the top (indicative of the sexualized god Pan or, from a Puritan view, Satan) and held, as was customary in medieval England, revels. Morton declared himself a Lord of Misrule.

Morton understood the sexual implications of his permissive agenda. In one of his writings about Merrymount, he noted that "there was likewise a merry song made, which [to make their revels more fashionable] was sung with a corus, every man bearing his part; which they performed in a dance, hand in hand about the May-pole, whilst one of the company sung, and filled out the good liquor like Gammedes and Jupiter."[24] His invoking Gammedes (Ganymede) and Jupiter (the Roman name for Zeus) in Elizabethan culture was a clear reference to the archetypical male lovers in Greek mythology.

The reaction of the Puritans was immediate. William Bradford wrote in *Of Plimoth Plantation,* "They . . . set up a May-pole, drinking and dancing about it many days together, inviting the Indian women, for their consorts, dancing and frisking together, (like so many fairies, or furies rather,) and worse practices. As if they had anew revived & celebrated the feasts of ye Roman Goddess Flora, or ye beastly practices of ye mad Bacchanalians." While Morton and his rapidly growing small colony posed no direct threat to Plymouth Colony, Bradford felt challenged enough to attack Merrymount and arrest its leader. In 1629 Morton was sent back to England. Merrymount was dismantled and its community dispersed. In London, Morton wrote political tracts that accused the Puritans of many crimes, including a fear of the native peoples that manifested itself in near-genocidal behaviors.

Expulsion from the Bay Colony was a mild punishment compared to death. The Puritans did execute women and men who they believed posed a danger to the community's spiritual and political life. In 1658 the Massachusetts legislature passed a bill banning all Quakers from the colony under pain of death. Under this law, Mary Dyer and four other Quakers, known as the Boston Martyrs, were hanged on the Boston Common.

Unrepentant Quakers were jailed, as were others who contested Puritan doctrine. Ann Glover, for example, was an elderly Irish woman sold into slavery by Oliver Cromwell in 1650. She was a practicing Catholic who also spoke Gaelic. She was accused of being a witch—historically, in Europe, an accusation primarily aimed at women—and hanged on the Boston Common in 1688. Cotton Mather noted that she was "a scandalous old Irishwoman, very poor, a Roman Catholic and obstinate in idolatry." Within the gendered, parental hierarchy of the family in Puritan society, husbands and fathers were heads of households, and wives and children were beholden to them. This is why Puritans disapproved of Anne Hutchinson's preaching and were quick to accuse nontraditional women of witchcraft.

The strict laws of the Puritans regarding sexual and gender behavior described a "gold standard" of human behavior, the goal to which all women and men should aspire. Puritan theology understood that since humans were imperfect, no one could live up to this ideal. It was also unrealistic to punish everyone for every infraction. Common sense dictated that laws were enforced for the good of the community as it was understood at the moment. But the importance of striving for an ideal way of life applied equally to the communities formed by Puritan dissenters, such as Roger Williams, Anne Hutchinson, and Thomas Morton. Although Morton returned to the colonies and died there in 1647, he could never realize his vision of a more open, even utopian, society, because the constant tension between control and liberation, the state and personal liberty, could not fully accommodate "extremes."

In understanding the historical ramifications of laws that control sexual behavior, it is useful to remember that no universal baseline of appropriate sexual or gender behavior exists. "Sexual deviance" is often the cultural and political wild card used to demonize people who do not conform to certain sexual norms. Its accusation can be used by mainstream culture against marginalized groups or between marginalized groups themselves. We see throughout American history that restrictions against LGBT people are enforced "as needed" to maintain the contemporary status quo—a clear example of Alan Bray's concept of society as a process. Regardless of the status quo, process denotes adjustment, change, experiment, all in the name of an ideal way of life that is different for everyone. The Puritans, like most English dissenter groups, had been accused of envisioning "the world upside down." Puritanism was, in this sense, a revolutionary movement.

PURITY AND DANGER

Bradford's intense antagonism to Merrymount cannot be explained simply by his disapproval of the maypole and Morton's sexual behaviors. It was Morton's social egalitarianism, his openness to treating the Algonquians as relative equals, and his theological liberality that set him decisively apart from the Puritans. Bradford's actions are understandable placed in a broader, historically complex tapestry of European and British history and the emergence of what British historian R.I. Moore calls the "persecuting society." Moore argues that during the eleventh and twelfth centuries, European society underwent a profound and powerful transformation in which certain minorities, such as lepers, Jews, heretics, witches, "sodomites," and prostitutes, were stigmatized and persecuted *as groups* and often physically separated from society. This physical isolation, which took the form of ghettos for Jews and social banishment of lepers, was often the precondition for a wide range of harsh punishments, including death.[25]

Moore argues that a series of fundamental social changes—including the rapid growth of towns and cities, broad changes in agricultural distribution networks, and a radical shift in how hierarchical power was distributed—created this new set of social classifications. Its purpose was to create clear social and cultural boundaries that would stabilize society by safely containing groups designated as dangerous pollutants. This fear of pollution was less about sex or death than about power and social standing. As Moore notes, "Pollution fear . . . is the fear that the privileged feel of those at whose expense their privilege is enjoyed."[26] The colonists' seizing of native peoples' lands was not in self-defense, but for economic gain, resulting in the fairly rapid development of colonial capitalism.

In the European mind, the non-gender-normative and non-sexually-normative body—however defined in each period and circumstance—was the dangerous body, the less-than-human body, even the disposable body. This wedding of draconian moral judgment to the need to separate and punish led to violence, particularly sexual violence, that was to shape attitudes in future centuries. Throughout history, sexual and gender deviance have always been used as reasons for almost all cultures, no matter how progressive, to deny certain people full rights as citizens.

In this view, the founding of modern society was predicated on the creation of minority groups whose only purpose was to be vilified as unclean and persecuted for the illusion of a comprehensive sense of societal safety. This idea, based on anthropologist Mary Douglas's widely accepted theory of purity and danger, is helpful in explaining broad trends in European and American culture.[27] The idea of purifying religious and secular thought and society was at the heart of Puritan identity. These ideas were continuous with the long European tradition of a persecuting society and emerged at a time of grave political and religious disruption that neatly dovetailed with the impulse to stabilize society through persecution. Throughout American history there is a pattern of persecuted groups, like the Puritans, treating other outsider groups in a similar manner.

Sodomy laws play a key element in structuring ideas about acceptable and unacceptable behavior in U.S. culture, and in structuring society itself, because gender and sexuality are often the prime axis by which society distinguishes between "purity" and "danger." These statutes are a legal device regulating all sexuality, not just same-sex activity. Their norms include not just sexual behavior but gender expectations as well. It is not acceptable, therefore, for a biological male to be penetrated by another male, nor is it acceptable for women to engage in anything other than reproductive sexual activity. This is why the legal act of "sodomy" has no articulated, stable meaning—why in some laws it is labeled "unmentionable."

Early colonial life in the northern continent was a mass of contradictions. It was extraordinarily intolerant, yet often surprisingly lax. The European settlers' relations to the native peoples ranged from murderous genocide to a complex series of eroticized relationships. While Europeans brought with them a persecuting society, the manifestations of that society took many forms. One of the lasting legacies of colonial social and legal culture was the application of laws prohibiting and punishing sexual activity between people of the same sex. Treating some sexual behaviors differently because potentially they had less impact on the community had a twin effect on future American culture. It gave rise to the social (and eventual legal) concept of "consenting adults" and to a domestic-based idea of privacy that offered protections to some people at certain points in history.

This concept of privacy, however, had another, damaging, impact on future social convention and law. By assigning sexuality to a private sphere, it prevented any public acknowledgment or discussion of almost all sexual activity. Thus it laid the groundwork for same-sex sexual behaviors and identities to be hidden and even considered shameful. While the Puritans rejected what they saw as sexual license or overt licentiousness in British culture, they fully accepted the role of sexuality and sexual desire in everyday life. This sharp divide—not exactly a contradiction, although it may have appeared so later, as sexual mores in American culture became more lenient—has remained a basic tenet of America's cultural life. The tension between the needs and demands of society and the decisions of an individual to live her or his life as part of, yet separate from, the community informed the four centuries that followed Europeans arriving in this foreign land.

TWO

SEXUALLY AMBIGUOUS REVOLUTIONS

The transition from the colonial period to the Revolutionary era, during which a daring political experiment took root, led to the emergence of a new nation. Fundamental to this new nation was the reshaping of ideas about gender and sexual behavior as they related to the political concept of the citizen.

The period from the Pilgrims' landing to the early eighteenth century was a time of enormous population growth. In 1700 the Anglo-European population in the Northeast was 250,000. By 1720 that number had almost doubled to 475,000. This surge in population was accompanied by the rapid growth of cities—by 1725 the population of Boston was over 12,000, nearly doubled from 6,700 in 1700; Philadelphia was home to 10,000 people. New York, although growing rapidly, had just 7,000 residents (by 1800 it would have 60,000). In 1760, colonists numbered 1.5 million—six times the population at the turn of the century.

This expansion of colonies and people meant that the influence of Puritanism was waning. Many of the newer colonies were founded on non-Puritan beliefs.

In 1682 Charles II granted wealthy English Quaker William Penn a large tract of land west of what is now New Jersey. Penn named it Sylvania for its densely wooded terrain, and then renamed it Pennsylvania after his father. (Like many of the colonies, Pennsylvania was a commercial venture that was intended to turn a profit for its investors, in this case through the trading of furs and lumber.)

Penn's charter for the new colony reflected his progressive Quaker views. There was freedom of religion for all who believed in God, and a constitution that called for two "houses" of government and that allowed, in the spirit of a Quaker meeting, "open discourse." Most important, Penn treated the native peoples of the area—primarily the Lenni Lenape, called the Delaware tribe by the Anglo settlers—with respect, buying land from them rather than attacking and taking it. Pennsylvania grew quickly as Quakers from all over Europe settled there, joined by Catholics, Amish, Mennonites, and Jews. Penn designed Philadelphia—the city of brotherly love, denoting many faiths—between 1682 and 1684. Within fifty years it was the second largest urban area in the colonies. Progressive Quaker views on religious freedom and abolition—and later, sexual freedom—would be a strong influence on American political thought.

This rapid growth and diversity meant that the social and religious cohesiveness of the early colonies was lost; the Puritans' strict social demands on the individual were waning and being questioned. The infamous Salem witch trials of 1692 and 1693, in which twenty people were executed and five more died in prison, were a grim manifestation of the excesses of the Puritan imagination. However, the Massachusetts General Court issued a public apology for the trials five years later and eventually granted monetary compensation to the families of those executed. The 1682 Pennsylvania sodomy law did away with the death penalty for sodomy and replaced it with a whipping, six months of hard labor, and the forfeiture of a third of the accused's estate. (Thirty-two years later Pennsylvania made sodomy a capital crime again, reflecting changing demographics and belief systems.)

The growing assemblage of people, social structures, and political entities fostered a sense of pluralism unique to the colonies. But this pluralism did not reconcile the tension between the freedom of the individual and the need for a strong state formally embodied by the personal moral rectitude of the Puritans.

SLAVES AND CITIZENS

Despite the progressive inclination of some colonies, the persecuting society persisted. Colonists continued their sexualized treatment of native people, sodomy laws proliferated, and the legal, economic, and cultural institution of slavery was introduced into the colonies. It is impossible to understand American history—including the position of LGBT people—without acknowledging the overwhelming, debilitating effect that slavery has had on this country. From the mid-seventeenth century, organized, profit-driven slavery influenced all aspects of American life. Slavery struck at the heart of the ideals of individualism, personal liberty, and equality that were present, in sophisticated and rudimentary forms, at the birth of the colonies. Slavery was integral to how the colonies, and later the Republic, continued to reconceptualize individual freedom, race, property, and the rights and responsibilities of citizenship.

From the sixteenth to the nineteenth century, over 650,000 Africans were brought to North America as slaves. However, this is a relatively small number compared to the twelve million Africans who were transported and sold, mostly in the Caribbean and South America, in the mid-Atlantic slave trade, also referred to as the first Middle Passage.

Slavery arose in the colonies hand in hand with both European and African indentured servitude, which was commonplace. In the seventeenth and eighteenth centuries more than half of all white European (mostly British) immigrants to the colonies were indentured servants. These were often rural people who, dispossessed of their land and unemployed, were living in poverty in English cities. Their indenture, a contractual agreement with the person or firm who brought them to the colonies, lasted five years, after which they were free.

In the mid to late seventeenth century, laws in the colonies began to change. In 1654 a Virginia court declared that John Casor, an African servant, was legally a slave for life. Gradually, African indentured servants became legally treated as slaves, with no possibility of ending their servitude. This shift occurred for a number of complex reasons, the most pertinent of which is that Africans, in contrast to indentured whites, had no outside social and cultural support systems of other Africans in the country and thus were more easily enslaved.

Contemporary European societies had not promoted or regulated persecution on this large a scale. By 1860, the slave population in the United States had grown to four million, a third of the population in the fifteen (out of thirty-three) states that sanctioned slavery. In some states slaves were in the majority. In 1720, just under 70 percent of South Carolina's population was enslaved.

Slavery was also tied to religious belief. Virginia ruled in 1682 that

> all servants . . . which shall be imported into this country either by sea or by land, whether Negroes, Moors, mulattoes or Indians who and whose parentage and native countries are not Christian at the time of their first purchase by some Christian . . . and all Indians, which shall be sold by our neighboring Indians, or any other trafficking with us for slaves, are hereby adjudged, deemed and taken to be slaves to all intents and purposes any law, usage, or custom to the contrary notwithstanding.[1]

Lawmakers in the colonies were constructing a separate class of nonwhite, non-Christian people to be an economic bulwark of free labor. They had several reasons: a growing landowning class that did not want the competition of a new class of freed indentured servants; a shift, mostly in southern states, to agricultural products such as tobacco and cotton that were labor intensive; and a massive westward expansion of colonies that needed labor.

Except for Quakers, most colonists did not consider slavery contradictory to Christian theology. Its proponents justified the practice by citing verses in the Hebrew Bible and the Gospels, including Genesis 9:25–27, in which Noah's grandson Canaan is condemned to slavery: "Cursed be Canaan! The lowest of slaves will he be to his brothers." The biblical justifications for slavery, not unlike the biblical justifications for the condemnation of same-sex sexual activity, were used to both enforce draconian laws and justify extraordinarily harsh punishments.

Because slaves were deemed to be "property," slaveholders had unlimited legal power over them, including the right to sell them for profit and separate them from their loved ones. Thus slaves were denied the basic right of maintaining relationships with their biological and chosen families. Slave owning was not simply a matter of personal property, but was woven into the social fabric of the Republic. For example, laws held slave owners accountable for not punishing runaway slaves, since such behavior was seen as a threat to public safety.

It would be inaccurate and unwise to make strict parallel claims for the oppression of slaves and gay people. But the extensive legal and social effects of slavery have shaped the social and political context of America today. The acceptance of slavery as a philosophical concept and political reality laid the groundwork for the justification of "othering"—designating a group of people as "different," placing them outside of the legal, social, and moral framework granting full citizenship. As was the case for both native people and religious dissenters, othering is the enactment of Moore's persecuting society and Douglas's sequestering of the impure from the pure. The template of othering in slavery has two main effects that apply to LGBT people and other minorities.

First, slavery constructed a legal system that mandated noncitizenship for slaves (which, after slavery was abolished, evolved into second-class citizenship for African Americans). This denial of citizenship, however, did not release slaves from the obligation of obeying the law, which was often enforced more harshly on them than on full citizens. While racialized slavery—abolished by the ratification of the Thirteenth Amendment to the Constitution in 1865—is clearly the extreme example of noncitizenship, its hierarchical legacies are applied to other marginalized groups throughout U.S. history.

Second, the widespread acceptance of legalized slavery reinforced and normalized mainstream society's ideas about moral and sexual inferiority. Just as early Spanish settlers accused native peoples of a natural inferiority and intrinsic sexual immorality, white colonists, even if they were not slaveholders, presumed that Africans were less than human and incapable of moral Christian behavior. To the Europeans, native people and Africans who looked and behaved differently from them were dangerous to the accepted morality of the dominant culture, and therefore they were treated with varying degrees of moral and social scorn.

Accusations of sexual immorality often took two forms. The first was the charge of dangerous hypersexuality. In the second—and counterintuitive—form, the sexual outcast becomes the object of repressed sexual fantasies of the mainstream culture. This was certainly the case in America, in which dominant culture's sexual fantasies were projected onto the sexuality of the enslaved Africans. These myths included prodigious sexual desire in African women and men and, in the post–Civil War years, the idea that all African men were capable of sexual violence and rape. These projections were used by the dominant group as reasons to maintain their position of physical and social power. A primary reason, for instance, why slave owners depicted enslaved women as hypersexual was to justify their right to rape these women. This presumed hypersexuality was the excuse for white men to be sexual with enslaved women and the reason they needed to be controlled.

The articulation of these sexual fantasies raised enormous anxiety in the dominant culture, thus making the minority group the target of more physical violence. Under slavery, this violence manifested itself in a pervasive culture of sexual humiliation, sexual harassment, and rape, all used to control and subjugate Africans. Projected sexual fantasies tell us nothing about the Africans or their descendants, but a great deal about the women and men who held them. By othering, European colonists began constructing a new national identity and citizenship premised on a massive displacement of their own sexual and gender anxieties onto marginalized groups.

This mixture of erotic fascination and anxiety is embedded in the numerous Indian captivity narratives, such as the best-selling 1682 memoir *A Narrative of the Captivity and Restoration of Mrs. Mary*

Rowlandson, that were hugely popular from the late seventeenth century to the end of the nineteenth century. These works—usually about European women captured by, then forced to live with (and often marry) native people—excited and titillated European readers, as the "innocence" of "white women" was threatened by the ravenous and dangerous sexuality of nonwhite men. (William Bradford saw a similar threat at Merrymount with the intermarriage of white men and Native American women.)

This othering of Native Americans was a major way that colonists conceptualized sexuality and same-sex relationships. In a complex mixture of displaced sexual idealization and fear, Native American characters appear as eroticized demons and ghosts in European American literature from the mid-seventeenth century on. In the popular colonial and European American imagination, these Native American characters embodied the overt sexuality and "natural" desire that the Europeans lacked or repressed. These fantasies of native people were, in essence, a critique of what was considered by majority culture to be normative sexual desire and behavior. This idea of nonwhite people possessing a "natural" or uninhibited sexuality—recalling, in a more positive way, how the early Spanish conquistadors saw native people—is inherently racist. Nevertheless, by the mid-nineteenth century it had evolved to become foundational to how America culture was to conceptualize male-male relationships.[2]

Ideas about the "natural" and the "civilized" are often at the heart of how a culture classifies people, groups, and actions. Sexual activity between people of the same sex is often described as "unnatural" in religious and legal discourse—it is contrary to what "nature" or "natural law" intended. This is why sodomy statutes often refer to "unnatural acts." European and colonial society considered itself "civilized" when contrasted with nonwhite peoples. Yet the othering of a behavior or identity as dangerous may, under certain ambiguous conditions, make it more desired. In this way, the "unnatural" became "natural" only when enacted by an already "civilized" white person. This is an example of purity and danger congealing around sexuality and gender.

FROM PURITANISM TO ENLIGHTENMENT THOUGHT

We now refer to the extraordinarily radical political, cultural, and scientific ideas of the eighteenth century, collectively referred to—using a phase coined in the mid-nineteenth century—as the Enlightenment. In Europe, the Enlightenment drastically transformed intellectual life, majority consciousness, and social structures. Its effect on the colonies was profound, since it led directly to the American Revolution and the establishment of the Republic with the writing of the Declaration of Independence and the Virginia Declaration of Rights in 1776.

At heart, the Enlightenment was a rejection of the age of faith—belief and acceptance of ideas and concepts without evidence. The Enlightenment grew out of the new scientific methods of thinkers such as Isaac Newton, who "proved" the existence of gravity in his 1684 *On the Motion of Bodies in an Orbit,* and René Descartes, who in his 1637 *Discourse on the Method* helped invent rationalism, a philosophical system that prioritized logic to arrive at its conclusions. One of the most important claims of the Enlightenment was the insistence that every human being had equal worth, dignity, and personal integrity. However, many of the Enlightenment thinkers who formulated these radical ideas did not apply them to everyone, harboring prejudice against nonwhites, Jews, and women even as they argued for equality. Some even constructed "scientific" evidence to rationally prove a biological inequality.

Some colonialists embraced one of the most radical ideals of the Enlightenment: John Locke's concept of the separation of church and state. For millennia, religious and political structures had been inextricably bound together. The Papacy forced kings and emperors to enact Catholic policy; monarchies were predicated on the divine right of kings; civil legal systems were based largely on canon law. That is why sodomy—in Catholic and Protestant theology, a sin—was written into civil law. The First Amendment's religion clauses—"Congress shall make no law respecting an establishment of religion, or prohibiting the free exercise thereof"—marked a critical and significant turning point in how the United States would be governed. Certainly the thinking of colonialists such as Thomas

Jefferson, Thomas Paine, Benjamin Franklin, and John Adams was enormously influenced by Enlightenment philosophers such as John Locke, Voltaire, and Jean-Jacques Rousseau. Almost all of the men who wrote the foundational documents of the new American political system were deists—they believed in a supreme being but not necessarily in organized religion, and they rejected the belief that the scriptures were divinely inspired. They envisioned the laws of United States to be, in true Enlightenment tradition, based on reason and equality.

There was one aspect of continental thought that had no impact on how the founders viewed sexuality. By the mid-1780s many European countries were enacting penal reform to recodify confusing and repetitive statutes and bring laws more in line with contemporary thinking. Sodomy laws were in direct conflict with principles of the Enlightenment that called for personal sexual autonomy. But despite a clearly articulated separation of church and state, the colonies never abolished their sodomy laws.

This was not true in France, which abolished its sodomy law using Enlightenment precepts. In 1789—more than a decade after the American Declaration of Independence—the French National Assembly produced the Declaration of the Rights of Man, boldly stating that true civil liberty included the right "to do anything that does not injure others."[3] By 1791 this progressive thinking reached its logical conclusion when the Constituent Assembly abolished punishments for crimes "created by superstition, feudalism, the tax system, and despotism." These included blasphemy, heresy, witchcraft, and sodomy, all crimes that were distinctly related to the persecuting society throughout European history. The only crimes connected with sex punished under the new French legal code were rape, child prostitution, and the selling of obscene pictures. This extraordinary legal reform had wide-ranging effects when, in 1810, it was incorporated into the Napoleonic Code. As a result, it was implemented in all French colonies and wherever Napoleon established governments in Europe and the Americas.

In the context of the European Enlightenment, such a reform makes sense. Writers such as Denis Diderot, Jean-Paul Marat, Montesquieu, and Voltaire had written about the need to decriminalize personal sexual behavior (which they saw as an ethical decision, not a criminal one), even if they personally thought sodomy was wrong or unnatural. (Voltaire's famous quip about his own forays into male-male sexual activity displays Enlightenment ambivalence: "Once, a scientist; twice, a sodomite.")

Why did the American revolutionaries not follow France's example? Benjamin Franklin and Thomas Jefferson attended dinner parties in Paris with some of these philosophers. The notion of sexual autonomy even rearticulated, for Enlightenment thinkers, the Puritan concept of individuality and care of the self and body. Yet not only did the thirteen original colonies keep their sodomy laws, they maintained, elaborated on, and enforced them for the next 212 years. Was it that the United States, composed of colonies rooted in many conflicting religious and civil polities, would be unable to agree on a nonambivalent way to conceptualize sexual behavior? Or was it that a country premised on dissent from England had to continue to assert its identity as such?

A crucial response to this question—which is central to thinking about lesbian, gay, bisexual, and transgender people—is that during the Revolutionary era, American culture was undergoing significant and complicated transformations regarding gender. Gender was understood by the majority of Americans as a stable system that had its roots in Genesis 5:2: "Male and female created he them; and blessed them, and called their name Adam." Gender is a primary organizational focus in any culture. In the newly formed United States—predicated on revolutionary ideas, yet deeply flawed in the execution of them—concepts of gender would undergo major changes that evidenced this ambivalence. The presentation of a firm, masculine authority as the face of the new American citizen exposed the tension of wanting to be free and needing to assert control.

INVENTING THE AMERICAN MAN

One of the most important changes of the Revolutionary era was the invention of a new form of American masculinity. As the colonies claimed their political independence from Great Britain, it was clear they would have to establish a new, distinct culture that would reflect their own political ideology. One of the ways they did this was to consciously invent a new "American man" who represented all of the new virtues of the Republic and had little connection to the traditional Englishman. This new American man was bold, rugged, aggressive, unafraid of fighting, and comfortable asserting himself. This model was in complete contrast to the Englishman, who was stereotyped as refined, overly polite, ineffectual, and often effeminate. The new American man was personified in popular myth-making by rural colonists such as Ethan Allen, who fought the British in Vermont and New York State, and John Paul Jones, the Scottish-born naval mastermind who famously said in battle, "I have not yet begun to fight."

This new action-oriented American man already existed in some form, due to the conditions of survival on the frontier. The Revolution was well fought by the colonists because they were an armed society and "just about every white man had a gun and could shoot."[4] The new American man, a mythic prototype defined by his heroic actions in the colonial militia, was also a prototype of the citizen. Not only were slaves unable to join a militia, but so were friendly native Americans, free Africans, white servants, and white men without homes. These restrictions ensured that the prototypical American man was of a certain class, ethnicity, property, and citizenship status.

A prime example of this fabrication of American manhood is Royall Tyler's 1787 *The Contrast,* the first American-written play produced in the United States. A traditional comedy of manners, the play pitted the foolish, duplicitous, American-born but British-identified Mr. Billy Dimple—a "flippant, pallid, polite beau, who devotes the morning to his toilet . . . and then minces out"—against the play's hero, the very American Colonel Manly, who is all that his names implies. *The Contrast* is insistently didactic and aimed at creating a new American citizen-based culture. The play's prologue states its political purpose: "Exult, each patriot heart!—this night is shewn / A piece, which we may fairly call our own; / Where the proud titles of 'My Lord! Your Grace!' / To humble Mr. and plain Sir give place."

At the play's end, as he is called a coward for refusing to fight with Dimple, Manly explains:

> Yes, Sir. This sword was presented to me by that brave Gallic hero, the Marquis De la Fayette. I have drawn it in the service of my country, and in private life, on the only occasion where a man is justified in drawing his sword, in defence of a lady's honour. I have fought too many battles in the service of my country to dread the imputation of cowardice. Death from a man of honour would be a glory you do not merit; you shall live to bear the insult of man and the contempt of that sex whose general smiles afforded you all your happiness.[5]

In one grand speech, Tyler connects the colonial revolution to American manhood, national pride, personal honor, and different-sex desire.

This is, in part, why the United States did not abolish its sodomy laws. Highly gendered societies reinforce traditional ideas about gender through regulating sexual behavior. In the fervor of those revolutionary years and the promotion of a national masculinity, the idea that sodomy laws might be abolished might have been understood, even by Enlightenment men, as counterproductive.

But the creation of a prototype American man presented a host of broader questions and problems. If there was a new American man, did there also have to be a new American woman? Would she be as bold and adventurous as her male counterpart? There is no question that colonial and Revolution-era women worked hard and exhibited enormous physical and psychological strengths; they often ran homes and businesses when men were off fighting. Life was filled with everyday hardships as the country grew and the Revolutionary War continued for eight years. Yet in the traditional Puritan equation of different-sex relationships in a family, a man's strength was defined, enhanced, and complemented by a compliant woman. At this point the myth of the new American man—and the nation's new gender roles—become less coherent. Like all strictly delineated systems of gender, the new American models could not represent the diverse lives of actual people.

The evolving American culture was filled with enormous anxiety over the meaning of gender roles. First, many of the men who conceptualized this new country were not good examples of the new American man. George Washington, Thomas Jefferson, James Madison, John Adams, and Alexander Hamilton, with their fine manners, powdered wigs, large estates, and voluminous libraries, were far closer to the image of the wealthy, aristocratic, educated Englishman from which the country was distancing itself. Second, the women in this circle were also well educated and frequently spoke their minds, contrary to the subordinate role women were thought to hold in society. During the 1776 Continental Congress, Adams and his wife, Abigail, wrote one another frequently, and she was direct in her concerns:

I long to hear that you have declared an independency. And, by the way, in the new code of laws which I suppose it will be necessary for you to make, I desire you would remember the ladies and be more generous and favorable to them than your ancestors. . . . If particular care and attention is not paid to the ladies, we are determined to foment a rebellion, and will not hold ourselves bound by any laws in which we have no voice or representation.

That your sex are naturally tyrannical is a truth so thoroughly established as to admit of no dispute; but such of you as wish to be happy willingly give up the harsh title of master for the more tender and endearing one of friend.[6]

John Adams dismisses her concerns with a joke: "We dare not exert our power in its full latitude. We are obliged to go fair and softly, and, in practice, you know we are the subjects. We have only the name of masters, and rather than give up this, which would completely subject us to the despotism of the petticoat . . ." But it is clear that the new American nation and the new American man valued free white men above women and all other men.[7]

Abigail Adams was not the only woman with these ideas. Over the next decade, women lobbied for suffrage, only to be consistently denied the right to have a voice in their government. While some states allowed female suffrage for a short while, this quickly changed. Women were denied suffrage in New York in 1777, in Massachusetts in 1780, and in New Hampshire in 1784. In 1787 a constitutional convention allowed the states to decide on suffrage; all states but New Jersey denied women the right to vote. New Jersey revoked female suffrage in 1807. In 1867 the Fourteenth Amendment stipulated specifically that suffrage is the right of male citizens alone.

JUST FRIENDS

In societies in which gender and power are inexplicably intertwined, often little respect is given to people who desire their own sex or who do not conform to accepted gender expectations. Same-sex relationships and desires, however, manifest themselves in various, often more socially acceptable, ways. This is especially true in the complicated interplay between companionship, community, and eroticism in people's lives. The clearly defined separate social spheres for women and men—both the public and the private for men, and most often the domestic for women—give rise to clearly defined same-sex cultures, usually referred to as "homosocial." This term does not necessarily imply an erotic or sexual component—although those could, and often do, exist—but rather describes a social construct that emerged in specific ways during the eighteenth century.

Homosocial space at this time gave birth to distinct same-sex relationships that were referred to in popular and literary culture as romantic or intimate friendships. These friendships were important to the women and men who engaged in them—often as important and long-lasting as traditional heterosexual marriages —and were an accepted, praised, and significant social institution. Alan Bray argues that these friendships were largely a product of the Enlightenment—that the ideas of egalitarianism, brotherhood, and rational love (as opposed to uncontrolled, passionate love) helped contribute to a new concept of deeply committed, emotionally passionate friendship between members of the same sex.[8] It is possible that some of these friendships embodied similarities to our contemporary ideas of romantic and sexual relationships. In many ways they were understood as a beneficial and complementary alternative to marriage. A major function of heterosexual marriage was to regulate sexual activity that would lead to reproduction, but this new idea of friendship, for men as well as women, often provided a more enlightening, expressive outlet.

We can easily find evidence of "romantic friendships" in the lives of both famous and common people. Feminist historians have uncovered extensive, complex networks of female friendships in the eighteenth and nineteenth centuries and examined what they meant, not only to the individual women but to the society in which they lived.

Personal allegiance could be political allegiance, but not necessarily national allegiance. Women involved in these friendships understood the social significance and resonance, which sometimes challenged social norms, of their deep and intense connections. Sarah M. Grimke, the abolitionist and feminist, signed her letters to her beloved Mary Parker "thine in the bonds of womanhood." Grimke—understanding the implications of "bonds" in slavery— used the phase to signify the deep connection between herself and Parker and how they were bound together as women, as well as oppressed together as women.

The writers' language also situates them in the realm of the erotic. In the first decade of the nineteenth century, Eunice Callender of Boston wrote to her cousin and intimate friend Sarah Ripley (whose letters, she wrote, "breathe forth the sentiments of my soul"): "Oh could you see with what rapture . . . all your epistles are open'd by me . . . then would you acknowledge that *my* Friendship at least equals your own, and yours I believe is as true as pure a flame as ever warmed the breast of any human Creature." [9]

This language was common within male romantic friendships as well. Daniel Webster wrote to James Hervey Bingham in an 1804 letter: "Yes, James, I must come; we will yoke together again; your little bed is just wide enough; we will practice at the same bar, and be as friendly a pair of single fellows as ever cracked a nut."[10] Such intensity and devotion were emblematic of how these relationships reflected the newly professed equality and fraternity of society and the nation. The Marquis de Lafayette wrote affectionately to George Washington on June 12, 1799, during the height of the Revolution:

> My Dear General . . . There never was a friend, my dear general, so much, so tenderly beloved, as I love and respect you: happy in our union, in the pleasure of living near to you, in the pleasing satisfaction of partaking every sentiment of your heart, every event of your life, I have taken such a habit of being inseparable from you, that I cannot now accustom myself to your absence, and I am more and more afflicted at that enormous distance which keeps me so far from my dearest friend.[11]

Because of their intensity, intimate friendships could be as complicated as any sexual relationship, and not always smooth, as we see in this letter from LaFayette to Washington, written a few months after the previous one:

> My dear general—From those happy ties of friendship by which you were pleased to unite yourself with me, from the promises you so tenderly made me when we parted at Fishkill, gave me such expectations of hearing often from you, that complaints ought to be permitted to my affectionate heart. Not a line from you, my dear general, has yet arrived into my hands, and though several ships from America, several despatches from congress or the French minister, are safely brought to France, my ardent hopes of getting at length a letter from General Washington have ever been unhappily disappointed: I cannot in any way account for that bad luck, and when I remember that in those little separations where I was but some days from you, the most friendly letters, the most minute account of your circumstances, were kindly written to me, I am convinced you have not neglected and almost forgotten me for so long a time. I have, therefore, to complain of fortune, of some mistake or neglect in acquainting you that there was an opportunity, of anything; indeed, but what could injure the sense I have of your affection for me. Let me beseech

you, my dear general, by that mutual, tender, and experienced friendship in which, I have put an immense portion of my happiness, to be very exact in inquiring for occasions, and never to miss those which may convey to me letters that I shall be so much pleased to receive.[12]

Lafayette's second letter to Washington can be read a communication from a hurt, angry lover. We have no conclusive evidence that George Washington and the Marquis de Lafayette were sexually involved as lovers—nor, as historian Charley Shively points out, do we have any evidence that they were not—but what we do know is that the two men had an intensely emotional, companionate friendship with erotic overtones. Their relationship can only be understood in the context of a national fight for freedom from political oppression and the ideals of the Enlightenment. Passionate same-sex friendships were often public and acknowledged by the culture in which they thrived. As public relationships, they influenced and were influenced by the political culture of the time.[13]

REVOLUTIONARY GENDER

In 1778 an anonymous contributor to the *Worcester Spy* wrote that the newly formed American people had "broken the line that divided the sexes."[14] At the end of the eighteenth century, three very different people—two real and one fictional, all of them born women—captured the pubic imagination for breaking that divide.

The first was Jemima Wilkinson, a charismatic evangelist who was born a Quaker in 1752. In 1775, during a series of debilitating illnesses and fevers, she believed that Christ entered her body and that she was now neither female nor male, but was commanded to bring her ministry to the new country. She renamed herself "Publick Universal Friend," refused to use the pronouns "she" or "he," and dressed in gender-neutral clerical garments that made her sex unreadable (although contemporary accounts state that many in her audience saw her as male). Wilkinson's gender presentation, as well as her theological message—she preached complete sexual abstinence, strict adherence to a narrowly defined interpretation of the Ten Commandments, unqualified universal friendship, and the apocalyptic vision of the harshest Hebrew Bible prophets—made her a sensation throughout Rhode Island, Pennsylvania, and Massachusetts. In the mid-1780s the popular press and pamphlet culture covered her sermons in detail and placed particular emphasis on her sexually ambiguous persona. She had a huge following that verged on a cult and eventually started her own religious settlement in central New York State.

Deborah Sampson Gannett's public career was as noted as Wilkinson's. She was born in 1760 outside Plymouth, Massachusetts. In May 1782, dressed as a man, she enrolled in the Continental Army under the name Robert Shurtliff. She fought in several battles until she was discovered, after being wounded in 1783, to be a woman. She received an honorable discharge and in 1785 married Robert Gannett. In a few years' time they had three children. Sampson Gannett was relatively unknown until 1797 when, in conjunction with the writer Herman Mann, she published a semifictional narrative of her time as a cross-dressed Revolutionary soldier. It was titled *The Female Review: or, Memoirs of an American Young Lady, Whose Life and Character Are Peculiarly Distinguished—Being a Continental Soldier, for Nearly Three Years, in the Late American War*. The work was a straightforward tale that touched on the author's possible homosexuality through descriptions of titillating, affectionate interactions with women. Sampson Gannett's intention in publishing the narrative was to gain public attention for her attempt to be awarded a military pension.

In 1802 Sampson Gannett commenced a series of public lectures about her life. She spent much of her time on stage—after stating that she could not explain why she chose to cross-dress and join the Continental army—extolling traditional gender roles for women. Near the end of the presentation, she left the stage, returned dressed in her army uniform, and executed complicated and physically taxing military drills. Her presentation was extremely popular in Boston, and she repeated it in other New England cities. In 1816, after years of petitioning and with help from Paul Revere, Sampson Gannett was finally awarded the full pensions she deserved by both the state of Massachusetts and Congress.

The Female Review and Sampson Gannett's public performance were popular because her dual public image as a brave soldier and a traditional woman tantalized the post-Revolutionary audience. By consciously refusing to be cast firmly in either gender role, Sampson Gannett insisted that she would be both and neither at the same time.

This transgressive approach to gender identity was also present in an 1815 work of fiction titled *The Female Marine, or the Adventures of Miss Lucy Brewer.* Most probably written by Nathaniel Hill Wright, an obscure Boston literary figure, it is a breathless, first-person narrative that frequently references Sampson Gannett's life. *The Female Marine* tells the story of a young woman who is seduced, impregnated, loses her child, and then is forced to work in a Boston brothel. She escapes and, dressed as a man, spends three years on the USS *Constitution* as a sailor. After many adventures, including potential romantic entanglements with women, she marries well.[15]

The Female Marine was so popular that it brought forth five sequels, testifying to the enormous reader interest in cross-dressing literature. These sequels included a self-defense from the madam of the brothel in which Lucy had been sequestered and a new story of male impersonation by a character named Almira Paul.

The public interest in the topic of female transvestism was not isolated to stories about these three strikingly different women. Late eighteenth-century American literary and popular culture was obsessed with this new notion of the cross-dressed female warrior.[16] Novels such as Charles Brockden Brown's *Ormond, or The Secret Witness*; the memoir of famous cross-dressing British sailor Hannah Snell, a popular version of which was published in *Thomas's New-England Almanack*; several plays based on the life of Joan of Arc; numerous broadsides of popular ballads detailing the exploits of cross-dressing female soldiers and sailors—all were extraordinarily popular with audiences.

These sermons, books, lectures, pamphlets, novels, plays, and ballads struck a chord with the new American audience. Female and male readers saw themselves at the center of a whirligig, a quickly evolving culture that was breaking from the old world but not yet settled in the new. Howard Zinn points out that "between the American Revolution and the Civil War, so many elements of American society were changing—the growth of population, the movement westward, the development of the factory system, expansion of political rights for white men, education growth to match the economic need—that changes were bound to take place in the situation of women."[17] Certainly the examples of Wilkinson, Sampson Gannett, and the fictional Lucy Brewer all point to new, if not explicitly articulated, freedoms that were opening for women in a country that was expanding on an almost daily basis. But they also are an indication of new ways of looking at gender.

In highly public ways, these three women opened a liminal space in which new ideas and constructs of gender and sexual behavior could be discussed. In news reports and public presentations, both Wilkinson and Sampson Gannett were mythologized—even fictionalized as much as Lucy Brewer. Historian Susan Juster claims that Wilkinson is best understood as a "spiritual transvestite."[18] She makes the point that Wilkinson took seriously Paul's claim in Galatians 3:28 that "there is neither Jew nor Greek, there is neither slave nor free man, there is neither male nor female; for you are all one in Christ Jesus." In this sense, Wilkinson's "transvestism" is indeed spiritual. But it is also gendered. It can easily be understood as a purely American phenomenon that blurs the line between male and female while at the same time creating the perfect U.S. citizen— literally the Publick Universal Friend—who is both religious and secular. This image supports and yet contradicts the Revolution's new gender roles, as well as the concept of separation of church and state central to the Constitution. To be neither male nor female, to experiment with coded representations of lesbianism, to banish—as Wilkinson did—traditional pronouns was a radical embrace of new articulations of public sexuality and understanding of gender.

Can we call Jemima Wilkinson, Deborah Sampson Gannett, or Lucy Brewer transgender or transvestite? Not by the standards and the vocabulary of their time. These women, however, helped set the groundwork for a national culture that was open to experimentation in gender and sexual identity. The connecting line moves backward as well as forward. It applies to the Enlightenment-influenced passionate friendships and the nationalized gender roles for women and men of the Revolution. Some of these new manifestations of gender behavior offered alternatives to social expectations, but they can also be seen as the building blocks to a more concise dichotomy between the public and private as a form of gender regulation.

The reality of the persecuting society never completely vanishes from U.S. history. It becomes increasingly refined. In the colonies, social and political persecution of certain groups was relatively indiscriminate, making few distinctions among individuals within a minority group. Gradually, by the beginning of the nineteenth century, we see a growing cultural schism occurring between the private and the public, which was largely the reason people were able to explore nontraditional gender roles. It was permissible for women and men to have passionate private friendships, which may have included an erotic or sexual component, as long as they conformed to accepted gender norms in public. It was acceptable for women such as Sampson Gannett to transgress gender norms in public as long as they adhered to traditional norms in their personal relationships.

This increasing split in public spheres and private spheres was a major shift in how sexual behavior and gender—and also citizenship—were conceptualized. Full citizenship was, and to a large degree still is, predicated on keeping unacceptable behavior private. This complicated relationship between the public and private is at the heart of LGBT history and life today.

THREE

IMAGINING A QUEER AMERICA

Through the Revolution, Americans developed a firmer sense of themselves as a nation. As the century moved forward, the process was complicated by the abolition of slavery, a huge increase in Asian and European immigration, and debates about the enfranchisement of women. By the 1870s many minority groups in America had cohesive collective identities, and individuals within those groups saw themselves as Americans. These collective and individual identities, sometimes race- or immigrant-based, were frequently rejected by those who were here earlier and saw themselves as the "real Americans." The challenge of how diverse peoples could form a single American identity resulted in tremendous institutional and individual violence against people whose identities or actions were viewed as threatening to mainstream culture.

At the center of this violence is the Civil War, fought between 1861 and 1865. As terrible as this war was, America was already familiar with violence. In the War of 1812, the Republic fought the British for almost three years. The fighting was brutal. Fatalities for both sides mounted to 24,181 from combat and rampant disease, with 8,184 combatants wounded.

Three decades later, in the midst of U.S. westward expansion, Mexico declared war on the United States in response to the U.S. annexation of Texas. Fought between 1846 and 1848, the Mexican War claimed the lives of 6,863 soldiers and 14,126 civilians. In addition, along with the endless, and sometimes deadly, violence perpetrated on African slaves, extraordinary violence was used to put down numerous slave rebellions. As the country expanded to the west and the south, hundreds of thousands of native peoples were forcibly evacuated from their homelands and relocated in the West. Thousands of these native peoples died during the relocation, and thousands more died resisting.

Violence was intrinsic to the expansion of the United States, in a process known by the self-aggrandizing euphemism "manifest destiny." As the Federal government rapidly acquired land—the Louisiana Purchase occurred in 1803, the Mexican Cession in 1848, and the purchase of Alaska from Russia in 1867—the size of the United States more than tripled in just over forty years. For the growing white population of the United States, the early years of the nineteenth century were still heady from the excitement of the Revolution. There were ongoing crises, but also a sense of fresh possibilities and new ideals of personal and national freedom. The Revolution had been conceptualized and run by colonial men of wealth—it was essentially a transfer of power from the European imperial elite to the local elite—but its radical ideals took root in society. This new spirit is best exemplified in the rise of soldier, and later president, Andrew Jackson in the 1820s. Jacksonian democracy, an early populism, extended the vote to all white men, not just property-owning white men. Jackson's championing of the common man—a rejection of both the "civilized" behavior of the Englishman and the eastern "city man"—extended and expanded the revolutionary masculinity of the War of Independence.

EXPANSION: THE WEST

Jackson stood in bold contrast to the founding fathers. He, along with Daniel Boone, Jim Bowie, and Davy Crockett, represented the new American hero and was mythologized in popular culture for his masculine adventures. These iconic men who refused to follow society's rules were emblematic of the era's westward expansion. America was not only the land of the free, but the land of fewer rules.

Certainly the women and men who migrated westward in the nineteenth century lived under far fewer rules, including those governing gender and sexual behavior. Because of harsh living conditions, the absence of strict legal policing, and relaxed demands of accepted propriety, gender norms in the West were markedly different from those in the East. For men, this meant being able to embody the image of the American man who was bold, adventurous, and often uninhibited in his behaviors, including sexual behavior. Not all men in the West adhered to this image; there were tradesmen, preachers, and schoolteachers as well as men who worked the mines and the plains. Still, the early and mid-nineteenth century West promulgated the image of an independent man who did not need civilization, women, or even overt heterosexuality to define his manhood.

For women, westward expansion often meant a release from the enforced gender restrictions they faced in the East. Wives and mothers in the western territories often did not conform to urban gender expectations, since they were running farms or ranches. Many women took on jobs traditionally held by men. Martha Jane Cannary Burke, known as Calamity Jane, was an innkeeper and an army scout. "Stagecoach Mary" Fields, a former slave, gained fame as a stagecoach driver, the first African American driver for the U.S. Post Office. There is extensive documentation of women who dressed and passed as men. Charlotte Darkey Parkhurst, known as One-Eyed Charley or Six-Horse Charley, was an expert stagecoach driver who turned to ranching and lumbering when her job was eliminated by the railroad. San Francisco's Jeanne Bonnet was repeatedly arrested for cross-dressing and petty theft; at the end of her short life, she organized prostitutes to leave their work and make a living shoplifting.

Life on the western frontier was frequently sex-segregated, creating homosocial communities and relationships. Brothels, for instance, which thrived in towns such as Deadwood and Rapid City as well as cities such as San Francisco, resulted in complicated female-centered social groups as the women who worked in them offered one another comfort and safety. Little concrete evidence can be found of sexual relationships among men or women within these communities. Such relationships, even if tacitly acceptable, would have been illegal and thus unacceptable or dangerous to record.

There is, however, strong evidence in fiction and poetry of the frequency of intense male-male relationships. (Less evidence exists for women's same-sex relationships in the West, perhaps because women had less access to publishing.) Jonathan Ned Katz documents the implicit eroticism in these relationships in Western poet Badger Clark's "The Lost Pardner":

> We loved each other in the way men do
> And never spoke about it, Al and me,
> But we both knowed, and knowin' it so true
> Was more than any woman's kiss could be.
>
> We knowed—and if the way was smooth or rough,
> The weather shine or pour,
> While I had him the rest seemed good enough
> But he ain't here no more!
>
> What is there out beyond the last divide?
> Seems like that country must be cold and dim.
> He'd miss this sunny range he used to ride,
> And he'd miss me, the same as I do him.
>
> It's no use thinkin'—all I'd think or say
> Could never make it clear.
> Out that dim trail that only leads one way
> He's gone—and left me here!
>
> The range is empty and the trails are blind,
> And I don't seem but half myself today.
> I wait to hear him ridin' up behind
> And feel his knee rub mine the good old way.[1]

These verses, written in the early twentieth century, offer a glimpse of what a romanticized, homosocial world of the American West meant in American culture. Nineteenth-century American western culture produced the mythic cowboy whose iconic image resonates today as the prototypical American male.

This is a central paradox of U.S. masculinity. Masculinity has been increasingly defined by active heterosexual desire and relationships, yet is also defined by participation in an all-male homosocial world that has the potential for sexual interaction. This paradox is predicated on the idea that men are more free outside of the "civilizing" presence of women, who demand they behave in accord with artificial social standards. "Civilization," often signified by home and family, is contrasted with "the wilderness," which becomes a male refuge. As cultural critic Chris Packard notes, "The cowboy is queer; he is odd; he doesn't fit in; he resists community."[2] The myth of the American West often locates civilizing forces in the teeming, conformist, urban East—the antithesis of the natural wilderness. The mythic, lone cowboy, sometimes coupled with a "pardner," is emblematic of the revolt against not only social dictates and conformity, but also institutional heterosexuality.

The cowboy is culturally positioned as a man outside of the law. Clark's poem "The Outlaw" argues that the cowboy and the outlaw are the same. The internal struggle it conveys—metaphorically, a cowboy breaking a horse—is between the natural man, "the beast," and the civilized man.

> When the devil at rest underneath my vest
> Gets up and begins to paw
> And my hot tongue strains at its bridle reins,
> Then I tackle the real outlaw.
> When I get plumb riled and my sense goes wild
> And my temper is fractious growed,
> If he'll hump his neck just a triflin' speck,
> Then it's dollars to dimes I'm throwed.
>
> For a man is a man, but he's partly a beast.
> He kin brag till he makes you deaf,
> But the one lone brute, from the west to the east,
> That he kain't quite break is himse'f.[3]

"The Outlaw" is an example of the internal conflict between control and liberation, a struggle that also reflects the ambivalence of society at large. The relationship between the cowboy and his "pardner" is distinct from the idealized romantic friendship seen in the letters of Daniel Webster or Lafayette. The cowboy is an isolated man, and his intimate friendships have more to do with being away from civilization, as this excerpt from Owen Wister's 1891 short story "Hank's Woman" demonstrates. Here two intimate friends call off their futile attempts at fishing to go swimming:

> "Have yu' studied much about marriage?" he now inquired. His serious eyes met mine as he lay stretched along the ground.
>
> "Not much," I said; "not very much."
>
> "Let's swim," he said. "They have changed their minds."
>
> Forthwith we shook off our boots and dropped our few clothes, and heedless of what fish we might now drive away, we went into the cool, slow, deep breadth of backwater which the bend makes just there. As he came up near me, shaking his head of black hair, the cow-puncher was smiling a little.
>
> "Not that any number of baths," he remarked, "would conceal a man's objectionableness from an antelope—not even a she-one." . . .
>
> We dried before the fire, without haste. To need no clothes is better than purple and fine linen. Then he tossed the flapjacks, and I served the trout, and after this we lay on our backs upon a buffalo-hide to smoke and watch the Tetons grow more solemn, as the large stars opened out over the sky.
>
> "I don't care if I never go home," said I.[4]

This domestic scene, complete with making dinner, is "home"—literally "home on the range"—for the narrator, but a home removed from civilization and women. These men are outside of society's control, but feeling at home with themselves.

These sentiments in nineteenth-century American western literature increase in the later decades of the century, when the West was becoming more "civilized." They offered imaginative alternative models to heterosexuality and some forms of same-sex friendship. Clark's and Wister's writings, published just after the time when the Old West was the frontier between nature and civilization, exemplify how the associations between same-sex desire and frontier life became all the more powerful as reverberations in memory. Whatever the sexual and affectional lives of the cowboys, the decidedly nonheterosexual myths that grew about them became deeply entrenched in mainstream culture. The actual conditions that bred these myths, however, were much more systemic than two "pardners" alone on the range.

THE BEGINNINGS OF COMMUNITY

From its earliest days, San Francisco was known as a wide-open town: an urban space with few social restrictions and a high tolerance for illegal behavior, including same-sex sexual activity and deviation from gender norms. The roots of this reputation can be found in the mostly all-male culture of the gold rush. Saloons, dance halls, rowdy theaters, and brothels were plentiful and, except for a small number of female workers, were patronized only by men.

In 1846 the population of San Francisco—then called Yerba Buena—was just over five hundred. In 1948 gold was discovered at nearby Sutter's Mill in Coloma. The next year nearly 90,000 people journeyed to Northern California, only half of them from the United States. By 1855 the area's population had swelled by another 300,000. San Francisco's population grew correspondingly. In 1850 it had jumped to 25,000, a decade later it was 56,800, and by 1870 it had nearly tripled to 149,500. Housing consisted mainly of rooming houses and cheap hotels, augmented by all-male public baths. In 1849 there were only three hundred women, two-thirds of them prostitutes, in a population of 25,000.

In 1850 organized same-sex dancing was perfectly acceptable, as was entertainment featuring cross-dressing. The public social life in San Francisco was so vibrantly nonconformist that British adventurer Frank Marryat, in his 1855 memoir *Mountains and Molehills, or Recollections of a Burnt Journal,* dubbed it "Sodom by the Sea."

The racial and ethnic diversity of this nearly all-male population contributed to a culture of uneasy and frequently disrupted tolerance unique to the area and the time. Many men who migrated to California and San Francisco were from South America, China, and Europe. In 1870, when San Francisco was the eighth largest city in America, close to 60 percent of its citizens were of foreign birth. There was also a large influx of fugitive slaves and free Africans during this time; in 1867 African Americans could use public transportation, and by 1869 they could vote. Six years later, San Francisco schools were desegregated for blacks. Hispanic and Chinese communities were central to creating San Francisco's economic infrastructure and shaping its sensibilities in food, architecture, and popular culture.

But as the presence of immigrants grew, so did strong anti-immigrant sentiment. In the 1850s there was organized mob violence against people from Latin America. Anti-Chinese sentiment led to the passage of the federal Chinese Exclusion Act in 1882, which was enforced until 1943. Miscegenation laws were frequently enforced. Institutionalized racism against some groups was integral to social interactions, but was constantly being negotiated. In San Francisco, individual freedom was both enhanced and hampered by community structures. Its hospitality toward nonnormative sexual and gender expression had much to do with its constantly changing social structures.

A second reason that nonnormative sexuality and gender was relatively acceptable in San Francisco after 1849 was its thriving economy. The presence of large businesses such as Wells Fargo and the city's position as a major seaport made San Francisco a center of commerce, a status enhanced in 1869 by the completion of the transcontinental railroad. John D'Emilio argues that historically, LGBT communities benefit in societies predicated on free labor—that is, a non-family-unit-based economy in which unmarried women and men are able to sustain economic independence.[5] The boom economy of San Francisco in the second half of the nineteenth century is a prime example.

A closely connected idea is historian George Chauncey's argument that gay and lesbian communities found their earliest manifestations in poor and working-class cultures, because wealthier classes could maintain a greater degree of personal privacy.[6] For LGBT people, the luxury of privacy was antithetical to forming communities, which are, by their nature, public in bringing similar people together.

Even as it prospered economically, late-nineteenth-century San Francisco insisted on maintaining its identity as an outlaw culture. But not all San Franciscans embraced the idea of a wide-open town. In response to rising crime in 1851 and 1856, vigilante committees were formed to combat vice. These groups wielded, often by violence, enormous social and political power in efforts to curb what they saw as social anarchy and excessive sexuality. This tension between social and sexual freedom and the demands of mainstream society to control and contain these actions—essentially demanding that they remain private, often by use of violence—contributed to the shifting terms in the national debate about sexual behavior and gender. San Francisco provided, for the first time in U.S. culture, an idea of how a community of "outlaws" can form and what can happen when concepts of private and public become more integrated.

WRITING A NEW NATIONAL CULTURE: THE EAST

Paradoxically, as westward expansion made the country geographically larger, new technologies—the invention of the telegraph in the late 1830s, the growth of a national railway system, and the telephone in the 1870s—facilitated travel and communications, making the country smaller and more cohesive. In these conditions we see the eventual flourishing of a distinctly American intellectual and literary culture. Washington Irving's 1820 short story "The Legend of Sleepy Hollow" promotes the ideal of robust, decidedly heterosexual masculinity, as embodied by "Brom Bones" Van Brunt, over that of the lanky, effeminized schoolteacher Ichabod Crane. Both men are courting young Katrina Van Tassel until Brom Bones frightens Crane out of town. Irving's gender and sexual message is clear. Crane's first name means "inglorious" in Hebrew, which Bible-literate contemporary readers would know. And as literary critic Caleb Crain points out, much of the action of the story takes place by "Major André's tree." This is a reference to Major John André, the British officer—generally thought to be a lover of men—

who collaborated with Benedict Arnold and was hanged by George Washington as a spy in 1780.[7] For Irving, nearly four decades after the Revolution, the new, clearly heterosexual American man was an imperative.

In contrast to Irving, also in 1820, nineteen-year-old Harvard student Ralph Waldo Emerson was writing entries in his journal about Martin Gay, a fellow student three years younger to whom he was attracted. Two years earlier, when he had first seen Gay, Emerson wrote:

> I begin to believe in the Indian doctrine of eye-fascination. The cold blue eye of [Emerson deleted the name here] has so intimately connected him to my thoughts & visions that a dozen times a day & as often . . . by night I have found myself wholly wrapped up in conjectures of his character and inclinations. . . . We have had already two or three profound stares at one another. Be it wise or weak or superstitious I must know him.[8]

Crain notes that Emerson's attraction to Gay was a form of the nineteenth-century ideal of "sympathy." In this context, sympathy— a form of empathy that, as Crain writes, "allows us to feel emotions that are not ours"—is an expansive form of romantic friendship. The deeply felt connective emotion of sympathy allows one to not only value a friend for his or her emotional sincerity, but to take imaginative leaps toward understanding and sharing the emotions of another. This new understanding of the possibilities of shared emotion was likely inflected by the new America of wide-open western spaces, natural landscape, and the outlaw.

In 1837 Emerson published "Nature," an essay fundamental in defining transcendentalism: the distinctly American philosophy promoting individual spiritual transcendence through experiencing the material world, especially nature, rather than through organized religion. The next year, in his "American Scholar" speech, he urged his audience to rethink the idea of the American man (by which he meant humans) and to create an independent, original, and free national literature. Animated by the ideal of an expansive sympathy influenced by the "naturalness" of America, Emerson argued for an egalitarian society that values all of its members' individual contributions to a whole: the doctrine "that there is One Man,—present to all particular men only partially, or through one faculty; and that you must take the whole society to find the whole man. Man is not a farmer, or a professor, or an engineer, but he is all. Man is priest, and scholar, and statesman, and producer, and soldier."[9]

Emerson's vision of American equality, the basis for his strong antislavery and pro–women's suffrage beliefs, has roots in the Enlightenment and in his radical, nature-based vision of Christianity. But it is especially rooted in his ability to admit and emotionally explore his attraction to—his sympathy with—other men. Same-sex affection was integral to understanding the mutually beneficent dynamics of the individual in society. This egalitarian same-sex affection placed the rugged individualism of the Revolutionary man into a new context, not of conquering an American landscape but of emerging from it and being at one with it. This was the cornerstone of a new way of understanding gender, desire, and personal and social liberty.

The feelings Emerson had for Martin Gay (his journals indicate "sympathy" for other young men as well) did not stop him from marrying twice and fathering four children. Emerson did not easily embrace all aspects of this sympathy. In 1824 he wrote in his journal, "He that loosely forgets himself here & lets his friend be privy to his words & acts which base desires extort from him has forfeited like a fool the love he prized."[10] This is an example of an internal tension that reflected a larger tension between sympathy and overt sexuality: that is, moving from a private emotion to publicly expressing that emotion.

Emerson was not the only person dealing with this conflation of desires, emotions, and political ideas. A wealth of homoerotic sentiments are present in the poems and journals of Henry David Thoreau. Meditations on friendship run throughout his journal, and by the 1840s they became increasingly erotic: "Feb. 18 [1840]. All romance is grounded on friendship. What is this rural, this pastoral, this poetical life but its invention? Does not the moon shine for Endymion? Smooth pastures and mild airs are for some Corydon and Phyllis. Paradise belongs to Adam and Eve. Plato's republic is governed by Platonic love."[11] Thoreau's invoking of Endymion, Corydon, and Plato strongly suggests a homosexual subtext; the two mythological figures were iconic representations for same-sex male desire in Renaissance art, and the *Republic* was, in part, an analysis of male friendship and love. Thoreau is using friendship as a metaphor here. However, his attraction to the eroticized male body appears throughout his journals without mythological trappings, but rather with a decidedly transcendentalist bent:

> [June 12, 1852.] Boys are bathing in Hubbard's Bend, playing with a boat (I at the willows). The color of their bodies in the sun at a distance is pleasing, the not often seen flesh-color. I hear the sound of their sport borne over the water. As yet we have not man in nature. What a singular fact for an angel visitant to this earth to carry back in his note-book, that men were forbidden to expose their bodies under the severest penalties! A pale pink, which the sun would soon tan. White men! There are no white men to contrast with the red and the black; they are of such colors as the weaver gives them. I wonder that the dog knows his master where he goes in to bathe and does not stay by his clothes.[12]

Thoreau's message is that civilization, with its "severest penalties," is most unnatural. He is arguing that nature not only allows for "exposure" but is a space for racial equality, one wherein even the idea of "whiteness" is exposed as a lie. Alluding to classical literature and the European culture it inspired was a common method for nineteenth-century American intellectuals to discuss sexuality and sexual behaviors. Used consciously to reinforce ideas about American citizenship and democratic structures, the older culture safely places the sexuality at a distance.

Margaret Fuller, a leading figure in the transcendentalist movement and author of *Women of the Nineteenth Century*, the first major feminist publication in the United States, was also connecting to same-sex erotic intimacy and a new American ideal. In 1843, several years after viewing Danish sculptor Bertel Thorvaldsen's *Ganymede* at a Boston exhibition, Fuller wrote "Ganymede to His Eagle," a poem about the beautiful boy abducted by Zeus, in the form of an eagle, to be his lover and cupbearer. Here the cupbearer speaks to the eagle:

> Before I saw thee, I was like the May,
> Longing for summer that must mar its bloom,
> Or like the morning star that calls the day,
> Whose glories to its promise are the tomb;
> And as the eager fountain rises higher
> To throw itself more strongly back to earth,
> Still, as more sweet and full rose my desire,
> More fondly it reverted to its birth,
> For, what the rosebud seeks tells not the rose,
> The meaning foretold by the boy the man cannot disclose.[13]

Caleb Crain notes that Fuller is referring not only to the implicit homoeroticism of the original myth but, more important, to the eagle as "the emblem of sovereignty of the United States." Thus she consciously conflates mythological same-sex desire with the democratic progress of the nation. Fuller is indicating that the longing for freedom implicit in same-sex desire and sympathy cannot be fully expressed—the rosebud cannot tell the rose what it feels—because its power, at root political, emanates from being unspoken. In much of this literature is an underlying assumption that unspoken feelings are stronger than articulated ones. In 1839, at the age of twenty-nine, Fuller wrote to a woman friend of long standing:

> With regard to yourself, I was to you all that I wished to be. I knew that I reigned in your thoughts in my own way. And I also lived with you more truly and freely than with any other person. We were truly friends, but it was not friends as men are friends to one another, or as brother and sister. There was, also, that pleasure, which may, perhaps, be termed conjugal, of finding oneself in an alien nature. Is there any tinge of love in this? Possibly![14]

Emily Dickinson, who wrote explicitly about intimacy between women in the mid-nineteenth century, showed her large body of work to a handful of people and published fewer than a dozen poems. A member of a well-to-do Amherst, Massachusetts, family, she was unmarried, lived a reclusive life, and was passionately devoted to her friend Sue Gilbert (who later married Dickinson's brother Austin). The homoerotic content in Dickinson's poetry is notable for its time. The language breaks from that of romantic friendships and reflects the transcendentalist idea that desire is more powerful and true in its imaginative parameters:

> Her sweet Weight on my Heart a Night
> Had scarcely deigned to lie—
> When, stirring, for Belief's Delight,
> My Bride had slipped away—
>
> If 'twas a Dream—made solid—just
> The Heaven to confirm—
> Or if Myself were dreamed of Her—
> The power to presume—
>
> With Him remain—who unto Me—
> Gave—even as to All—
> A Fiction superseding Faith—
> By so much—as 'twas real—[15]

Dickinson's directness, like Fuller's letter, is remarkable; she clearly has complete access to erotic desires for other women. This is also true in her letters to Gilbert, of which over three hundred survive. She wrote the following just as Austin Dickinson was beginning his courtship of Sue Gilbert:

> June 11, 1852
>   Susie, forgive me Darling, for every word I say—my heart is full of you, none other than you is in my thoughts, yet when I seek to say to you something not for the world, words fail me.

If you were here—and Oh that you were, my Susie, we need not talk at all, our eyes would whisper for us, and your hand fast in mine, we would not ask for language—I try to bring you nearer, I chase the weeks away till they are quite departed, and fancy you have come, and I am on my way through the green lane to meet you, and my heart goes scampering so, that I have much ado to bring it back again, and learn it to be patient, till that dear Susie comes.[16]

What does it mean that Dickinson wrote poems, some explicit in their eroticism, that she never shared? Were they intended for a larger audience? Or did she simply write them for herself? There is no concrete answer. But Dickinson's quiet, domestic life was the reality for many women, and her poetic dictum "tell the truth but tell it slant" (Poem 1129) recognized that writing outside of prescribed codes was dangerous, especially for a woman.

For men, the social and political atmosphere of mid-century allowed for public expressions of same-sex desire when it was intertwined with democratic ideals of community and nation. Herman Melville's 1850 review of Nathaniel Hawthorne's *Mosses from an Old Manse* in *The Literary World* is written in the voice of a man reading Hawthorne's book in an empty barn:

A man of deep and noble nature had seized me in this seclusion. . . . The soft ravishments of the man spun me round about in a web of dreams. . . . But already I feel that this Hawthorne has dropped germinous seeds into my soul. He expands and deepens down, the more I contemplate him; and further and further shoots his strong New England roots into the hot soil of my Southern soul.[17]

Melville's articulation of erotic attraction for Hawthorne is extraordinary, even if coded. In a culture in which same-sex desire was not discussed openly, Melville's erotic words are completely absorbed into the American nation, from the North to the South. This vision, at once private, public, national, and emotional, is emblematic of how same-sex desire had become American.

The same-sex desires presented in literature were idealistic. In reality, same-sex sexual behavior was not always easily understood. The highly public marriage and highly private lives of Julia Ward Howe and Samuel Gridley Howe demonstrate how nineteenth-century domestic culture was shaped by the emotional and sexual complications of people's lives. Born in 1801 to a prominent Boston family, Samuel Howe was inspired by Byron to fight in Greece's 1820 revolution. Returning to Boston, he dedicated himself to abolition and the education of the blind, a radical idea at the time. He also formed a passionate friendship with Charles Sumner, later one of the most vocal antislavery voices in the Senate, that was central to his life. In 1843 Howe married Julia Ward, later a prominent writer, social reformer, and author of "The Battle Hymn of the Republic." While on his honeymoon, Samuel Howe wrote to Sumner:

> You complain of your lonely lot, & seem to think your friends will lose their sympathy with you as they form new ties of love, but dearest Sumner it is not so with me and in the days of my loneliness & sadness I never longed more for your society than I do now in my joy & in the whirl of London life: hardly a day passes but [I] think of you & long to have you by my side.[18]

For most of the marriage, Julia was emotionally estranged from her husband because of his attachment to Sumner. In the third year of wedlock, while raising two children, she wrote to her sister: "Where shall I go to beg some scraps and remnants of affection to feed my hungry heart? It will die if it not be fed."[19]

During this time Julia Ward Howe began writing *The Hermaphrodite,* an uncompleted novel that details the life and loves of Laurence, who is both woman and man. Laurence has "bearded lip and earnest brow . . . falling shoulders, slender neck, and rounded bosom" and tells Emma, a woman who falls in love with him/her, "I am as God made me." Howe uses the noted Greek sculpture known as the Sleeping Hermaphrodite as a central image in the work and, as Fuller did with classical allusion, uses it to convey a multiplicity of meanings. The bi-gendered Laurence is often confused about her/his life, but feels filled with enormous emotional and sexual potential that is, like the sculpture, sleeping. Although Emma calls Laurence a "monster," Howe's attitude to the character is kindly ambivalent. Later in the book, when Laurence has a passionate, unconsummated affair with sixteen-year-old Ronald, Howe is overtly sympathetic.

Scholar Gary Williams argues that *The Hermaphrodite,* which was not finished or published in Howe's lifetime, was her way of attempting to understand her husband's relationship with Sumner. Not having a specific language for a love between men that can coexist with a love between a man and a woman, Howe imagines a man-woman, in the classical mode, who is capable of both. Julia Ward Howe knew how to directly express what was wrong with her life. In 1854 she published *Passion-Flowers,* a book of poems that openly spoke of her isolation as a woman and mother in a difficult marriage. But *The Hermaphrodite* is not simply coded fiction about a personal problem. It is a manifestation of a culture in which gender role limitations and nontraditional sexual relationships were actively, albeit in a coded way, discussed as political issues. Howe's involvement with a wide range of social change movements— helping to organize the American Woman Suffrage Association, convening the first national meeting of women ministers, and, as editor of *The Woman's Journal,* advocating a feminist argument for peace—informs how she thought her views about gender and sexuality were a vital component of full citizenship.

SAME-SEX DESIRE AND THE DEMOCRATIZATION OF RACE

The influence of the transcendentalists and their bold philosophical and social views promoted a public discussion that treated issues such as race, science, reproduction, gender, and sexual activity outside the realm of religion. For many of the transcendentalists, science replaced theology as they embraced the new work in the natural sciences, including the theories of Charles Darwin. One of the transcendentalists' greatest political legacies—articulated by Thoreau, but embraced in various forms by most of his circle—was the concept of civil disobedience: an individual's legitimate resistance to legal authority when her or his standard of personal morality is compromised.

Throughout the century, the subject of race and racial difference was central to discussions of personal liberty and how the promised ideal of freedom could be manifest in a country that, amid institutionalized slavery, was becoming more diverse. These discussions happened in myriad venues: pamphlets, broadsides, sermons, lectures, novels, and theatrical dramatizations such as *Uncle Tom's Cabin*. Discussions of race did not focus solely on abolition. Leslie Fiedler's 1948 essay "Come Back to the Raft Ag'in, Huck Honey!" elucidates how American literature has a history of connecting same-sex male eroticism and interracial friendships between white males and men of either Native American or African descent. Such relationships appear in novels by James Fenimore Cooper, Herman Melville, and Mark Twain, among others. The association between male homoeroticism and race was not accidental and was easily integrated into American culture. Fiedler claims that these relationships are not just about race, but are reflective of a desired male flight from the "civilization" of women and the family into the freedom of natural wilderness.[20]

Sexuality and race are about bodies. In the nineteenth century, when both of these categories were hotly debated, they were inextricably bound with one another.[21] Firm categories of race were disrupted by the shifting lines between indentured servant and slave and between slave and freeman, and by the children of interracial couples. Intense same-sex friendships blurred the line between the romantic, the platonic, and the erotic. The categories of same-sex and opposite-sex relationships were consistently being redefined in relation to the categorization of race. Film historian Richard Dyer notes that same-race heterosexual relationships reproduce racial similarity.[22] Different-race relationships do not. Fear of mixed-race offspring led to a variety of legal statutes designed to control individuals' behavior connected to race, especially sexual behavior. These statutes included miscegenation laws that prohibited marriage between people of different races; the first American miscegenation law was passed in 1664 in the colony of Maryland. They also included a wide range of Jim Crow laws, passed mostly in the late nineteenth and early twentieth centuries, that mandated segregation.

The joint construction of the categories of race and sexuality had implications for people who desired those of the same sex. Because same-sex couples could not have children, their relationships, while illegal under sodomy laws, were less scrutinized under race laws than heterosexual relationships and could often go unnoticed if the parties involved were discreet (as was always mandated by the sodomy laws). Because it was not reproductive—and thus, ironically, was safer—same-sex interracial coupling was often the subject of certain genres of fiction or travel literature. These works set a cultural standard in gay male writing and iconography in which interracial erotic relationships were a central theme. As an embodiment of the "sympathy" of social equality, as well as erotic desire, that is evident in Emerson and Thoreau, this literature became a place in which ideas about citizenship, especially in relationship to sexuality, gender, and race, could be publicly articulated and discussed.

Many of these homoerotic novels are considered canonical to American literature (even as the same-sex eroticism is rarely discussed). Herman Melville's *Moby-Dick* (1851), as well as *Typee: A Peep at Polynesian Life* (1846) and *Omoo: A Narrative of Adventures in the South Seas* (1847), are discussed in high school and college English classes. Charles Warren Stoddard's books, such as *South-Sea Idyls* (1873), *A Trip to Hawaii* (1885), and *Island of Tranquil Delights* (1904), popular when published but infrequently read today, also contain explicit homoerotic content. These same themes, to a lesser degree, can be found in works such as James Fenimore Cooper's *Last of the Mohicans* (1826), Richard Henry Dana Jr.'s *Two Years Before the Mast* (1840), and Mark Twain's *The Adventures of Huckleberry Finn* (1884). The prominence of these titles indicates that homoerotic themes continue to be part of a vital discussion in American culture.

Melville's novels, partially based on his South Pacific whaling ship expeditions, contain passages describing erotic feelings between sailors and island men. In *Omoo*, Melville writes:

In the annals of the island are examples of extravagant friendships, unsurpassed by the story of Damon and Pythias: in truth, much more wonderful; for, notwithstanding the devotion—even of life in some cases—to which they led, they were frequently entertained at first sight for some stranger from another island.[23]

In the next chapter, the narrator describes how he became the object of one native's affections:

Among others, Kooloo was a candidate for my friendship; and being a comely youth, quite a buck in his way, I accepted his overtures. By this, I escaped the importunities of the rest; for be it known that, though little inclined to jealousy in love matters, the Tahitian will hear of no rivals in his friendship.[24]

The relationship dynamic gets more complicated in *Moby-Dick,* when Ishmael, the narrator, half-willingly shares a bed at the inn with the South Pacific harpooner, Queequeg:

Upon waking next morning about daylight, I found Queequeg's arm thrown over me in the most loving and affectionate manner. You had almost thought I had been his wife. The counterpane was of patchwork, full of odd little particoloured squares and triangles; and this arm of his tattooed all over with an interminable Cretan labyrinth of a figure, no two parts of which were of one precise shade—owing I suppose to his keeping his arm at sea unmethodically in sun and shade, his shirt sleeves irregularly rolled up at various times—this same arm of his, I say, looked for all the world like a strip of that same patchwork quilt. Indeed, partly lying on it as the arm did when I first awoke, I could hardly tell it from the quilt, they so blended their hues together; and it was only by the sense of weight and pressure that I could tell that Queequeg was hugging me.[25]

In this passage, implicit homoeroticism is juxtaposed with the domesticity of the classic New England quilt. Melville has titled this
chapter "The Counterpane," so there is no question that he intends
for us to compare Queequeg's multicolored tattoos with the designs
of the quilt: they are one and the same, inseparable. The homoeroticism is not expressed as an exclusive identity, but rather as a marker
of democracy and American civilization, which is neatly folded
into the "uncivilized" Queequeg. Melville's use of the metaphors
of weddings and marriage throughout the book reinforces his vision of a republic resonant of interracial, same-sex relationships that
blend nature with civilization to the point of creating a "natural"
democracy.

Stoddard's work, two decades later, is laced with similar scenes,
often more overtly erotic in tone and description. Here the narrator
first meets Kána-aná:

> So Kána-aná brought up his horse, got me on to it in some
> way or other, and mounted behind me to pilot the animal and
> sustain me in my first bare-back act. Over the sand we went,
> and through the river to his hut, where I was taken in, fed,
> and petted in every possible way, and finally put to bed, where
> Kána-aná monopolized me, growling in true savage fashion if
> any one came near me. I didn't sleep much, after all. I think I
> must have been excited.[26]

After the narrator returns to the United States, he misses his chum
and muses on what it would mean to bring him to "civilization": "I
could teach him to dress, you know; to say a very good thing to your
face, and a very bad one at your back; to sleep well in church, and
rejoice duly when the preacher got at last to the 'Amen.'"[27] Stoddard
presents a complicated relationship between the sexual freedom that
Kána-aná represents and the narrator's desire to bring his friend to
"civilization," even as he admits that civilization is riddled with repression and hypocrisies. Like Melville, Stoddard is concerned with
finding a way to merge what he idealizes as sexual freedom and lack
of social constraint with the conventions of U.S. life. His attempt
remains all the more powerful as a radical ideal, not a reality.

Aside from fiction, few records document same-sex behaviors during this time. In his mid-century diaries, Philip C. Van Buskirk, an American marine, details mutual sexual interactions among sailors. They include mutual masturbation (called "going chaw for chaw") and anal intercourse, as well as sexual and romantic relationships between older sailors, often officers, and cabin boys as young as thirteen. In 1853 his diary records an older sailor's opinion about sex between men. While the sailor would punish men who had sex with men on land, he had no desire to do so at sea: "What can a feller do?—three years at sea—and hardly any chance to have a woman. I tell you . . . a feller must do so. Biles and pimples and corruption will come out all over his body if he don't."[28] The open sea, like the open range, by offering escape from social condemnation, allowed for the articulation of same-sex desire and made same-sex sexual behavior natural and even utopian. Leslie Fiedler rejects the idea that male-male sex occurred because men were isolated from women in homosocial places; he suggests instead that this all-male isolation was "sought consciously as an occasion for male encounters."[29]

Yet few of these same-sex erotic relationships among men at sea were interracial, furthering highlighting that when authors used the theme of same-sex, different-race eroticism, they did so to discuss the place of race in American society. Clearly, this theme resonated with readers. Melville's *Omoo* and *Typee* had a wide readership (*Moby-Dick* was not appreciated until the twentieth century), as did Stoddard's *South-Sea Idyls*. While romantic friendship, "sympathy," racial mixing, and the desire to flee civilization were literary conventions of the time, in Melville's and Stoddard's novels these themes becomes explicitly indicative of same-sex desire. In this context, Melville's allusions in *Omoo* to Damon and Pythias (common in nineteenth-century writing on male friendship) become clearly sexualized. In the early chapters of *Moby-Dick*, Melville mentions Sodom and Gomorrah as a clue to his subtext.

In the United States at this time, there was a strong, growing culture of women writers, such as Harriet Beecher Stowe, who wrote about race relations; none of them touch on same-sex, interracial erotic relationships. Perhaps social prohibitions against women writing sexually tinged material, or reader's expectations that subject matter concern the domestic rather than exulting the natural wilderness, prevented them from doing so.

Although depictions such as *Moby-Dick* and *South-Sea Idyls* modeled a progressive view of sex and race relationships, they also carried mixed messages. They were implicitly racist in "othering" men of color, routinely described as savages and barbarians. But they also value and praise these men for being "natural," untainted by the social and sexual repression that was embedded in American culture. Melville and Stoddard, because they were writing about same-sex couples, actively blurred these boundaries. Kooloo is both a "primitive" and a churchgoer; Queequeg's "savage" tattooed arm becomes the New England quilt; Kána-aná must be "civilized," but civilization is hypocritical, not natural. The same-sex-desiring American man feels the pull of freedom and persecution most keenly and is a ripe figure for exploring and understanding that dynamic. Whatever problems Melville and Stoddard betray in how they treat race, their work is clearly more complicated and nuanced than most of the contemporary political, public discussions about race in a country split by the fight over slavery.

FOUR

A DEMOCRACY OF DEATH AND ART

THE CIVIL WAR

The Civil War is literally and metaphorically at the center of nineteenth-century American life. In this war the remaining United States fought the Confederacy, states that had seceded from the Union over economic issues closely related to the rights of states to sanction slavery. Even in a century riddled with violence, the amount of death wrought by the conflict was extraordinary. The death tolls from the century's earlier two wars were 45,170; the Spanish-American War of 1898 would bring 11,570 deaths in battle, another 2,045 wounded, and 15,565 dead from disease. The Civil War eclipsed them all; it claimed 620,000 lives, or 2 percent of the American population at the time. Calculated for the U.S. population today, this number would be six million. Battles were often horrific, combining traditional forms of hand-to-hand combat with newly invented, more impersonal technologies such as the Gatling gun. The Civil War is the defining moment of the nineteenth century, and indeed of America. It staged on a national scale the ongoing conflict between freedom and enslavement that had wracked individuals, communities, colonies, and states for over three hundred years. It also exposed the underlying racial and gender-related violence that had been intrinsic to those everyday conflicts since the arrival of the first Europeans.

America was already a devout country—religious revivals of the Second Great Awakening, ending in 1840, had won 40 percent of the population over to some form of Christian evangelicalism—and the horrors of the war moved many to embrace their beliefs more deeply. Other Americans began to question traditional ideas about providence, the belief that life is guided by God. This questioning stance, reminiscent of the Deism of the founders and the European Enlightenment, as well as the transcendentalists, was reinforced by advances in the sciences—Charles Darwin's 1859 *On the Origin of Species* is the most notable—that were at odds with traditional religious beliefs.

Defenders of slavery and abolitionists both quoted Bible verses to make their arguments. As early as 1787, British politician and abolitionist William Wilberforce used the Bible to justify his cause. Both sides held considerable sway in a country still in the wave of massive conversions. Beneath the debate lurked the more substantial issue of biblical inerrancy, the belief that the Bible is literally true in every detail. The use of biblical texts to justify the persecution of a class of people within a secular democracy is still with us today, including the justification for legal prohibitions against same-sex sexual behavior, because scriptural rationales and the rhetoric of persecution continually set the terms of national discussions.

An immediate effect of the Civil War on LGBT lives and history was how it shaped ideas about gender; specifically, what it meant to "be a man." Historian Drew Faust notes that during the Civil War, manhood was "defined and achieved by killing." W.E.B. Du Bois noted in his 1935 *Black Reconstruction in America*:

> How extraordinary, and what a tribute to ignorance and religious hypocrisy, is the fact that in the minds of most people, even those of liberals, only murder makes men. The slave pleaded; he was humble; he protected the women of the South, and the world ignored him. The slave killed white men; and behold, he was a man![1]

The war was a rite of passage for young white men. Data for the Confederate army are sketchy, but many scholars claim that two million soldiers in the Union army were twenty-one or younger, and one million were eighteen or younger. The intense patriotism on both sides ensured that full gendered citizenship was measured by being an effective soldier, which meant being a ruthless killer. Violence by Confederate soldiers against captured "colored" Union troops was prevalent, as was mutilating the bodies of those who had been killed in action or executed. Brutality was also present in the Union army. On June 21, 1864, General William Sherman wrote to Edwin McMasters Stanton, Lincoln's secretary of war: "There is a class of people [in the South] . . . men, women, and children, who must be killed or banished before you can hope for peace and order."

The Civil War had deeply affected men's relationships to one another. Killing now defined a new type of American masculinity, but it also exposed men's physical and emotional vulnerability. In confronting their own mortality, men could explore, often with one another, new expressions of sexuality. This is seen most clearly in the writings of Walt Whitman. Considered by many to be the most notable nineteenth-century poet of American democracy, Whitman's poems and letters are a perfect example of affectional and sexual behaviors between men in this period.

Historian Charley Shively, among others, has documented Whitman's romantic and sexual relationships with numerous young men, and Whitman's work is crucial for understanding the centrality of male homoeroticism in nineteenth-century American culture.[2] Whitman's wartime writings, influenced by his experiences as a nurse on the battlefield and in hospitals, are vibrant examples of how the harm done to the male body shaped narratives of male same-sex desire. His "Hymn of Dead Soldiers" from *Leaves of Grass* is a prime example:

Phantoms, welcome, divine and tender!
Invisible to the rest, henceforth become my companions;
Follow me ever! desert me not, while I live.

Sweet are the blooming cheeks of the living! sweet are the musical
   voices sounding!
But sweet, ah sweet, are the dead, with their silent eyes.

Dearest comrades! all now is over;
But love is not over—and what love, O comrades!
Perfume from battle-fields rising—up from fœtor arising.[3]

This conflation of desire, death, and love epitomizes the horror of the war as well as new gender roles open to men. The stream of homoerotic sentiment in transcendentalist thought, along with the mandate to take the American concept of equality seriously, confirmed and sustained these feelings. The American man as capable killer was augmented by a new type of citizen who could, as part of his patriotic duty, empathize with and mourn the dead. These sentiments are present in many of Whitman's notes of his meetings with wounded soldiers and other young men:

The Army Hospital Feb 21, 1863 There is enough to repel, but one soon becomes powerfully attracted also.

Janus Mayfield, (bed 59, Ward 6 Camp[bell] Hosp.) About 18 years old, 7th Virginia Vol. Has three brothers also in the Union Army. Illiterate, but cute—can neither read nor write. Has been very sick and low, but now recovering. Have visited him regularly for two weeks, given him money, fruit, candy etc.

Albion F. Hubbard—Ward C bed 7 Co F 1st Mass Cavalry/ been in the service one year—has had two carbuncles one on arm, one on ankle, healing at present yet great holes left, stuffed with rags—worked on a farm 8 years before enlisting—wrote letter—for him to the man he lived with/ died June 20th '63[4]

There can be no doubt of Walt Whitman's intentions when he wrote *Leaves of Grass*, first published in 1855 and revised in five more editions before Whitman's death in 1892. Praised by Emerson for its echoes of transcendentalism, it is also overtly homoerotic. Stanza 5 from "Song of Myself" describes an act of oral sex with a personification of his own soul:

I believe in you my soul, the other I am must not abase itself
   to you,
And you must not be abased to the other.

Loafe with me on the grass, loose the stop from your throat,
Not words, not music or rhyme I want, not custom or lecture,
   not even the best,
Only the lull I like, the hum of your valvèd voice.

I mind how once we lay such a transparent summer morning,
How you settled your head athwart my hips and gently turn'd
   over upon me,
And parted the shirt from my bosom-bone, and plunged your
   tongue to my bare-stript heart,
And reach'd till you felt my beard, and reach'd till you held
   my feet.[5]

The eroticism of *Leaves of Grass* had far-ranging effects. In 1865 Whitman was fired from his job in the Department of the Interior. Influential anthologist and literary critic Rufus Wilmot Griswold labeled the poet a lover of men when, in an 1855 review, he wrote that Whitman was guilty of *Paccatum illud horribile, inter Christianos non nominandum* ("that horrible sin not to be mentioned among Christians").

Despite the criticisms—even Emerson found the "Children of Adam" poems too overtly sexual—Whitman's popularity and reputation grew with each new edition of *Leaves,* contributing to a social climate that made other expressions of same-sex male desire permissible. Theodore Winthrop, who died in battle in 1861 at the age of thirty-two and was a direct descendant of Puritan leader John Winthrop, wrote the posthumously published *Cecil Dreeme,* a satirical novel that flirted with same-sex relationships and fluid gender roles. Charles Warren Stoddard's *South-Sea Idyls* found a large readership in 1869. Noted poet Bayard Taylor's novel *Joseph and His Friend* was published a year later, and Frederick W. Loring's *Two College Friends* in 1871. Each of these authors moved away from idealizations of romantic friendship and closer to presenting conjugal love. Taylor wrote of his two protagonists in *Joseph and His Friend:*

> They took each other's hands. The day was fading, the land-scape was silent, and only the twitter of nesting birds was heard in the boughs above them. Each gave way to the impulse of his manly love, rarer, alas! but as tender and true as the love of woman, and they drew nearer and kissed each other. As they walked back and parted on the highway, each felt that life was not wholly unkind, and that happiness was not yet impossible.[6]

PERFORMING MANLINESS

New definitions of masculinity were not the only gender issue affected by the war. Many women passing as men fought for both sides in the Civil War. It is impossible to know the exact number—perhaps over a thousand—but we know the names of the most prominent. Some women enlisted with their husbands and fought side by side with them. Satronia Smith joined the Union forces with her husband, and after he died in battle, she continued fighting. Some, like male soldiers, enlisted out of intense patriotism. Loreta Velazquez, who served the Confederacy under the name Lt. Harry Buford, had enough money to finance her career as a soldier. She likely deeply believed in the South's political principles. Sarah Emma Edmonds joined the Second Michigan Infantry as Franklin Thompson in 1861. After fighting in some of the bloodiest battles of the war, she deserted in 1863 when, after coming down with malaria, she refused to be hospitalized and have her secret uncovered.

Undoubtedly, some women, bored and trapped by gender restrictions, may have enlisted to experience a more exciting life. Mary Ann Clark, as Henry Clark, joined the Confederate forces in 1861 after being abandoned by her husband. She fought for a year, then came home, only to join again after placing her children in a convent. She was captured a year later and returned home in a prisoner exchange. V. A. White, a well-to-do prostitute in Nashville, Tennessee, joined the Union army around 1862 as penance for her professional life, which she chose after having a child as an unmarried woman.

Still other women, most probably a small percentage, spent most of their lives passing as men. Enlisting was simply the logical course of action for them. Albert Cashier was a Union soldier who fought in over forty battles. Not until years later did anyone discover that he was biologically a woman, having been born Jennie Irene Hodgers in Ireland around 1844. Hodgers immigrated to the United States as a child, and after passing as a man for some time, joined the Union army in 1862 as Albert Cashier. After the war Cashier continued living as a man.

It is impossible to apply any single description to these women. Were some of them transgender? Albert Cashier may have been, but the women who cross-dressed and fought had a wide variety of reasons for doing so. Most apparently came from poor rural or urban backgrounds that prepared them for the excruciating life of a soldier. Without doubt, their "passing" was facilitated by the presence of so many young male soldiers, which allowed them, without beards and deep voices, to be seen as boys. If they took up gambling, chewing tobacco, swearing, and drinking, their passing was made easier. We know almost nothing about their time in the army, except that by necessity, they performed as well as any male soldier.[7] It would be naive to think that their fighting was not as brutally murderous as that of their compatriots. It would also be naive to believe that the women who fought for the Confederacy did not hold abhorrent views about race or did not partake in the savageries against captured black Union soldiers.

America was fascinated with these passing women. *Women of the War: Their Heroism and Self-Sacrifice,* a popular 1866 history written by Frank Moore, contained a full chapter on cross-dressing women soldiers. Loreta Velazquez published her memoirs in 1876. Satronia Smith married veteran John Hunt after the war, and her obituary mentioned her military service. Sarah Emma Edmonds Seelye, along with other women, received government pensions. Albert Cashier lived as a man until 1913, when at the age of 69 and failing mentally, he was admitted to Illinois's Waterville State Hospital for the Insane. When it was discovered that he was biologically a woman, he was forced to wear a dress until his death in 1915. Even though his secret was made public, his tombstone described him as "Albert D. J. Cashier, Co. G, 95 Ill. Inf."

ACTING FREE

Women who fought for equal rights and social change during this time sought justice with soldier-like conviction. Women in the United States had greater mobility than those in some European societies; after the Civil War, as a result of their involvement with the suffrage and abolition movements, they had greater access to public space than before. In 1848 the first national suffrage gathering was held in Seneca Falls, New York, igniting vigorous public discussion about women's rights. The struggle for suffrage became more organized after the war and gave women an institutionalized public voice.

In addition, new printing technologies increased the number of national newspapers and magazines. While there were already women editors (in 1828 six women began editing national and local periodicals), their numbers increased dramatically in the 1860s. Magazines aimed at women often had large audiences—Sarah J. Hale's *Godey's Lady's Book* had a readership of 150,000 in 1860—and were culturally and politically influential.[8] These magazines' messages were often sharply dichotomized. They promoted the joys of the domestic sphere as assertively as they insisted on the cultural and moral importance of women to the nation.

Women's new visibility as citizens and intellectuals was reinforced by the increased growth of women's colleges. Frequently called "female seminaries," these institutions were predicated on women being as intelligent as men. Their all-female environments were havens for romantic female friendships as well as female mentoring. These relationships did not happen without criticism. Lillian Faderman notes that in 1838, journalist Harry F. Harrington wrote in *The Ladies' Companion* that women who wanted a serious education were "mental hermaphrodites" and "semi women."[9]

This public discussion of women as disenfranchised citizens was an important step in creating the idea of women as a community. Implicit in this idea was the potential of same-sex desire to bind that community together. In the years after the war, there were many ways in which women who loved women were visible and had a decisive impact on society.

Charlotte Cushman, one of the most famous Shakespearian actors of the nineteenth century, was unabashedly open about her intimate relationships with women. She became famous at a time when the connection between gender and citizenship in America was becoming more complicated. Born in Boston in 1816, she was raised as a Unitarian; Ralph Waldo Emerson was the pastor of her church. By age twenty, she was acclaimed for playing vivid character parts and male roles. Cushman's Romeo (her sister Susan played Juliet) was so famous that a figurine of the balcony scene was manufactured by the noted British pottery company Staffordshire.

Cushman had a huge following and led a very public life. Beginning in 1848, she and writer Matilda Hays were publicly acknowledged as a couple. In 1852 they moved to Rome, where they were part of a loosely connected colony of artists, including Harriet Hosmer, Emma Stebbins, Edmonia Lewis, George Sand, Nathaniel Hawthorne, and Robert and Elizabeth Barrett Browning. Over the next few years, Cushman and Hays were involved in a series of affairs with other women. The affairs culminated in Hays's threatening to sue Cushman for the income she lost after giving up her own career to support her lover emotionally. Cushman then partnered with Stebbins (with whom she had been having an affair). That relationship lasted until Cushman's death in 1876. During this time she had other lovers, including Emma Crow, who was twenty-three years younger.

Cushman's fame allowed her social freedoms unknown to most women of the time. After her 1874 farewell performance in New York, twenty-five thousand people gathered outside her hotel and gave her a prolonged ovation. She was able to dress in a masculine fashion and be remarkably pubic with her affections. Elizabeth Barrett Browning noted in a letter that "I understand that [Cushman] and Miss Hays have made vows of celibacy and of eternal attachment to each other—they live together, dress alike . . . it is a female marriage."[10] In 1860 Cushman wrote to Crow, "Ah what delirium is in the memory. Every nerve in me thrills as I look back & feel you in my arms, held to my breast so closely, so entirely mine in every sense as I was yours. Ah, my very sweet, very precious, full, full of extasy."[11] Most important, having her own income allowed Cushman to travel, support other women artists, and create her own community. Cushman's determination to build a tight-knit friendship network—what artist and critic William Wetmore Story called "a Harem (Scarem) of emancipated females"—attests to the independence that women gained by earning an income and living outside of a heterosexual marriage.

In this context, Cushman's persona manifested the idea that women could be powerful, charismatic, and independent as well as womanly, charming, and idolized. Cushman's penchant for male attire, as well as her ability to convincingly play a man (and in the case of Romeo, a sexualized romantic young man) added to her ability to embody what was becoming a new prototype of American women. Theater historian Faye E. Dudden suggests that Cushman's Romeo "undermined the assumption that gender was natural, inborn, undeniable, and suggested instead that it was something assumed, learned, performed."[12] Cushman's visibility as a female performer of international renown also viscerally appealed to women. In 1858, at age twenty-six, Louisa May Alcott, author of *Little Women,* was so struck by Cushman that she noted in her diary she "had a stage struck fit"; later she based Miss Cameron, a character in *Jo's Boys,* on Cushman. Kate Field, later a noted actor and journalist, wrote at age twenty, "The other day upon returning from Boston after having been excited by Miss Cushman, I shut myself up and wrote some verses to her."[13] These young women, both unmarried and at the beginning of their careers, found inspiration in Cushman, as well as a clear vision of what was possible for them to achieve.

There are numerous documented instances of women living together as domestic partners and being socially accepted as a couple. The common term for this arrangement was "Boston marriage," suggested by the title of Henry James's 1886 novel *The Bostonians.* Such relationships were found throughout society. However, little documentation of working-class women who lived as couples exists, because there are fewer records of the lives of less-affluent people.

The letters of Rebecca Primus, who lived in Maryland, to her intimate friend Addie Brown of Hartford, Connecticut, written between 1854 and 1868, give us a sense of how a middle-class African American wrote:

> My Cherish Friend,
>
> My head is better today Last night it pain me very hard O My Dear dear Rebecca when you press me to your Dear Bosom . . . happy I was, last night I gave anything if I could only layed my poor aching head on your bosom O Dear how soon will it be I will be able to do it I suppose you think me very foolish if you do tis all the same to me. Dear Rebecca when I am away from you I feel so unhappy it seems to me the hours and days are like weeks and months.[14]

Even women who did leave a detailed record of their lives, such as Louisa May Alcott, were often not forthcoming about their erotic desires, or may have foregone romantic relationships to pursue their work. Alcott, who published twenty-nine books and story collections in forty-four years, told poet Louise Chandler Moulton in 1873 that she had remained a spinster "because I have fallen in love with so many pretty girls and never once the least bit with any man." A bold statement that gives few details. Like most of the reform-minded women in her circle, Alcott was an ardent feminist and questioned how women's relationships with men affected their place in society. In the 1870s she and friends, including Julia Ward Howe, recommended that women not use "Mrs." or "Miss" to avoid discrimination.[15]

Many women found, along with their affectional and sexual desires, that female partners were more conducive to their lives as educators and reformers. Boston marriages were prominent at women's colleges, where professors and administrators such as Jeannette Marks and Mary Woolley at Mount Holyoke, and M. Cary Thomas and Mary Garrett at Bryn Mawr, were famously coupled. These arrangements were instrumental in promoting women's higher education and mentoring female students. Other noted Boston marriages included upper-middle-class couples such as Annie Fields and writer Sarah Orne Jewett, Alice James (the sister of Henry and William James) and Katherine Loring, sculptor Anne Whitney and painter Abby Adelaide Manning, poet Amy Lowell (of the Boston Lowells) and actor Ada Dwyer Russell. These couples, all based in or around Boston, were only the most public in their time. Their visibility in a society that primarily values opposite-sex relationships is important. These women had, through social position, inherited wealth and access to powerful male figures, giving them substantial political and social clout in shaping discussions and public opinions. People with economic advantages were often social and cultural leaders, but never before were women, unattached to men, able to be this independent or so prominently involved with other women.[16]

It is impossible to ascertain whether women in Boston marriages, or any romantic friendships, engaged in sexual activity with one another. No direct documentation exists to prove that they did, just as such no documentation, except for the birth of children, exists for heterosexual relationships. There is no reason to presume that these women did not engage in any number of forms of sexual play, from caressing and fondling to genital orgasm. Some of their letters and journals certainly indicate that their passions were physical as well as emotional. It is clear that the tenderness and love these women had for one another was publicly accepted, even valorized, and that these relationships were integral to many social institutions.

NEW BODIES FOR THE BODY POLITIC

In the years after the Civil War, American artists, in direct response to so many war deaths, began representing the male body in new ways. The need to promote a single national identity after the war led to a plethora of patriotic artwork, much of which glorified politicians and soldiers and valorized the male body as heroic. Many of these works were sculpted by women—such as Harriet Hosmer, Edmonia Lewis, and Anne Whitney—who made their lives with other women. (Some other sculptors, such as Vinnie Ream Hoxie and Adelaide Johnston, were married, outspoken feminists.) Hosmer's colossal bronze statue of Senator Thomas Hart Benton; Anne Whitney's larger-than-life recreations of Charles Sumner, Samuel Adams, and Lief Erickson; Emma Stebbins's imposing statue of Horace Mann; Edmonia Lewis's marble sculptures of Colonel Robert Gould Shaw, John Brown, Ulysses S. Grant, and Abraham Lincoln—all glorified the patriotic American male body.

Viscerally, these imposing works of public art represented the gender of a new body politic: the strong, indomitable, progressive American man who symbolized freedom and resilience in the face of injustice—and who, if Whitman was correct, contained within himself the potential for an expansive same-sex desire. In the public discussion over the changing nature of American masculinity, these statues represent the antithesis of the persecuting society. That these representations were being created by women who were outside of traditional gender or sexual roles indicates that significant shifts had occurred in who had permission to represent American patriotism.

As these commanding masculine statues of politicians and generals were erected across the United States, other artists, almost all of whom were men who desired men, were creating a different image of American masculinity: the male nude. Classical Greek and Roman statuary had depicted the male nude, but until the Italian Renaissance, Anglo-European sensibilities had discouraged displays of the male body and genitals. Although this attitude was due in part to the Christian church's stigmatization of sexuality, it also stemmed from the fact that such representations often implied physical, psychological, and emotional vulnerability, which was viewed as unmasculine. But after the Civil War highlighted the vulnerability of the male body, and as public discussion of same-sex male desire became more common, images of male nudity were considered increasingly acceptable. In the 1870s, English art critic John Addington Symonds wrote about Michelangelo's and da Vinci's nudes, explicitly associating them with contemporary male-male desire. At the same time, in Sicily, German photographer Wilhelm von Gloeden began taking photographs of local young male peasants in "classical" poses. His work with clothed models garnered popular attention in Europe and America.

Von Gloeden's more explicitly erotic photos of nude males, many of them in sexually suggestive poses, also gained attention among American and European men who identified as lovers of men. In the 1880s, Philadelphia painter and photographer Thomas Eakins did extensive work with the male nude, including a series of photographs of a probably eighteen-year-old Billy Duckett, who was intimately involved, and lived for five years, with Walt Whitman. (Eakins also took formal photographs of Whitman, including a traditional "wedding portrait" of Whitman and Duckett.)[17] *The Swimming Hole*, Eakins's famous 1885 painting of five youths bathing nude on a lake, echoes Whitman's images of an eroticized pastoral scene from "Song of Myself":

An unseen hand also pass'd over their bodies,
It descended tremblingly from their temples and ribs.

The young men float on their backs, their white bellies bulge to
    the sun, they do not ask who seizes fast to them,
They do not know who puffs and declines with pendant and
    bending arch,
They do not think whom they souse with spray.[18]

Boston-based photographer F. Holland Day, considered by art historians to be one of the founders of American photography, also worked with the male nude at this time. Day's publishing company, Copeland and Day, printed works by the English Decadents, including works by same-sex-loving Oscar Wilde and Aubrey Beardsley. In 1898 Day's nude portrait of Thomas Langryl Harris, *Study for the Crucifixion*, was the first frontal male nude to be publicly exhibited in Boston. Day, like von Gloeden, was interested in men of color. Some of his most noted works were of his chauffeur, Alfred Tannyhill, as an Ethiopian chief and in other poses that combined a forthright sexuality with dignity.[19]

Renowned society painter John Singer Sargent, also in Boston at this time, was exploring the male nude in his public art and private albums. His use of Thomas E. McKeller, an African American elevator operator he befriended, as the model for many of his black-and-white nudes speaks to Sargent's impulse to rethink racial paradigms, even as he is caught in them. Day, von Gloeden, and Sargent are part of a tradition of negotiating sexuality and race through art, one that stretches back to Thoreau, Melville, and Stoddard. Art historian Trevor Fairbrother points out that Sargent's male nudes have a sensuous quality, often reclining in positions associated with the female nude.[20] This pose is in direct contrast to patriotic statuary.

Technology and consumer capitalism helped bring some of these artists' images to a broader public. Inexpensive and easily available photographic prints—called studio cards—were now available through mass reproduction, and copies of artworks could be easily obtained by middle-class and even working-class people. This meant that art, once owned only by the wealthy, was becoming democratized and democratizing in a new way.

Most art historians agree that von Gloeden had sexual relationships with men and that Day, Eakins, and Sargent had romantic, if not physical, relationships with men. Women and men who desired their own sex had not found a significant level of freedom in America. But these female and male artists were able to live with a certain amount of visibility, with privileges the ordinary person did not have.

POLITICS AND POETICS

Walt Whitman, now internationally famous, had become the most visible advocate of "manly attachment" or "adhesiveness," two of the words he used to describe male same-sex desire. As such, he was a focal point for other men who felt similar desires. Whitman received many letters from the common man, as well as from noted American figures such as Emerson, Thoreau, and Charles Warren Stoddard; English writers such as Oscar Wilde, Bram Stoker, and John Addington Symonds; and Edward Carpenter, a socialist and political organizer who, in an interview much later in his life, claimed to have had sex with the poet. The connections between the intellectually and artistically adventurous Whitman and his British counterparts, Symonds and Carpenter, are a vital link in LGBT history.

Carpenter and Symonds were politically and socially animated by developments in Germany. There, some thinkers were articulating a new way to think, legally and socially, about women and men who desired their own sex. In 1862, Karl Heinrich Ulrichs, who had trained as a lawyer and a theologian, published (under a pseudonym) *Forschungen über das Rätsel der mannmännlichen Liebe* (*Researches on the Riddle of Male-Male Love*), a collection of essays that explained same-sex attraction through the lens of philosophy and medicine. In these essays Ulrichs coined the term "urning" to describe a man who is attracted to other men. By 1867 he was boldly arguing in the German courts to abolish laws that forbade consensual same-sex activity.

In 1869, Karl-Maria Kertbeny argued in a series of pamphlets that Prussian laws punishing same-sex sexual activity contradicted the "rights of man" and a natural human desire. In these pamphlets he coined the word "homosexual." The invention of this word—which quickly gained currency in European legal, cultural, and medical circles—was a turning point in American LGBT history; but it was a turning in a particular direction. "That horrible sin not to be mentioned among Christians" was given a "scientific" name that grew out of a legal reform movement. The new name emerged as the primary tool through which homosexuals in Europe would try to alleviate many of the social problems they faced.

Sexology, which emerged from the writings of Ulrichs and Kertbeny, was one of the main impetuses of the legal reform movement addressing homosexuality. This nonjudgmental science was a new way of understanding sexual desire and activity. It attempted to explain sexual desire in a variety of ways, largely as a science of taxonomy. Viewing different forms of sexuality as scientific classifications allowed reformers to claim that homosexuals must be treated as full citizens, since they were born that way.

In 1870, Ulrichs published *Araxes: A Call to Free the Nature of the Urning from Penal Law*. Using Enlightenment language, he mixes legal rhetoric about natural rights with moral arguments about the responsibilities of the state:

The Urning, too, is a person. He, too, therefore, has inalienable rights. His sexual orientation is a right established by nature. Legislators have no right to veto nature; no right to persecute nature in the course of its work; no right to torture living creatures who are subject to those drives nature gave them.

The Urning is also a citizen. He, too, has civil rights; and according to these rights, the state has certain duties to fulfill as well. The state does not have the right to act on whimsy or for the sheer love of persecution. The state is not authorized, as in the past, to treat Urnings as outside the pale of the law.[21]

The rhetoric of Ulrichs and Kertbeny is antithetical to the universality of Whitman's concept of emotional and romantic wholeness. Whitman's vision included female and male desire, but he emblematically wrote about male-male relationships as being at the core of sexualized citizenship:

Come, I will make the continent indissoluble;
I will make the most splendid race the sun ever yet shone upon;
I will make divine magnetic lands,
    With the love of comrades,
    With the life-long love of comrades.

I will plant companionship thick as trees along all the rivers of
    America, and along the shores of the great lakes, and all over
    the prairies;
I will make inseparable cities, with their arms about each other's
    necks;
    By the love of comrades,
    By the manly love of comrades.

For you these, from me, O Democracy, to serve you, ma femme!
For you! for you, I am trilling these songs,
    In the love of comrades,
    In the high-towering love of comrades.[22]

Whitman's inclusive, utopian vision was more liberating from political and legal structures and understandings than the views of Ulrich or Kertbeny, who argued for explicit legal changes. It is notable that Whitman wrote extensively about same-sex desire and garnered only a modicum of criticism. Perhaps this is because he did not use scientific terms such as "homosexual." Whitman's vision of erotic justice depended on ideas of sexual and legal equality as much as Ulrich's and Kertbeny's did, but Whitman's term "comrade," like "manly attachment" and "adhesiveness," drew on the American transcendentalist strain of individualism and freedom.

Carpenter and Symonds were also influenced by Whitman's conflation of sexual freedom and citizenship. Symonds's first major work, privately printed in 1883, was a historical analysis of same-sex male love titled *A Problem in Greek Ethics*. It was followed by a contemporary political analysis, *A Problem in Modern Ethics*, in 1891. As a critic, Symonds was interested in manifestations of same-sex desire in classical art and literature and how they could be used to argue for personal freedom under the law. Along with Symonds's work, Edward Carpenter's 1894 pamphlet *Homogenic Love and Its Place in a Free Society* and his 1908 book-length *The Intermediate Sex: A Study of Some Transitional Types of Men and Women* were fundamental in constructing a language and a mode of political thinking that would eventually form the modern LGBT movement.

Carpenter, a committed socialist, saw sex-law reform as part of a much larger project to address the social and legal inequalities faced by women, nonwhite people, the poor, prisoners, and anyone denied full citizenship. He conceptualized sexuality as a powerful, progressive political force and argued—in a clear articulation of what Melville and Stoddard demonstrated in their fiction—that same-sex desire, because of its outsider status, could help facilitate solutions for social problems. Carpenter writes in *The Intermediate Sex: A Study of Some Transitional Types of Men and Women:*

Eros is a great leveller. Perhaps the true Democracy rests, more firmly than anywhere else, on a sentiment which easily passes the bounds of class and caste, and unites in the closest affection the most estranged ranks of society. It is noticeable how often Uranians of good position and breeding are drawn to rougher types, as of manual workers, and frequently very permanent alliances grow up in this way, which although not publicly acknowledged have a decided influence on social institutions, customs and political tendencies.[23]

Carpenter's political theory of same-sex eros as a force for social equality was informed by both Whitman's poetic vision of sexual liberation and Ulrich's legal arguments. Whitman's profound impact on Carpenter and Symonds is a prime example of how American thinking about sexual freedom, intimately connected to uniquely American concepts of democracy and citizenship, influenced European political thought.

Whitman greatly influenced Carpenter and Symonds, but as famous as he was, his views on sexuality did not change America. Perhaps Whitman's liberatory philosophy was so expansive and radical that it was difficult for large numbers of people in America to accept it on its own terms. It might have been, in a counterintuitive sense, too deeply American in its view of citizenship and sexuality. Whitman himself was purposefully ambivalent. In 1889, Symonds finally, after hinting at it for years, forthrightly asked Whitman whether "comradeship" actually referred to the love between men. Whitman dodged the answer with a near-hysterical retort, claiming that such an interpretation was "terrible," "morbid," and "damnable." He went on to state, highly implausibly, that "tho' always unmarried I have had six children." While same-sex desire is articulated beautifully in his verse, Whitman could not vocalize about his own life. Perhaps he felt that his grand ideas about sexuality, citizenship, and democracy could not actually exist in an America that, even with the progress it had made, was still splintered by deep social divisions and violence.

But his ideas had other champions, such as free love advocate Victoria Woodhull, who in 1872 was the first women to run for president of the United States. Her arguments are sustained philosophical attacks against the state's regulation of sexuality and affection. In an 1871 speech cowritten with anarchist Stephen Pearl

Andrews, "And the Truth Shall Make You Free: A Speech on the Principles of Social Freedom," she states:

> Yes, I am a Free Lover. I have an inalienable, constitutional and natural right to love whom I may, to love as long or as short a period as I can; to change that love every day if I please, and with that right neither you nor any law you can frame have any right to interfere. And I have the further right to demand a free and unrestricted exercise of that right, and it is your duty not only to accord it, but as a community, to see I am protected in it. I trust that I am fully understood, for I mean just that, and nothing else.[24]

The free love movement in America tried to realize these ideas about individual freedom and freedom from the state, but could do so only within small utopian communities.

As the century was drawing to a close, tensions surrounding the question of what it meant to be an American dominated the political sphere. The devastation and trauma of the Civil War had profoundly shaped the social and political issues of the century. Ironically, the war both codified and reshaped existing gender roles, and both heightened and lessened the role of religion in public life. It made possible the Emancipation Proclamation, which freed all slaves, but also set the stage for new manifestations of the persecuting society. They would include the continued violent persecution of the descendants of the enslaved Africans—historian Sherrilyn Ifill estimates that five thousand African Americans were lynched between 1890 and 1960, over one lynching a week for sixty years—as well as a new wave of attacks on European and Asian immigrants.[25]

In the end, the Civil War maintained the Union—uniting, to use Lincoln's domestic metaphor, a "house divided against itself." But it was difficult in this context to realize a larger sense of equality, let alone liberation. America was about to enter the Progressive Era, yet in many ways its culture was to became even more divided and more persecuting as it grew.

FIVE

A DANGEROUS PURITY

THE LANGUAGE OF POLITICS

In the second half of the nineteenth century, with rapid expansion and a constant influx of immigrants, the United States was in a state of volatile change. The country was expanding, but also growing internally as people began to move to cities. The second Industrial Revolution, spurred on by enormous technological innovations—advances in the uses of electricity, the internal combustion engine, the mass manufacturing of steel, new chemical substances used to mass-produce consumer goods—created a need for a large labor force. Ten million immigrants came to America to work in factories. The wealth generated by this economic and social revolution helped create a class structure dominated by a new upper class defined by capitalist, not inherited, wealth. Its excesses and social profligacy were disparagingly labeled "the Gilded Age" by Mark Twain and Charles Dudley Warner.

The nation was now composed of people who varied in race, ethnicity, class, and identities. The making of a strong middle class allowed some economic and class mobility. This expansiveness reflected Walt Whitman's vision, posing a challenge and an opportunity for conceptualizing a similarly inclusive and American idea of sexuality.

Whitman's utopian sexual democracy was not in sync with the reform politics of late nineteenth-century America, nor was it useful for political organizing at the time. With the exception of a few progressive thinkers like Victoria Woodhull, social change movements of the nineteenth century, such as abolition and suffrage, did not consider sexual expression integral to their vision. For many women reformers, male sexuality was the problem, not the solution. The suffrage movement was focused not only on gaining women's political independence, but on reforming an economic system that required women to have sex with men, in or out of marriage, in exchange for financial support. (The struggle for suffrage ended in 1920 with the ratification of the Nineteenth Amendment.) Historian Beryl Satter notes that even progressive women "agreed with more conservative women activists that male lust damaged society, and that female virtue would improve it."[1] They saw unrestrained male desire as the cause and effect of widespread gambling, alcoholism, and prostitution, all of which threatened women's homes and families, public decency, and personal freedom. Most women reformers endorsed accepted ideas about male sexual restraint and female purity as necessary to American social progress, a concept that had roots in the Second Great Awakening of the early nineteenth century.

The social purity groups that formed in response to urban growth and new ideas of personal freedom were confronting real problems such as public violence, domestic abuse, and the abandonment of pregnant women, all of which stemmed largely from alcoholism. The Woman's Christian Temperance Union (WCTU), founded in 1874, and the Anti-Saloon League, founded in 1893, are the most famous of hundreds of groups whose efforts eventually led to Prohibition, enacted with the passage of the Eighteenth Amendment in 1919. Temperance advocates had long claimed that drinking was intimately linked to prostitution and sexual immorality. They were correct. Many saloon owners would rent rooms to prostitutes or keep brothels above their businesses. Organized prostitution was often a family business, and saloons and brothels were run by married couples.[2]

Other reformers focused more on problems in the private sphere. Early nineteenth-century diet reformist Sylvester Graham believed that alcoholism and sexual urges were brought on by unhealthy food, in particular meat and food additives. He invented healthy, or "pure," whole-grain breads and crackers designed to curb lust, particularly masturbation, which he believed contributed to blindness. At the beginning of the twentieth century, John Harvey Kellogg urged sexual abstinence and believed that "neither the plague, nor war, nor small-pox, nor similar diseases, have produced results so disastrous to humanity as the pernicious habit of onanism," by which he meant masturbation. He advocated whole grains and invented the corn flake to grapple with these urges.

These dietary theories seem quaint today. Social purity groups, however, had a tremendous effect on how America publicly conceptualized and discussed sexuality. Their work stigmatized certain forms of sexual expression well into the twentieth century. The social purity movement continued a line of thought that traces back to the Puritans' entrenchment of individual restraint and persecution as values fundamental to their vision of a "city upon a hill." Traditional Christianity taught that reproduction was the only rationale for sexual activity and that all nonreproductive sexuality was sinful. There was little theoretical difference, in this thinking, between same-sex and different-sex oral and anal intercourse. Separation of sexuality from reproduction struck at the heart of how society was organized and threatened social progress.

The tension between securing personal freedom for individuals and the social purity movement's desire to protect people was strongest in urban areas. The economic, religious, and individual freedoms that many in the United States valued were most often found in cities. The everyday public life of cities, often rowdy and unpredictable, created new and conflicting value systems. These often centered on issues of employment, living arrangements, dining, same-gender and different-gender socializing, entertainment, and appropriate dress, demeanor, and manners. Women and men who were concerned about morality increasingly saw cities as centers of sin, drinking, drug use, sexuality, and general unhealthiness. They were not necessarily wrong. In the mid to late nineteenth century—when tenements and apartment buildings were rapidly being built and single-family homes were being converted to rooming houses to accommodate the mass influx of single women and men—it was nearly impossible to distinguish brothels from boardinghouses. Even the New York City census stopped trying; in the 1850s it had listed the city's most noted brothels, but by the late 1870s they were identified simply as rooming houses.[3]

Social reformers wanted to broadly and publicly address what they saw as dangerous immorality. The best way for them to do that was through the law. In 1873 Anthony Comstock, a member of the National Purity Party and a United States postal inspector, founded the New York Society for the Suppression of Vice, which continued until the 1940s. It was the prototype for similar organizations, such as Boston's Watch and Ward Society, founded in 1878 (and active in suppressing books until the 1950s). These groups advocated legal censorship to improve public morality. In 1874 Comstock successfully lobbied for a federal law, the Comstock Act, that banned from the U.S. mail "obscene, lewd, or lascivious" material, which included some anatomy books as well as all birth control and sex education material.

Over the next three decades, hundreds of similar social purity groups formed, including the Union for Concerted Moral Effort (founded in 1891), the National Union for Practical Progress (founded in 1894), the American Purity Alliance (founded in 1895), and the National Congress of Mothers (founded in 1897). Although these groups were concerned with a wide range of topics, their most vocal pronouncements were often on issues of "dangerous" sexuality, such as prostitution, nonmarital sex, and masturbation. The statement of principles for the Union for Concerted Moral Effort argued that "recognizing the moral law as the supreme law of the universe, we believe that its supremacy should be enforced in all of the affairs of life."[4] Mrs. Anna Rice Powell of the American Purity Alliance wrote in 1896:

> While our first active efforts were directed against the legalization of vice, it soon became apparent that this was but a symptom of a deep seated disease in the body politic, which could not be cured without constitutional treatment; and that the people must be made to feel the need for it.[5]

Along with banning gambling and lotteries as harmful to the home, these groups lobbied to criminalize prostitution, remove paintings of nudes from saloons, ban books with immoral content, and censor objectionable material in stage plays, music halls, and the newly emerging motion pictures. Satter points out that members of social purity groups were deeply suspicious of most new forms of communication technology, even newspapers, which would "'daily enter the home' [and] would plant the 'first seeds of morbid desire and impure sentiment' in innocent minds."[6] They argued that children were at great risk and required proper moral guidance and protection from harm, including being shielded from harmful images and suggestions that would stunt their growth into mature, moral, heterosexual adults. Charles Loring Brace, who founded the Children's Aid Society in 1853 to help place abandoned and vagrant youth in new families, did so because he worried that "homeless boys and newsboys waste their time going to theaters."[7]

The protection of the home was paramount for the social purity reformers. The home and motherhood were sacred and profoundly necessary for the construction of a pure society. Lucinda Banister Chandler, founder of the Moral Education Society of Boston, was a popular thinker and writer whose pamphlets "A Mother's Aid" and "The Divineness of Marriage" were significant in shaping social purity thought. In "Motherhood, Its Power over Human Destiny" she writes, concerned about expectant women reading debased literature, that moral and physical "deformities" of children were the result of the pregnant mother experiencing "polluting intrusions."[8]

Social purity groups' history and philosophy linked them to other reform movements. Almost all supported women's suffrage, and many were part of the abolition movement. Yet each of these movements was different, and eventually they had conflicting goals. The social purity groups, for example, were predicated on social control, while the abolition and women's suffrage movements were overtly liberatory. Many women and men lived with contradictions between the ideas and goals of the multiple movements to which they belonged.

As misguided as many of the social purity groups' actions seem to us now, they—as much as the abolitionists—were trying to create a just society. Unfortunately, their basic assumptions about desire and gender, as well as their actions, did more harm than good.

CONCEPTUALIZING RESISTANCE: LABOR, RACE, AND SEX

As new social opportunities opened up in America in the decades after the Civil War, women and men had access to new pleasures. New ways of thinking about sexuality and gender informed all parts of their lives. Their political thinking shaped their discussions and approaches to sexuality. In the Gilded Age of urban influx, newly freed African Americans, and a growing middle class, social and sexual beliefs were tied to socioeconomic status. While the social purity reformers were battling what they saw as a crisis in public morality, the last two decades of the nineteenth century also witnessed the rise of labor organizing to combat the horrific conditions in factories and mines.

Beginning in the 1890s, labor organizer Mary Harris Jones, known as Mother Jones, fought for workplace safety, a fair wage, and humane working hours. She did not support suffrage, since she saw it as an upper-class women's concern and thought more attention should be paid to the lives of poor women. The labor movement, less concerned about a woman's proper place in society, was deeply committed to gender issues in the workplace. Famous for her fiery speaking, Mother Jones raged in a 1910 speech about the treatment of young women who worked as "slaves" in the Milwaukee breweries:

> The foreman on those breweries regulates the time, even, that the girls may stay in the toilet room, and in the event of overstaying it gives him the opportunity he seems to be looking for, to indulge in indecent and foul language. . . .
>
> While the wage paid is 75 and 85 cents a day, the poor slaves are not permitted to work more than three or four days a week, and the continual threat of idle days makes the slaves much more tractable and submissive.[9]

Jones and other labor organizers, many of whom were women, were interested in empowering women, not protecting them—a position that struck at the heart of the social purity movement's ideas about womanhood and domesticity.

While both the labor and social purity groups were abolition-ist, there were disagreements on race politics. Many people in the social purity movement were wedded to a model of racial purity that placed the "white race" above all others. They imagined the dangers of race and sex to be strikingly similar. Often they linked nonwhite races to sexual impurity and immoral sexual behaviors, including unrestrained sexual desire, rape, and "unspeakable acts" (a euphe-mism for same-sex sexual activity). Racial purity was intrinsic to their quest for purifying American culture and ensuring their class status.

M. Carey Thomas—who was passionately involved with women her entire adult life and who, as president of Bryn Mawr, profoundly shaped women's education in the United States—believed in white racial superiority. She refused to allow any Jewish faculty mem-bers at the school and frequently questioned the ability of nonwhite people to be educated. Frances Willard, also involved in passionate female-female relationships, voiced sentiments indicative of social purity politics in an 1890 newspaper column about temperance, Northern immigration, and race in the South:

> I think we have wronged the South, though we did not mean to do so. The reason was, in part, that we had irreparably wronged ourselves by putting no safeguard on the ballot-box at the North that would sift out alien illiterates. They rule our cities to-day; the saloon is their palace, and the toddy stick their sceptre. It is not fair that they should vote, nor is it fair that a plantation negro, who can neither read nor write, whose ideas are bounded by the fence of his own field and the price of his own mule, should be entrusted with the ballot. . . . The Anglo-Saxon race will never submit to be dominated by the negro so long as his altitude reaches no higher than the personal liberty of the saloon.[10]

Willard's words did not go uncontested. Ida B. Wells, the African American activist who was a central leader in antilynching cam-paigns of the time, accused the temperance leader of "condoning fraud, violence, murder, at the ballot box; rapine, shooting, hanging, and burning; for all these things are done and being done now by the Southern white people."[11]

Wells was decisive in exposing the murderous physical reality that logically resulted from Willard's political principles. Her words also highlight how the tension between progressive reform and the social purity movement continued to yoke together race and sex as the battlefield on which an American sexuality was defined. In *The Souls of Black Folk* (1903), his defining look at race relations in the United States, W. E. B. Du Bois stated that "the problem of the Twentieth Century is the problem of color line." The problem of the color line had always been intertwined with the problems of sexuality and gender.

The African American and newly identified "homosexual" communities were shaped, in part, in reaction to mainstream oppressive ideologies predicated on ideas about social purity. The terms "homosexual" and "heterosexual," which emerged from the European medical-legal discourse, had a firmer claim on the public discourse and imagination than did Whitman's "comrade." They fit perfectly into the social purity movement's increasingly pseudo-scientific thinking that negatively categorized groups and behavior. Jonathan Ned Katz documents how the American medical establishment quickly used these new ideas to pathologize and further criminalize women and men who engaged in same-sex sexual activity.

The word "homosexual" was first used in the United States in an 1892 article by Dr. James G. Kiernan, a noted Chicago neurologist, in which he stated that homosexuals were persons whose "general mental state is that of the opposite sex." Later in the article he discussed two cases of women murdering their lovers:

> Sexual pervert crimes of all types are likely to increase, because of newspaper agitation of the subject, among hysterical females, from a desire to secure the notoriety dear to the hysteric heart. All such cases should be carefully scrutinized, and the mere existence of the alleged perversion should never be admitted as proof of irresponsibility. . . . Each case should be tried on its own merits, and the exact mental state of the accused determined.[12]

Kiernan's article was followed by many others on the subject of homosexuality. Kiernan's messages are mixed: homosexuality is linked to crime, but it may not be the cause of the crime. Cultural historian Lisa Duggan analyzes the racializing of sexuality in one of the cases Kiernan discussed. She traces the practice of lynching to institutionalized violence against perceived deviance from traditional gender and sexual roles.

In 1893 Dr. F. E. Daniel, editor of *The Texas Medical Journal*, gave a speech, later reprinted multiple times, titled "Should Insane Criminals or Sex Perverts Be Permitted to Procreate?" He argued that it is more humane to castrate sex criminals than to execute them or spend public money on imprisonment.[13] This reasoning is a logical outcome of the social purity movement's desire to curb all forms of lust and restructure society on an ideal of sexual and reproductive purity. Daniel explicitly placed his arguments in the context of creating a "sanitary utopia" based on both purity and applied eugenics, a theory and practice of the late nineteenth and early twentieth centuries designed to improve society through elective human reproduction.

The "sanitary utopia" of the social purists was the nightmarish opposite of the utopian visions of the more radical strands of the labor movement and the African American civil rights movement. All three emerged in response to the circumstances of mid-nineteenth-century America. The latter two embraced two different political languages, both of which stood in stark opposition to the ideology of social purity. Some labor organizers embraced anarchism, a wide-ranging political philosophy that espoused, as an alternative to government, the option of self-regulation by citizens. Most African Americans, however, sought more protection from the state against lynching and other forms of racial violence. They also looked for more inclusion in the state to attain equal status with white people.

A similar divide can be seen in the struggle of same-sex-desiring people: the broad project of sexual liberation (which would free people from the bonds of sexual repression) and the legal reform movements (which would fight to change laws that prohibit or repress certain sexual acts, behaviors, or identities). The decisive difference between the two political philosophies affected how Americans constructed political movements concerning sexuality, especially homo-sexuality. The stark difference between them is evident in two major political events that occurred at the end of the nineteenth century: the 1886 Haymarket riot and the Supreme Court case *Plessy v. Ferguson*. Each event would have political reverberations throughout the twentieth century.

In May 1886, labor organizers planned a week of national rallies in major cities to support the eight-hour work day. (At the time, workers were expected to be on the job a minimum of twelve hours a day.) At least 400,000 women, men, and children went on strike or marched. Most of the rallies were peaceful, but in Chicago, police shot and killed two workers at a local factory. The next day, labor supporters met in Chicago's Haymarket Square to protest police violence. During the rally, a pipe bomb was thrown at police officers, who then shot into the crowd. Chaos ensued, leaving eight dead. Eight anarchists were arrested for murder; four were hanged. The case, now considered a miscarriage of justice, created an international furor. It became a symbol of state suppression of legitimate political activism and a rallying cry for grassroots organizing.

In 1892 Homer Plessy, with the support of the Committee of Citizens, an all-black New Orleans group that promoted racial justice, refused to sit in the "colored" car of the East Louisiana Railroad. In a 7–1 decision handed down in *Plessy v. Ferguson* on May 18, 1896, the Supreme Court affirmed racial segregation in the United States through the concept of "separate but equal." This decision reaffirmed the concept, embedded in slavery, that certain classes of individuals did not have complete equality under the rule of law. Plessy's actions and the ensuing court case were a harbinger of the future use of civil disobedience to resist unlawful authority, as well as of the limits of the legal system.

The Haymarket incident and the Plessy case illustrate two fundamental American models for organized political resistance. The labor movement's model of organizing is grassroots based and relies on challenging state authority with demands for justice. (The violence at the Chicago rally was not part of this model; it was initiated by the police.) This model functions outside of the accepted, legally sanctioned social and judicial system; it claims its authority in a code of ethics based on human dignity and the innate worth of the individual. In 1984 Audre Lorde, a black lesbian feminist theorist and poet, would state this idea as "the master's tools will never dismantle the master's house." The second model of resistance, as seen in *Plessy v. Ferguson*, is predicated in the belief that the existing system can fix itself when challenged through proper channels of social or legal appeal. It acknowledges, however, that the existing system is often constructed to avoid such appeals, and allows for breaking the law—Henry David Thoreau's concept of civil disobedience—in order to correct the injustices. Although Plessey's civil disobedience was effective in bringing the case to court, it would not be until 1954, in *Brown v. Board of Education*, that the Supreme Court outlawed segregation.

These alternative models have been the bedrock for the LGBT liberation and equal rights movements that began to come into existence in 1950. The structures of racial prejudice and resistance to racism have profoundly shaped how Americans have conceptualized and responded to most problems of social inequality. In this context, questions of sexuality and gender inequality have been fitted into paradigms created to understand racial prejudice. The movement to free homosexuals from oppression has become predominantly a legal, rights-based movement. This approach has largely eclipsed the idea of a sexual liberation movement and narrowed its vision to a simple struggle for legal equality.

Many American anarchist theorists, including Emma Goldman, Alexander Berkman, Ben Reitman, Benjamin Tucker, and Leonard Abbott—all of whom drew inspiration from Whitman—were in the forefront of addressing the role of sexuality in U.S. society as a political issue. They believed that it was unethical for the state to have any role in personal affairs. Benjamin Tucker wrote in his 1895 *State Socialism and Anarchism* that anarchists "acknowledge and defend the right of any man and woman, or men and women, to love each other for as long or as short a time as they can, will, or may. To them legal marriage and legal divorce are equal absurdities."[14] Tucker's ideas dovetail with those of Victoria Woodhull. According to Terence Kissack, Tucker believed that "anarchists look upon attempts to arbitrarily suppress vice as themselves crimes."[15]

Emma Goldman wrote several times about homosexuality. Here she describes a conversation with Dr. Eugene Schmidt in Paris in 1900:

> I told the doctor of the indignation I had felt at the [1895] conviction of Oscar Wilde. I had pleaded his case against the miserable hypocrites who had sent him to his doom. "You!" the doctor exclaimed in astonishment, "why, you must have been a mere youngster then. How did you dare come out in public for Oscar Wilde in puritan America?" "Nonsense!" I replied; "no daring is required to protest against a great injustice."[16]

Margaret Anderson, who with her lover Jane Heap edited the experimental literary journal *The Little Review,* was a close friend of Goldman's in the mid-teens. Anderson suggested that, as historian Margaret Marsh puts it, "homosexuality might be a more normal form of sexual behavior than heterosexuality" and that "she and her friends represented the link between the anarchist-feminist idea of sexual liberation as one component . . . of a society of freely cooperating individuals."[17]

These anarchist writings about homosexuality are a radical break from most thinking in the late nineteenth and early twentieth centuries. They argue that sexuality is natural and positive, that sex can be solely about pleasure and, if consensual, should not be the subject of any laws. These basic precepts about sexuality, and homosexuality, that are present today in the LGBT movement—both its liberatory and civil rights sides—find their roots in anarchist thinking.

The labor movement profoundly influenced the LGBT movement by conceptualizing workers not as individuals, but as a class of people who are treated unjustly. The early labor organizations—in particular the Industrial Workers of the World, also known as the Wobblies, which had over one million members in 1923—conceptualized a worldwide movement based on identity and group status. This concept is the historical basis for the thinking of Harry Hay (whose membership in the Wobblies was formative to his political education) when he founded the Mattachine Society, an early homosexual rights group, in 1950.

Comparisons of other political movements to the LGBT movement are always inexact. Homosexuals are not a specific racial or ethnic group. They are not a class bound by a type of employment or harmed by a similar economic injustice. In organizing politically, homosexuals predicate their group status on a presumption of shared injustice. As individuals, their experiences are so varied that any all-encompassing type of organizing is difficult or inapplicable. In many ways the LGBT movement is unique; it is able to draw upon, but not totally conform to, other forms of political organizing.

THE POLITICS OF LANGUAGE

If the nascent LGBT movement was to organize itself and be taken seriously by the law, it needed language with authority. Anarchists understood the power of words. In the 1880s Angela and Ezra Heywood, who published the free love journal the *Word*, argued that the use of plain Anglo-Saxon words such as "cock," "cunt," and "fuck" would demystify sexuality, reduce individual shame, and liberate women. (In 1873 Ezra Haywood had been sentenced to prison for using the U.S. Postal Service to mail copies of his free love pamphlet *Cupid's Yokes*.)[18] This political position was antithetical to the social purity movement, which sought to suppress sexual speech.

In the midst of these extremes, the new discipline of sexology gained authority through language. (Sexology was, to some degree, an extension of the Enlightenment's desire to prove everything rationally.) The scientific discovery of "homosexuality" generated language that promoted more open discussion about the subject. Ironically, it immediately led to a clear articulation of negative stereotypes about homosexuals. For the first time in U.S. history, same-sex-desiring people could now feel diseased.

The most common sexological theory of same-sex desire was that it was the result of physical, emotional, or psychological "inversion." In other words, the gender of persons who desired their own sex was somehow reversed. When a man desired a man, it was actually a woman—presumably existing within the man's body—who was desiring a man. When a woman desired a woman, it was actually a male essence within the woman's body who felt that desire.

This metaphysical explanation, accepted as scientific (at this point of the emergence of psychology as a science), had a substantial effect on the public imagination for the next fifty years. It became how many people understood the phenomenon of same-sex desire. Theories of inversion were published widely, and sexologists were understood by the average person to be the experts on a "new science." The idea of the "invert," or "third sex," also quickly and profoundly informed two popular and lasting stereotypes: the mannish lesbian and the effeminate homosexual man. (Although there were preexisting stereotypes of the effeminate male, sexological taxonomy invented him as a *homosexual* man.)

Anthropologist Esther Newton notes that the concept of the masculine woman who loves other women made emotional sense to both homosexuals and heterosexuals, because it played into the popular idea that if sexual desire is masculine, then a woman who desires a woman must be mannish.[19] Lillian Faderman argues that the mannish lesbian was a break from the concept of romantic friendship, because her masculinity gave her access to sexuality. This new step in how mainstream culture understood sexual attraction between women made the concept of the romantic friendship—so integral to personal and social acceptance of both female and male same-sex relationships—impossible.[20] The mannish lesbian was also used in the popular imagination to "explain," as well as demonize, the new twentieth-century woman who was active in the public sphere, including the suffragette. The mannish lesbian was not, however, conflated with the well-known concept of the "passing woman"—a woman who dressed to pass as a man, like the Civil War soldiers—which was understood as a masquerade, not an identity.

The early sexologists created a space for homosexuals to tell their stories. This new form of "scientific" autobiography allowed women and men to clearly describe their sexual histories. The following autobiography of a patient was included in "Sexual Crimes," an 1894 article by Charles Gilbert Chaddock, a leading American neurologist:

The knowledge that I am so unlike others makes me very miserable. I form no acquaintances outside of business, keep mostly to myself, and . . . do not indulge my sexual feelings . . . . I do not want to create the impression that my feelings for my own sex are weak, for they are strong; but I have heretofore had sufficient will-power to restrain them. . . . My desire . . . has always been to handle the genitals of those for whom I feel affection and to have them do the same to me.[21]

The existence of forthright personal narratives that overtly admitted to same-sex desire was a major advance toward a public homosexual identity. The link between medical discourse and openly pro-homosexual literature is clear in this excerpt from Edward Prime-Stevenson's 1906 *Imre: A Memorandum*. Prime-Stevenson wrote the novel under the pseudonym Xavier Mayne and had it privately printed in Naples. Here Oswald, the main character, tells his life story to his lover:

From the time when I was lad . . . I felt myself unlike other boys in one element of my nature. That one matter was my special sense, my passion for the beauty, the dignity, the charm, the—what shall I say—the loveableness of my own sex. I hid it, at least so far as, little by little, I came to realize its force. For, I soon perceived that most other lads had no such passional sentiments.[22]

In his widely read 1912 *Prison Memoirs of an Anarchist*, Alexander Berkman, who was Emma Goldman's lover, offers an example of how same-sex desire need not be explained through sexological language. In the book, he wrote at length about male homosexuality in prison. His series of portraits of intensely emotional male-male relationships, some of which include sexual intimacy, are extraordinary for the time. In the chapter "Passing the Love of Woman" (the title is a common literary reference to the relationship between the biblical David and Jonathan and to male homosexuality), after Berkman relates his own experience of a passionate male-male friendship, a friend and fellow prisoner named George tells Berkman about his relationship with a younger man:

> For two years I loved him without the least taint of sex desire. It was the purest affection I ever felt in my life. It was all-absorbing, and I would have sacrificed my life for him if he had asked it. But by degrees the psychic stage began to manifest all the expressions of love between the opposite sexes. I remember the first time he kissed me. . . . Never in my life had I experienced such bliss as at that moment. It's five years ago, but it thrills me every time I think of it. . . . From then on we became lovers.[23]

Berkman's *Memoirs* brought anarchist theories, as well as radical sexual ideas, to a wide range of readers. Unlike others who wrote about sexuality at the time, Berkman explicitly discussed the reality and importance of masturbation. His was also one of the first books to discuss the homosexual behavior of young men, who as a group would not be acknowledged until later in the century.

True-life accounts could easily reinforce ideas about gender and defined categories of sexual orientation. *Autobiography of an Androgyne* was a 1919 memoir by Earl Lind, who also called himself Ralph Werther and went by the name Jennie June when dressed as a woman. In this remarkable book, the author understands his condition as being congenital:

> As to my own feminine characteristics, I have been told by my intimate associates from boyhood down to my middle forties—when this book goes to press—that I markedly resemble a female physically, besides having instinctive gestures, poses, and habits that are characteristically feminine. My schoolmates said that I would make a good-looking girl and that kissing me was "as good as kissing a girl."[24]

Lind identifies himself as a "fairie," an "invert," a "homosexual," and an "androgyne" and compares himself to the Sleeping Hermaphrodite, the famous Greek sculpture that inspired Julia Ward

Howe's *The Hermaphrodite*. But in contrast to Howe's use of the image, which opened up an imaginative and expansive space for being sexual, Lind's use was based in a scientific typology that medicalized his sexuality. For the time, Lind's medicalization of himself was extreme: in his early thirties he had his testes removed because he feared that his "emissions" were causing him health problems.

Sexology generated a broad-based public discussion about the need for sex education and legal birth control, both of which helped bring reproductive choices to women. It is not a coincidence that the emergence of an affirming, clearly defined homosexual identity coincided with social changes that gave women freedom over their bodies. The connection between the advance of widespread sex education and birth control and the acceptance of homosexuality was clear to Mary Casal. Her 1930 autobiography (which describes events three decades earlier), *The Stone Wall*, is one of the few written accounts by a lesbian in the early twentieth century:

> People are now daring to talk about birth control, and important provisions are being made for the execution of such methods. . . . There is no suffering comparable to unsatisfied sex desire, not any condition that brings about such dire results. . . . The time is coming when a man's love for a man and a woman's love for a woman will be studied and understood as it never has been in the past.[25]

The dissemination of information about sexuality and reproduction, almost all of which was in a heterosexual context, was an important development in a culture in which sexuality had not been discussed openly. The emergence of a homosexual identity that increasingly refused criminalization and discrimination—what Prime-Stevenson called "any intelligent civilization's disrespect"—related directly to the newly emerging reproductive rights movement. Both embodied a social ideal that reflected the integrity of the human body and the integral importance of sexuality to the citizen. Most important was the radical idea, literally embodied in homosexual activity, that sex and reproduction can be completely separate, that sex can be enjoyed without the fear of pregnancy.

This distinction between sexual activity, pleasure, and reproduction threatened the social purity advocates, who prized motherhood and the family. Ironically, even those who advocated sexual freedom were often not immune to social purity ideology. Margaret Sanger, for instance, who was highly influential in forging a national movement for birth control and family planning, held racist, eugenicist views about nonwhite people. And while a firm believer in women controlling their bodies, she was not a sexual liberationist. She believed that "every normal man and woman has the power to control and direct his sexual impulse. Men and woman who have it in control and constantly use their brain cells thinking deeply, are never sensual."[26] Like the staunchest advocates of the social purity movement, she was against masturbation, which she saw as a "revolting disease." And physical masturbation was not the only menace:

> In the boy or girl past puberty we find one of the most danger-ous forms of masturbation, i.e., mental masturbation, which consists of forming mental pictures, or thinking of obscene or voluptuous pictures. This form is considered especially harm-ful to the brain, for the habit becomes so fixed that it is almost impossible to free the thoughts from lustful pictures.[27]

Sanger's views on masturbation, seemingly at odds with her more progressive stands on sexuality, were intimately connected with the gradual formation of a "pure" race through eugenic practices. Sanger's objection arose from her claim that masturbation can, especially for women, be physically addictive and replace sexual intercourse, thus harming the chances of genitally sound and racially pure reproduction.

The emergence of sexology as a public way of discussing sexuality increased the anxiety about the rise of urban culture. Moral guides for young women and men were increasingly popular at the turn of the century, when many youths were moving to cities. Such guides were often published by church groups, with a religious message complementing the sex advice. They turned sex education into sex regulation. Their messages echoed social purity ideologies about what made sexuality dangerous: women were susceptible to it, and men were irresponsible with it. (Implicit in these warnings was that sex was dangerous for women because it "ruined" them for marriage, which was the only condition within which they could survive economically.) These books, while concerned with the dangers of intemperate drinking, gambling, public dancing, and music halls, were often obsessed with sex.

The 1929 *Helps to Purity: A Frank, Yet Reverent Introduction on the Intimate Matters of Personal Life for Adolescent Girls* by Rev. Fulgence Meyer, OFM, was explicit in its warnings against masturbation. Meyer noted that "this unnatural and abominable sin of self-abuse is committed by a girl when she voluntarily excites and stimulates her sexual nature in a degree to bring on complete sexual satisfaction." He went on to note that "sexual gratification is allowed only in the virtuous sexual conduct between husband and wife" and that "sinful lovemaking, or. . . immodest touches by oneself or another, of the same of the opposite sex, or even of animals, or by some other unjustified method, is always a mortal sin."[28] Meyer was careful to stipulate that immodest actions are possible with either the same or the opposite sex, indicating that the possibility of homosexual behavior was commonplace and easily articulated by religious instructors.

Medically based marriage guides of the early twentieth century, such as the 1926 best seller *The Doctor Looks at Love and Life* by Joseph Collins, MD, gave similar messages. Collins was in favor of less sexual repression and rejected religious morality in favor of scientific fact. He was sympathetic to the struggles women faced, arguing that the "problem" of frigidity may well be caused by male selfishness. He also viewed "natural homosexuals"—those born that way—as "victims of fate," but his arguments were complicated:

> There are many persons who indulge in unnatural sexual relations who are not homosexuals. They are the real degenerates. There are many potential and actual homosexuals whose intercourse with persons of their own sex is confined to emotional and intellectual contacts. . . . They are not degenerates. . . . They are victims of Fate, the only ones who do not

excite our compassion; and all because we cannot distinguish
between the work of God and Satan.[29]

In contrast to men, women, in Collins's view, more often fell into
homosexuality through "bad habits, kisses, embraces, tender inti-
macies, feeblemindedness and evil companionship."[30] Echoing the
earlier religious instruction books and their concerns about leisure
time, Collins believed that homosexuality in women "flows from
idleness, boredom and loneliness, and its victims are as a rule un-
der- or oversexed."[31] Despite his relative (for the time) tolerance,
he ultimately believed that "we should rid ourselves of the notion
that we are the keepers of the natural homosexual, but we should
hearten ourselves to prevent and cure those who accidentally or
deliberately acquire vicious sexual habits."[32] Collins devoted forty
pages to discussing homosexuality, an indication of its importance
in 1920s culture.

Marriage manuals were best sellers because the average American wanted to read and think about sexuality. Americans discovered
that the changes wrought by the sexology movements allowed them
to have discussions not possible before. Changes in book distribution, the low cost of mass book production, and increasing literacy
rates made this information easily accessible to a huge, diverse readership. Not all Americans could agree on the specifics of sex education, but most agreed that the topic should be discussed. As Estelle
Freedman and John D'Emilio point out, "[B]y the 1920s circumstances were present to encourage acceptance of the modern idea
that sexual expression was of overarching importance to individual
happiness."[33]

This "modern idea" was antithetical to the social purity movement, since one person's sexual expression was another's mortal sin.
The vision of social purity was fueled mainly by women and men
who were attempting to gain full citizenship for women through
suffrage and other reforms. Some, such as Frances Willard, had lives
centered on other women. Unfortunately, this vision was essentially
denying full citizenship to others, especially racial minorities. The
social purity movement also reinforced social standards that were
directly antithetical to sexual freedom and directly harmful to many

women and men who desired their own sex. These standards, predicated on traditional heterosexual ideals of gender, were written into laws clearly delineating what was legally pure and impure. That was the language of politics. The politics of language, in contrast, allowed for an individual interpretation that was not based on absolutes. People wanted to read about sex so that they could imagine, in private, their sexual lives. This was the underlying fear about masturbation and its connection to sexual fantasies.

The articulation of sexual desire was the first step in building a consciously constructed community of individuals who desired others of their own sex. The hope for this community is expressed implicitly in the patient's story from Chaddock's "Sexual Crimes" article and explicitly in Prime-Stevenson's novel *Imre*. In both instances, the narrator's identity radically changes when he realizes that he is not alone in the world. The attraction of reading such material in private was similar to the attraction single people had to cities in which they could find freedom. Aided by cities and the imagination, this sense of individual freedom would complicate the divide between public and private and blur the line between purity and danger.

SIX

LIFE ON THE STAGE/LIFE IN THE CITY

As early as 1802, Washington Irving noted that American theater "promoted flirtatious fantasies for all."[1] He might have added that such fantasies were the root of both social change and social discord. This deep sense of disruption inherent to fantasy was the greatest fear of many in the social purity movement. Fantasies might never come to light, but fantasy—or more broadly, desire—was impossible to police; it existed mainly unseen.

Public entertainment—including the "legitimate" stage, as well as burlesque, vaudeville, nickelodeons, movie theaters, and other amusements—was understood by many public moralists to be an environment of sexual promiscuity, criminal activity, and gambling. The impulse to prohibit theatrical productions has a long, and largely unsuccessful, history in the United States; Samuel Adams believed the theater weakened civil and personal virtue and argued vigorously to ban theaters in Boston in the late eighteenth century. The accelerated growth of urban theatrical venues in the early decades of the twentieth century reignited this impulse. The association between prostitution and the theater was strong, as were the connections between theaters and sites of both street- and residence-based prostitution. The reality was that some actors were prostitutes, and theater culture often had its own standards of personal and sexual morality.

For public moralists, the problem was not just that theaters bred immorality and crime, but that they let the imagination flourish. The theater was a central form of entertainment in urban areas and provided titillating alternatives to traditional ideas about gender and sexuality. This had been true for decades. In the early 1860s, poet and actor Adah Isaacs Menken, a Jewish convert of African American and Creole parentage who was a close friend of Walt Whitman's and had both female and male lovers, became internationally infamous when she took the lead role in *Mazeppa*. At the show's climax, Menken, playing a young man, appeared mostly undressed and rode a live horse across the stage. Menken was a prototype of the socially dangerous "unruly woman" who refused to conform to accepted norms of gender and sexuality.[2] By the late 1860s, British dancer and performer Lydia Thompson's troupe, the Blondes, brought *Ixion,* a parody spectacle of Greek myths and contemporary politics that featured highly sexualized female cross-dressing, to New York. The show caused an enormous stir when it influenced middle-class women to dye their hair blonde, a drastic violation of social norms.

Menken and Thompson were important precursors to twentieth-century theater's evolving identity of the "invert" and the homosexual. Kirsten Pullen suggests that Thompson, wearing tights, a corset, and short pants, "talked like a man but walked like a woman. She was neither male nor female, but in the words of William Dean Howells, 'an alien sex parodying both.'"[3] Such a description parallels the medical discourse of sexology in the early years of the twentieth century: these performers have "inverted" the sexes.

For social moralists, the theater promoted instability and immorality by allowing deviations from sexual and gender norms to materialize on the stage. The tremendous growth of theater culture in cities aggravated this threat. As gender bending became common on the stage, the sheer theatricality of the inversion made it, as Howells states, a parody: rather than reinforce sexology's negative view of the "third sex," the theater destabilized and even normalized it. Homosexual audiences, who understood both the threat of the "inverted" image and how the parody operated, could appreciate the performance as both.

This complicated social interaction must be understood in two contexts. Urban demographics were changing; in a departure from the rural ideal of the extended family, cities now included increasingly large numbers of single women and men. And the entertainments presented in theaters and in films were undergoing major changes in content—changes that made Adah Menken and Lydia Thompson look tame and unthreatening.

ALONE TOGETHER IN THE BIG CITY

The growth of American cities in the early twentieth century intricately shaped the development of the homosexual community and individual's lives by radically altering female and male gender roles and sexual behaviors. Until now, the heterosexual family unit, even in an urban environment, had been viewed as the standard. Unmarried people of all ages resided, and functioned economically, with their biological families. As the United States shifted from an agricultural economy to one predicated on industry and a service economy, many young women and men left small towns and farms to look for work and a new life in cities. The rise of communities of single women and men presented new models of how individual's lives might be led. It also generated new structural models of public socializing that had an enormous impact on urban culture.

This paradigm shift in American culture had a major effect. A society that defined the ideal relationship—and the only proper, moral sexual relationship—as reproductively heterosexual within legal marriage now had to come to grips with the reality that other life arrangements were possible and increasingly prevalent. Indeed, nonmarried single-gender groups were creating spaces and situations that concretely led to the formation of communities of people who sexually desired their own sex. They often identified themselves as such and built a visible culture around these spaces.

The sheer number of single men and women during this time illustrates their potential impact on urban life. In 1890, single men in Chicago numbered 170,571. Of these, 151,362 were between the ages of fifteen and thirty-four. A similar situation existed in Boston, which had 74,112 bachelors; 63,031 of them were aged fifteen to thirty-four. Thirty years later, these communities were much larger: single men in Chicago numbered 362,178, of whom 287,796 were between fifteen and thirty-four; Boston had 111,245 single men, of whom 97,845 were between fifteen and thirty-four.[4] The figures for single women living in cities were also high. In 1910, 24.8 percent of Chicago women aged twenty-five to thirty-four were unmarried; in Boston the figure was 38.9 percent.[5]

While cities had always provided living accommodations for the unmarried, the new wave of single people—many of whom had immigrated to cities from rural areas—mandated many more. The options included boarding with a family and sharing a life with them, living in a boardinghouse that provided meals, or renting a room, or even just a bed, in a rooming house in which food was not served. Large cities such as New York also saw the construction of apartment buildings designed especially for unmarried people.

Work spaces were often segregated by gender, and so were living conditions. Working women, even with lower-middle-income salaries, also had the option of single-gender residential hotels. (There were mixed-gender residential hotels as well.) By 1915, there were fifty-four women's residences in New York City run by nonprofit organizations, some housing up to one hundred women.[6] The advantage of these arrangements was that women were freed from the traditional "woman's work" of shopping, cooking, laundry, and often even cleaning. In the 1930s two-thirds of the women living in the city's residential hotels were single.[7]

While most of these residences catered to middle- and lower-middle-class women and men, all cities contained much cheaper lodgings for men who had extremely low-wage jobs or worked only occasionally. These cheap lodging houses, sometimes called flophouses, were usually located in poor parts of a city. In 1915, an area of only a few blocks in San Francisco's South of Market area housed over forty thousand male workers.[8]

There were also single-gender organizations such as the Young Men's Christian Association. Founded in Great Britain in 1845, its mission was to provide not only inexpensive rooms and food, but the moral instruction and wholesome companionship that a young man away from his Christian home would need to combat the corrupting influence of the city. Because the mind, soul, and body were viewed as one, moral instruction was often instilled through physical exercise, which was almost always done in groups and included nude swimming. The first YMCA in the United States was built in Boston in 1851. The organization's growth was so rapid that by 1940 there were a hundred thousand YMCA rooms (often with beds for two or more men) throughout America.

The Young Women's Christian Association, founded in Great Britain in 1853 and incorporated in the United States in 1907, provided similar residences for women. In the early decades of the century, the YWCA also provided employment bureaus and job counseling. As was true of most housing in the United States at the time, YMCAs and YWCAs were racially segregated. Both organizations ended their national policy of segregation in 1946, but desegregation was not implemented on all local levels until the 1970s.

While the ideals of the YMCA emphasized individual moral uplift, other reform movements focused on the collective. Feminist social activists in the settlement house movement were intent on constructing communities that placed the power of the individual in the wider realm of social change. The settlement house movement, founded in London, aimed to bring together middle-class and lower-income people in an urban group-living situation. Settlement houses attempted to build community in working-class neighborhoods, providing lodging, meals, adult and child education, exercise, and cultural programs. They also prioritized the sharing of knowledge and skills among their residents and the community.

Jane Addams and her companion Ellen Gates Starr founded Hull House, the first U.S. settlement house, in Chicago in 1889. (Later in her life, Addams would be partnered with Mary Rozet Smith, a major benefactor to Hull House.) Addams, born in 1860, was a product of late Victorian American culture. She believed deeply in some of the traditional ideas about sexuality and gender, even as she herself transgressed them in her own life and work.

Addams's most radical idea, and one that was at the heart of the settlement house movement, was expanding the notion of family to include broader, diverse social groups that needed to "combine" for a common goal. Julie Abraham notes that Addams's vision of "combining" is a "joining of the personal and the political." Addams was interested in a project that was at once "a deeply personal enterprise and a release from the personal," an expansion into what

Addams herself called, in *Democracy and Social Ethics*, "the larger life . . . which completely surrounds and completes the individual and family life." This was a profound advance in thinking about how society could be organized.[9]

Along with literary readings, art studios, music rooms, and a gymnasium, Hull House offered a place for socialist labor organizers to meet. Addams felt strongly that labor organizing was necessary to ensure that workers had safe conditions, worked reasonable hours, were paid fairly, and gained some satisfaction from their work. All of these women social activists were deeply interested in understanding the connections between industrialization and community, focusing on how they affected women and children. Many of the activists came from privileged backgrounds similar to those of the social purity reformers. But while the latter were interested in protecting, regulating, or controlling individual behavior, the former were committed to sustaining a healthier relationship between the individual and community. Addams's parents were wealthy, and although she encouraged socialist involvement in Hull House, she insisted that she was not "technically" a socialist because she did not subscribe to all of its tenets. Yet Julie Abraham claims that Addams's work at Hull House essentially "affirmed the 'socialism' that Wilde, Carpenter, and others drew from Whitman."[10]

Two factors define the complicated lives of these women, regardless of whether they were erotically or romantically attracted to other women. The first is that they were frequently connected to one another through a large, close-knit network of relationships that sustained them personally and professionally. The second is that they often focused on social issues that affected women and children. Historian Blanche Wiesen Cook argues that "networks of love and support are crucial [for] women to work in a hostile world . . . frequently the networks of love and support that enable politically and professionally active women to function independently and intensively consist largely of other women."[11]

The life of Lillian Wald is a prime example of these complex networks. Born in 1878 into a comfortably middle-class family in Cincinnati, Ohio (they later moved to Rochester, New York), Wald drew on Jewish and social justice traditions of caring for the poor.

As a nurse in the 1890s, she worked with immigrant orphans in New York's Lower East Side, but quickly initiated more comprehensive community health programs. She and her close companion Mary Brewster, also a nurse, moved into the neighborhood and lived with the people with whom they worked. In 1893 Wald coined the term "public health nurse" and founded the Henry Street Settlement, using the four-year-old Hull House as a template.

Henry Street was a nexus of women-centered activity and friendships. Such noted reformers as Ysabella Winters, Anne Goodrich, Florence Kelly, Helene MacDowell, and Lavinia L. Dock "worked together on all projects, lived and vacationed together for over 50 years, and, often in company with the women of Hull House, traveled together to Europe, Japan, Mexico, and the West Indies."[12] While it is always difficult to understand the complete context of personal correspondence, this letter to Wald from her intimate friend Mabel Hyde Kittredge, a wealthy New York socialite who spent years working in Henry Street, displays deep emotion:

> I seemed to hold you in my arms and whisper all of this. . . . If you want me to stay all night tomorrow night just say so when you see me. . . . Then I can hear you say "I love you"— and again and again I can see in your eyes the strength, and the power and the truth that I love.[13]

In the following letter to Wald, Alice Lewisohn recalls a trip that the two took, along with Alice's sister Irene and Ysabella Waters, during their time in Henry Street:

> Why attempt to tell a clairvoyant all that is in one's mind? You know even better than I what those months of companionship with you and Sister Waters have meant. For way and beyond even the joys of our wanderings I have some memories that are holier by far than temples or graves or blossoms. . . . Much of my heart to you![14]

The cultural and social influence of Henry Street was interwoven with the new city. The growth of contemporary urban culture and the interconnectedness of leisure, work, and politics were direct results of homosocial community building. Unmarried women, freed from caring for home, husband, and children, were a vitalizing force behind these major shifts in American life and thought. Under Wald's leadership, Henry Street thrived, adding the Neighborhood Playhouse in 1915 and Henry Street Music School in 1927. These additions connected homosocial communities with the city's burgeoning arts and entertainment scene. Kathy Peiss charts how urban entertainments aimed at female consumption—including dance halls, community-based girls' clubs, theater, movies, and "refined vaudeville" (an important advance from vaudeville's roots in saloon culture)—provided real outlets for women, particularly working-class women, to gain a more active role in public life. Peiss notes that while many of these activities, such as public dancing, were aimed at promoting heterosexual relations, they were often facilitated through homosocial activity and bonding, which ensured a larger degree of safety in group activities.[15]

Howard Chudacoff notes that single-gender male communities in clubs, bars, and other venues for leisure activities helped give rise to a culture of bachelorhood that existed from the late nineteenth century well into the twentieth. Participation in all-male sports teams, in events such as boxing matches (often with all-male spectators) and in physical exercise such as calisthenics and swimming, reinforced a single-gender culture that created emotional and physical male intimacy not found in heterosexual family environments.[16] Like Hull House and Henry Street, male-segregated spaces and the acceptance of bachelorhood as an appropriate social status for young men were catalysts for same-sex community formation.

The social purity movement's impulsive regulation of sexual desire and promotion of healthy bodies through gender, class, and racial segregation had an unintended consequence: the use of single-gender residences and recreational venues as meeting places for homosexual women and men. George Chauncey charts how the YMCA, especially through the 1920s and 1930s, became a visible and internationally noted place for homosexual men to find one another for sex and socializing. He notes that by the 1930s some gay men joked that YMCA meant "Why I'm So Gay."[17] The YMCA, and other all-male facilities that promoted socializing and health through (nude) swimming, calisthenics, and other forms of physical exercise, were logical places for homosexual men to meet one another. Historian John Donald Gustav-Wrathall describes how the friendships promoted by the YMCA "had an embodied element: a delight in one another's physical proximity, an awareness of each other's bodies, a sort of excitement that overtook them at the prospect of spending time together."[18]

Battles over inequality in race, sexuality, and gender are often articulated around questions of private and public space. Severely limiting access to public and social spaces and institutions through the legacy of "separate but equal" was one of the most effective and destructive means used by the dominant white culture to continue the subjugation of African Americans (and other people of color) in the decades that followed slavery. This model of segregation informs how we think about LGBT lives and communities when we examine the links between antiblack racism and the treatment of homosexuals during the twentieth century.

Like African Americans, many homosexuals moved to urban areas to live in communities of similar people. In these neighborhoods they could live openly and possibly more safely. This situation is strikingly illustrated by the African American aphorism of the 1920s: "I'd rather be a lamppost in Harlem than the governor of Georgia." Ironically, an unintended side effect of segregation was that African Americans, in the space that they were allowed, formed vibrant, thriving communities. These spaces gave birth to and nourished African American cultural expression. They were also centers of political activity. For similar reasons, homosexual communities such as Greenwich Village were crucibles of exciting culture and politics. Venues such as cafés, bars, clubs, and theaters, as well as events such as semipublic parties, dances, art shows, and literary readings, built and preserved a sense of sexual community.

The social acceptance on which these communities were predicated often manifested itself in complicated ways. Homosexuals and African Americans shared a sense of social stigmatization, marginalization, and criminalization. George Chauncey charts the growth of homosexual neighborhoods in New York, such as Greenwich Village and Harlem. Greenwich Village was in many ways accepting of people of color. Harlem, a primarily African American community, was accepting of homosexuals of color as well as some white homosexuals. Chauncey details how Harlem, the center of African American life in New York, became the site for both exciting artistic explorations of black culture and public manifestations of homosexual culture. Harlem's world of jazz clubs, speakeasies, cellar clubs, and low-end and upscale nightclubs (the latter frequented by wealthy white patrons) encouraged sexualized performances. In the early 1930s, performers such as African American Gladys Bentley, who performed dressed as a man, and "Gloria Swanson," a renowned Chicago drag queen who moved to Harlem to open his own club, were extraordinarily popular.[19] The sites of arts and entertainment that blossomed around African American and same-sex communities continued in the sexual tradition of nineteenth-century same-sex-loving artists to turn homosociality into sexual fluidity.

ENTERTAINING NEW IDEAS ABOUT GENDER

In the first four decades of the twentieth century, entertainment in the United States grew and diversified enormously. In the later decades of the nineteenth century, burlesque, a form of theatrical parody, was extraordinarily popular. Its main objective was to parody existing social norms, frequently gender norms. (The Latin root of "burlesque" is "burra," meaning "trifles" or "nonsense.") The popularity of burlesque—and later vaudeville, which presented a collection of acts, including burlesque, in a revue—greatly shaped American popular culture. This was even more true of film, which in the late 1920 and 1930s became the cheapest and most available form of entertainment in the country.

One of the effects of these entertainments was to subvert traditional ideas about morality, gender, sexual behavior, and sexual identity. Cultural theorists Peter Stallybrass and Allen White write about burlesque as promoting the "low other"; the same might be true of much of popular theater and film in America. Here the low other "is reviled by and excluded from the dominant social order as debased, dirty, and unworthy, but . . . is simultaneously the object of desire and/or fascination."[20]

Homosexual community developed, in part, through the public discourse of sexology and the invention of the "invert." Simultaneously, popular theater and film were subverting this pathologized image by challenging what "invert" meant. This conflict animated the career of the most noted male performer of these decades: William Julian Dalton, internationally famous as female impersonator Julian Eltinge. Born outside Boston in 1881, Eltinge began performing as a female impersonator in a local theatrical revue at age fifteen. By 1904 he was performing on the New York stage in musical comedies. Some stage performers dressed in women's clothing for a comic effect; Eltinge convincingly portrayed women who dressed beautifully and embodied the gender ideals of the day.

Eltinge played theaters all over the United States and Europe. He made his producer, Al Woods, so much money that in 1912, the businessman named his newly constructed Broadway playhouse the Eltinge 42nd Street Theater. Eltinge's popularity rested on his subversive ability, in a society "in which gendered behavior was understood as the natural, inevitable expression of physical sex," to expose these roles as culturally constructed. Little is known about Eltinge's personal life. Many historians now presume he was homosexual; making the matter more complex, he was also famous for aggressively promoting a masculine persona offstage.[21] Whatever his personal life, Eltinge easily promoted the idea that gender and sexuality were far more complicated than traditional standards held. The power and common sense of these new ideas is evident in "A Musical Comedy Thought," a short, comic 1916 poem by Dorothy Parker about Eltinge and British male impersonator Vesta Tilley:

> My heart is simply melting at the thought of Julian Eltinge;
> His vice versa, Vesta Tilley, too.
> Our language is so dexterous, let us call them ambi-sexterous—
> Why hasn't this occurred before to you?[22]

The implications of these theatrical presentations were far-reaching. If Julian Eltinge could transform himself from a virile man to a beautiful woman—a process that was thoroughly, even compulsively, documented in the popular press through drawings and photographs—what did this say about paragons of theatrical beauty such as the tall, stately, elegantly adorned, internationally famous Ziegfeld Girls, who were promoted as the glorification of perfect (white) American womanhood?

Other noted male performers were undermining the cultural presumption that "real masculinity" was "white masculinity." They did this by playing with stereotypes and preconceived notions of race and ethnicity. Vaudeville and Broadway comics such as Eddie Cantor and Bert Lahr, both of whom emerged from Jewish immigrant traditions of masculinity that often countered the idea of the aggressively heterosexual "all-American man," were famous on stage and screen for their brilliantly realized, nontraditional, and self-acknowledged masculine personas. Cantor, who often performed in blackface, referred to this character as a "cultured, pansy-like negro" who was "slight and effeminate, with white-rimmed glasses and mincing step."[23] Lahr's characters were equally flamboyant. His most famous role, as the Cowardly Lion in the 1939 *The Wizard of Oz*, is animated by the sheer joy of nonmasculine emotional display.

While the pansy was a stock figure in popular culture, this was not true of the female invert: the mannish lesbian, recognizable by her masculine clothing and short-cropped hair. She was present in some comic, visual images that lampooned her, but largely absent from popular culture's images of lesbians. Perhaps this is because the image was associated with progressive causes such as suffrage, and was specifically, not generally, subversive. In contrast, the pansy was rarely connected to public figures or overt political activity. Also, the stereotype of the mannish lesbian was relatively new (the effeminate man can be traced back to the European fop). For this reason—as well as because the pansy was more flagrantly sexual and instantly recognizable, fluttering his hands and fussing over women's clothing—the pansy image enjoyed much wider appeal.

Questions raised by sexology about gender roles and sex were also explicitly "staged," and this became part of a public discourse. The opening scene of Mae West's 1927 play *The Drag* has two characters openly discussing the ideas of Karl Ulrichs, and the play later examines the relationship of these ideas to medical practice. Even drama critics, writing for a broader audience, felt free to casually drop sexologists' names in print. Robert Benchley, in 1928, reviewed West's *Pleasure Man* and wrote: "The cast included Cases 1 though 28 in Volume Two of Havelock Ellis."[24] Popular Broadway musicals were replete with slyly mocking references to sexology, as demonstrated by this 1939 Dorothy Fields song, "A Lady Needs a Change," sung by Ethel Merman in *Stars in Your Eyes*:

> When Mr. Havelock Ellis tries to tell us
> Why we're so complex,
> I say "Mr. Ellis, what the hell is
> Scientific sex?"[25]

In the first two decades of the twentieth century, there were already distinct links in the public imagination between the theater, subversive gender performances, and homosexuality. In 1908 Maud Allan, a San Francisco resident, created international headlines with her erotic, scantily clad performance as the title character of Oscar Wilde's verse play *Salome*. The Maud Allan phenomenon generated anxiety in the American press. The *New York Times* editorialized in 1908 that "at the present rate [of Allan's European popularity] it is probable that Salome dances will invade the fashionable drawing rooms of New York . . . unless a halt is called."[26] Not surprisingly, men called for the censoring of Allan's dancing, but women loved the image of freedom it presented.

Ten years later Allan became an overtly political scandal when she instigated an internationally publicized British libel trial by suing conservative politician Noel Pemberton-Billing. He had claimed, in an article titled "The Cult of the Clitoris," that a legion of lesbian spies were hurting England's war effort: "In lesbian ecstasy the most sacred secrets of the state were betrayed." He then suggested that Allan's *Salome* was connected to the "systematic seduction of your British soldiers by the German urnings." Allan lost the case after Pemberton-Billing stated out loud what everyone suspected—that Allan was a "pervert"—and even linked her romantically with Margot Asquith, the wife of the former prime minister. The revelation may have contained some truth, as Asquith was sexually involved with other women at the time. The trial, with its sensational claims, was widely covered in the U.S. press, which agreed with the verdict.

Despite Allan's intentions, the popular press portrayed her theatrics, on and off stage, as representative of a pathological type. This newly defined pathologized identity, despite what some progressive sexologists intended, was a social and political threat that caused the public moralists to react. The immediate effect of this moral backlash was the enforcement of laws that censored productions on the stage. The New York Society for the Suppression of Vice lobbied aggressively to clean up the Broadway stage and was particularly vigilant against homosexual themes and characters. In 1922 it urged the city to close Sholem Asch's classic 1907 Yiddish drama *The God of Vengeance* because of its setting in a brothel and its lesbian content. In February 1927, the society instigated the shutting down of Arthur Hornblow Jr.'s drama *The Captive,* which had been running since the previous September, because of its overt lesbian theme. The society, a private organization, worked closely with the district attorney, who had the New York City police raid the theater and serve arrest warrants to the actors. Two months later, the Republican-run state assembly passed a law that prohibited theatrical performances "depicting or dealing with the subject of sex degeneracy, or sex perversion." It also instituted the Wales Padlock law, which allowed police to close a theater for a year if the owners were convicted of presenting a play that violated obscenity laws. (The Wales Padlock law remained on the books, largely unenforced, until 1967.)

The society's power came from the support of organized religion and the legal system. New York's governor, Al Smith, as well as the mayor, district attorney, and police chief, all had close ties to Roman Catholic clergy. Protestant clergy were also supportive. Before *The Captive* was raided, the *New York Morning Telegraph* reported that "one thousand Protestant clergymen of the Great New York Federation of churches yesterday passed a resolution to back up the District Attorney in his drive against objectionable plays."[27] Later that year, Mae West's play *Sex* was closed by the authorities and she was sentenced to jail. Her play *The Drag,* featured homosexual characters and an onstage drag ball, played in New Jersey and Connecticut but did not open on Broadway under direct threat of being immediately closed. While relatively few plays were closed or producers prosecuted, the Society for the Suppression of Vice, politicians, and clergy had a chilling effect in preventing homosexual images or themes from reaching the stage.

The questions about gender and sexuality that were raised on the New York stage were also being posed in Hollywood. Throughout the 1920s, the film industry was known for its culture of sexual permissiveness. One reason was the interplay between the new film industry and the established theater; many performers came to Hollywood from vaudeville, burlesque, and the legitimate stage. Another was that Los Angeles, like San Francisco, had social and cultural roots that embraced personal freedoms and a healthy respect for individual differences.

Throughout the 1920s and early 1930s, although there were few restrictions on Hollywood films, overt representations of lesbians or gay men were rare. Occasionally a star such as Marlene Dietrich, known for her affairs with both women and men, would cross-dress in a film such as the 1930 *Morocco*, and in the 1930s performers such as Edward Everett Horton and Eric Blore consistently played pansy characters. Performers' personal lives, however, were not particularly private. Lillian Faderman and Stuart Timmons document that in the 1920s "the lesbian cavortings of silent film stars such as Evelyn Brent, Nita Naldi, Pola Negri, and Lilyan Tashman" were an open secret. The homosexuality of Ramon Novarro, William Haines, and directors James Whale and George Cukor were known within the industry and rumored among the general public.[28]

The taint of Hollywood's gender and sexual nonconformity is clear in the attacks on extravagantly emotional heterosexual heartthrob Rudolph Valentino. An editorial in the *Chicago Tribune* in 1926 railed against a powder dispenser in a men's room at a public ballroom and traced its genesis to Hollywood:

A powder vending machine! In a men's washroom! Homo Americanus! Why didn't some one quietly drown Rudolph Guglielmo [*sic*], alias Valentino, years ago? . . .
Do women like the type of "man" who pats pink powder

on his face in a public washroom and arranges his coiffure in a public elevator? Do woman at heart belong to the Wilsonian era of "I Didn't Raise My Boy to Be a Soldier"? What has become of the old "caveman" line?[29]

The editorial makes clear that American masculinity is a political issue when it compares the powder puff to the threat of radical movements, in particular communism: "Is this degeneration into effeminacy a cognate reaction with pacifism to the virilities and the realities of the war? Are pink powder and parlor pinks in any way related?" The connection, clearly articulated here, between gender or sexual nonconformity and political nonconformity was often lurking behind censorship campaigns.

Alarmed by the increasing sexual content of films and the industry's "immorality," public moralists took a stand in the late 1920s. Threatening to invoke government censorship, mainstream Protestant and Catholic groups allowed the industry to set up a system of self-regulation, the template of which was generated by a group of Catholic laymen and clergy. Adhering to conservative Catholic theology, this group presented William Hayes, the head of the industry's trade association, with a highly restrictive code of subjects and themes to be avoided. The censorship process would occur during film production, ensuring that there was little chance of questionable material even being filmed.

The regulations stipulated that "pictures shall not imply that low forms of sex relationship are the accepted or common thing," thus mandating that adultery and nonmarital sex could never be presented in a neutral or positive manner. They also stated that all references to "sexual perversion" were forbidden. This new set of restrictions, the Production Code (often referred to as the Hayes Code), was formally adopted by the industry in March 1930. Starting in July 1934, all films were required to have a certificate stating that they adhered to the standards of the code before they were released. For almost two full decades, until individual film directors challenged the code in the mid-1950s, there could be no mention of homosexuality or many other taboo topics in a Hollywood film.

The censors won in Hollywood, but the gender and sexual subversions that outraged them were appearing elsewhere as well. This is seen most clearly on the vaudeville stage. Vaudeville was an important social space where the concept of the new American woman—economically independent, sexually free, not necessarily heterosexual, and refusing to conform to social standards of beauty—was visible. As threatening as these images were, they were also enormously popular. Eva Tanguay was the most popular entertainer in the first decade of the century, earning more than $3,500 a week. Her elaborate production numbers glorified her as she eschewed all traditional femininity: she displayed manic energy, did not shape her body with rigid corsets, and had a mop of hair that she would shampoo with champagne on stage. She was nicknamed the "I Don't Care Girl" after her theme song:

> They say I'm crazy, got no sense,
> But I don't care . . .
> You see I'm sort of independent,
> Of a clever race descendent,
> My star is on the ascendant,
> That's why I don't care.
>
> I don't care! I don't care!
> What they may think of me.
> I'm happy-go-lucky,
> Men say I'm plucky,
> So jolly and carefree.[30]

Tanguay's stage presence was innately political in its depiction of women, and women involved in fighting for suffrage were avid fans. Other extremely popular female vaudeville performers, such as Trixie Friganza, the "queen of fat comedy," ridiculed contemporary ideas of beauty. Friganza was herself an ardent proponent of suffrage, routinely giving speeches on the topic at rallies.[31]

There was an increasingly evident overlap between female performers who embodied the "new woman" and the emerging subcultures of lesbian and gay men. Marie Dressler, who started in vaudeville and by the early 1920s began making films in Hollywood, was known for her fat, sympathetically comic characters, almost always working-class and Irish, who gloried in their physical and cultural distinctiveness. Dressler did not particularly hide the fact that she had female lovers. She was part of a friendship network of women who loved women, including Bessie Marbury, a powerful theatrical agent who reshaped theater in the United States, and her lover Elsie DeWolf, a noted decorator and social leader. Dressler was politically active; she worked with socially prominent heiresses Anne Morgan and Anne Vanderbilt to establish the American Women's Association, an organization that provided a home and support for professional women in New York City. (Morgan and Vanderbilt were intimate friends and frequently lived with de Wolf and Marbury in the latter's villa in France.)[32]

Lillian Faderman notes that many women prominent in New York theater, such as Beatrice Lillie, Jeanne Eagels, Tallulah Bankhead, and Libby Holman, established public reputations as sexually adventurous women with both female and male partners. Their association with respectable Broadway theater gave them economic security as well as the social freedom to live their lives outside the cultural and sexual mainstream.[33]

This freedom was enticing to many homosexuals and heterosexuals who fantasized about living alternative sexual lives and frequented places to experience what that might be like. Post-Prohibition San Francisco hosted a wide range of gender-transgressive nightclubs—often featuring vaudeville performers as well as female impersonators—and a highly visible sexual culture that included lesbians and homosexual men.[34] The prevalence of theatrical female impersonation and drag in San Francisco led growing numbers of ostensibly heterosexual tourists to visit the bars and nightclubs usually frequented by homosexuals.

On the East Coast, Harlem clubs were frequently visited by white heterosexuals who were looking for sexual and social excitement not found in predominantly white, "respectable" neighborhoods. This semi-institutionalized crossing over of individuals from the dominant culture into a "strange" subculture (often located in a racially or sexually segregated ghetto) was called "slumming," and it both excited and disconcerted the slummer. It allowed someone who was usually an "insider" to become, for a period of time, the "outsider" in another culture. It was also a conduit through which lesbian and gay male culture interacted with, and was introduced into, mainstream culture.

Slumming facilitated physical and emotional relationships between people in these two cultures. Historian Chad Heap recounts that in 1933, "a queer girl" at Chicago's Ballyhoo Café hostilely informed a heterosexual patron that "queer people despise jam people," the latter phrase being homosexual jargon for heterosexuals.[35] Yet despite the resentment that some homosexual patrons might have felt, slumming provided the outsiders with a bracing look at difference. One of the most popular singers on Sunset Strip was Bruz Fletcher, who sang his own songs at the fashionable Bali nightclub. The lyrics of "The Simple Things" told outsiders that they were guests in a way that was charming enough to make them feel comfortable:

I want a cozy little nest, somewhere in the West
Where the best of all the worst will always be.
I want an extensive, expensive excursion
To the realms of "in," "per," and "di"-version.
It's the simple things in life for me.[36]

While most of these clubs were predicated on entertainment, they also served other community functions. Heap notes that in 1931, Chicago's Dil Pickle Club, which had roots as a bohemian club frequented by labor activists and anarchists, hosted a talk by Magnus Hirschfeld, a noted German sexologist who was openly homosexual and lectured on the topic.[37]

A PRIVATE/PUBLIC CULTURE EMERGES

Cities, providing anonymity as well as diversity, promoted a new blurring of traditional ideas about privacy. George Chauncey charts the vital, public "fairy" culture that thrived in New York's Bowery and Greenwich Village in the 1920s and 1930s. As ideas of public space changed, homosexuals found public streets and parks useful for meeting one another. These public places became a space to enact formerly private aspects of life. Earl Lind, in his 1919 *Autobiography of an Androgyne,* describes at length an active homosexual culture, often centered around the role of fairy or pansy, in New York City earlier in the century. Harlem Renaissance writer Richard Bruce Nugent wrote about public homosexuality in his 1932 novel *Gentleman Jigger:*

> In Washington Square he sat and watched the people pass. Lithe Italian hoodlums in exaggerated clothes creased to razor sharpness, with dark, sallow skin and oiled hair, strutting with clicking heels and a cocky grace. . . . Painted boys who ogled the hoodlums hungrily and lowered their eyes in false modesty and brazen coquetry as they passed, leaving trails of perfume. . . . A hoodlum would say "hello, sweetheart," and then turn to his companions and pass some remark that would cause them to laugh loudly.[38]

This emerging street culture was present in New York's Harlem and Greenwich Village, but also in other major cities. Public cruising often relied on sexology's inversion stereotypes, which Nugent portrays here, to make same-sex desire legible. Making desire visible, however, could also elicit violence.

Bars, clubs, and night spots that catered to a homosexual clientele, even if nonhomosexuals were there slumming, were frequently targets for police raids instigated by public outrage or by politicians promising to make public spaces "safe" for women, children, and families. More dangerous to homosexuals, however, were the legal and moral crusades that emerged in the late 1930s. These climaxed in the summer of 1937, when widespread panic broke out over alleged sexual psychopaths who would harm and murder children. The frightening image of the sexual psychopath was clearly linked to the emerging figure of the male homosexual. These campaigns were connected to the local police assaults on homosexual venues in Los Angeles.[39]

The crusades against homosexuality had a tremendous impact in other cities as well. In September 1937, J. Edgar Hoover, the director of the FBI (who was emotionally, if not sexually, involved with his assistant, Clyde Tolson), wrote an article called "War on the Sex Criminal" that was published in the *New York Herald Tribune* and widely reprinted. Hoover's article was clearly inciting fears of the more public homosexual:

> The present apathy of the public toward perverts, generally regarded as "harmless," should be changed to one of suspicious scrutiny. The harmless pervert of today can be and often is the loathsome mutilator and murderer of tomorrow. . . . The ordinary offender [turned] into a dangerous, predatory animal, preying upon society because he has been taught he can get away with it.[40]

These attacks, always in coded language that never mentioned "fairy," "pansy," or "homosexual," were primarily aimed at homosexual men. Illinois, California, Michigan, Minnesota, and Ohio almost immediately passed "sexual psychopath laws," and other states followed. Over the next decade, more waves of "sex panics" spread across the country and similar laws were passed. The laws differed in detail from state to state, but usually allowed the courts to incarcerate suspected "sexual psychopaths" for undetermined periods of time in mental institutions. These laws were broadly written, and the definition of "sexual psychopath" always remained vague so that it could be applied as indiscriminately as possible.

Sexual psychopath laws, clearly influenced by social purity concerns, almost always presumed children were being victimized. By the mid to late 1940s, "during the nationwide campaigns against sexual psychopaths, the terms *child molester, homosexual, sex offender, sex psychopath, sex degenerate, sex deviate,* and sometimes even *communist* were used and became interchangeable in the mind of the public."[41] The conflation of vague "sexual deviancy" with homosexuality and child molestation set up what was to become a widely accepted myth: that male homosexuals were innately driven to seduce or sexually assault male children. This myth was a strong influence in shaping the public discussion about homosexuality well into the twenty-first century.

The more public homosexuals became, the more they were believed to threaten society. Many women and men felt that personal, and even community, safety would more likely be secured by fighting for a right to personal privacy rather than a right to public security. This emphasis on privacy dovetailed with the accepted sentiment, and mandate, that all sexuality was private. Mandated privacy of sexual expression was what social purity activists, vice squads, and religious leaders were attempting to achieve in their attacks on all public manifestations of desire and fantasy in popular culture. What they could not ban or eradicate, however, was the individual, private imagination. Certainly women and men who read sex and marriage guides had their sexual curiosity piqued and were encouraged to think about these matters in greater detail. One of the unintended effects of these publications was the rise of public discussions about what roles sexuality, sexual behavior, and gender played in people's lives.

Fictional depictions of homosexuality were becoming common during these decades. While some of them were censored, the private act of reading a book was less upsetting to the guardians of public morals than the more theatrical, and public, manifestations of homosexuality. European works such as Marcel Proust's 1922 *Cities of the Plain,* Thomas Mann's 1912 *Death in Venice* (published in the United States in 1925), and Radclyffe Hall's 1928 *The Well of Loneliness* were influential in shaping American ideas about homosexuality. The character Stephen Gordon, a masculine woman who loves other women, in *The Well of Loneliness* became the prototype of the mannish lesbian. The novel was banned in England and published in the United States after a lengthy court battle. Its extraordinary popularity affirmed widespread interest in the subject of homosexuality, as well as how strongly the idea of the "invert" had taken root.

The concept of the "tragic" male invert was so pliable that Americans Charles Henri Ford and Parker Tyler, in their 1933 *The Young and the Evil,* made him the center of a quirky, madcap romance.

Published in Paris because of its blithe acceptance of homosexual sex and comic tone, the novel was banned for years in the United States and Great Britain, where customs offices confiscated and burned copies. Lesbian and gay male themes also surfaced in popular American novels, such as Nella Larsen's 1929 *Passing* and Blair Niles's 1931 *Strange Brother,* both set in Harlem, and Gale Wilhelm's critically acclaimed *We Too Are Drifting* (1934) and *Torchlight to Valhalla* (1938). Gay male themes were prevalent in lowbrow novels, such as André Tellier's 1931 *Twilight Men* and Lew Levenson's 1934 *Butterfly Man,* but also in more literary works, such as Kay Boyle's 1933 *Gentlemen, I Address You Privately* and Djuna Barnes's 1936 *Nightwood.*

Readers encountered the ideas of sexologists through fiction. Novels with homosexual themes—which drew on and often described homosexual subcultures—would routinely mention sexologists and their works. Blair Niles's 1931 *Strange Brother,* set in Harlem's ambisexual nightclubs and homosexual milieu, mentions so many authors and their books—Edward Carpenter's *Love's Coming of Age,* John Addington Symonds, Havelock Ellis—that it functions as a basic reading list on homosexuality. Foreman Brown's 1933 *Better Angel,* written under the pseudonym of Richard Meeker, notes that Kurt, its main character, has read Ellis, Carpenter, Freud, and German playwright Frank Wedekind's *Spring Awakening,* which included a positive portrayal of homosexual love between teenage boys. Sometimes the references in popular writing are simply allusions; the "modern" poet Helen Havelock in Tellier's *Twilight Men* is a clear reference to the sexologist.

The popularity of these books indicated that many people were interested in homosexuality. In a cultural climate that fostered fear of public homosexuality, the privacy of reading even popular material on the subject holds political significance, reinforcing the idea that personal and community safety can be secured through privacy. This was a different model than the fight for access to public space for which many in the African American community were waging. Most movements for social change were not open to explicitly discussing homosexuality.

Despite the vibrancy of homosexuality in popular culture in Harlem's clubs and streets, most of the homosexuals involved in the Harlem Renaissance were not open about their sexuality outside of their art. There was overt and covert hostility to homosexuality within some of the African American community—more overt in the middle class, who were more concerned about social respectability.[42] Even the insightful W. E. B. Du Bois seems to have been both bewildered by and oblivious to the issue. He dismissed his longtime, highly valued coworker, Augustus Granville Dill, from the *Crisis,* the official magazine of the NAACP, after Dill was arrested in a men's room for a homosexual encounter. (Du Bois later apologized in his autobiography.) Yet he also encouraged his daughter Yolande to marry the brilliant Harlem Renaissance poet Countee Cullen, who was widely thought to be homosexual and who, three months after the wedding, sailed to Europe with his best man, the bisexual Harold Jackman. (Yolande followed a month later.) The message here was the same for African Americans as it was for homosexuals: if you are seeking political gains, then the requirement is to appear appropriate in public.

One model that marginalized groups often follow in order to gain social acceptance is to produce culture that will be acknowledged and valued by people outside the group. The Harlem Renaissance was a "civil rights enterprise masquerading as an arts movement." Noted white literary critic Carl Van Doren emphasized the importance of black voices when he stated in 1924 that "what American literature decidedly needs at the moment is color, music, gusto, the free expression of gay or desperate moods. If the Negroes are not in a position to contribute those items, I do not know what Americans are."[43] Across art forms and races, homosexuals had a similar relationship to mainstream culture. They also formed community and gained visibility through the arts and popular culture. In some ways this eased the road to full citizenship for both African Americans and homosexuals. The road, however, was not a smooth one, as both homosexual and black cultural production—in particular, black-originated music such as jazz—was frequently attacked by moralists as overly sexual, provocative, and dangerous.

The insistence on policing images of homosexuality and gender deviance in public, as well as the bodies and spaces with which they were associated, was a manifestation of social and cultural anxiety. This anxiety was less about an individual play or film than about larger changes in social structure and mobility of deviant types. Stallybrass and White note that "what is *socially* peripheral is so frequently *symbolically* central." Social leaders, clergy, and legislators focused on manifestations of homosexuality in the so-called social periphery of the "low other" because they were able to, in varying degrees, regulate and control them.

They could not, however, as easily control how women and men chose to live their lives now that urban areas were growing and offering a plethora of choices, from living to leisure. Complicating this situation was the reality that as homosexuals themselves were moving away from the social periphery toward the symbolic center of mainstream life and culture, many nonhomosexuals were valuing homosexual-created forms of art and entertainment. The presence of same-sex-desiring people in single-gender urban spaces led to the blossoming of a homosexual arts scene. This newly defined and influential subversive culture began to change mainstream culture in myriad ways.

SEVEN

PRODUCTION AND MARKETING
OF GENDER

The hectic vitality of the United States between 1900 and 1940 can clearly be seen in the rise of the population, which grew from 76 million in 1900 to 131.7 million in 1940. In 1910, 26.1 million people lived in metropolitan areas, as opposed to 65.9 million in nonmetropolitan areas. By 1940 those numbers had shifted to 63 million people living in cities and 68.7 in nonmetropolitan areas.

In this radical reshaping of the country, American cities became centers of commerce and industry. They were also becoming centers of influential artistic production, the clearest examples being the modern theater and publishing industries in New York and the film industry in Hollywood—venues that were extraordinarily influential in shaping contemporary, progressive attitudes about gender and sexuality.

The emergence of the new, strange, ambiguous, intermediate third sex—the invert—led American culture to clearly define the physical, social, and cultural parameters of the first and second sexes. Officially, homosexuality was condemned, although it was certainly an object of fascination and was often tolerated in urban areas. In addition to the sexual anxiety it caused, homosexuality also generated confusion about gender that had to be addressed. Heterosexuality was painstakingly constructed by the medical profession. Homosexuality was scrutinized, pathologized, and policed. But this was not enough. One clear, proactive response to the potential confusion and threat of the invert was the invention and promotion of the strong, forceful, muscular male as an icon of white heterosexual masculinity.[1]

The form and impact of this response must be understood in the context of American economics and consumerism. Each was a fundamental force in the lives of U.S. citizens. Together they were the basis for what would increasingly be called "the American way of life." This new national economic condition was largely a result of the economic systems and substantial amount of capital created by the entrepreneurs of the Gilded Age. These men, called "robber barons" by their critics, acted ruthlessly and often illegally, but laid the foundation for the United States to be at the forefront of the world economy. More important, these economic changes also produced a culture in which personal identity was formed not just through gender, race, sexual identity, and class, but through consumption.

As people migrated from rural areas to urban centers, there was a profound shift in economic and consumption patterns. The United States was slowing turning from a culture of production to one of consumption—a process that would reach its apotheosis in the 1950s. This culture shift is illustrated by the success of the assembly line (often attributed to Henry Ford, but actually based on ideas from employees) and the production of the Model T car. Efficiency and relative worker safety made the Model T so inexpensive that by 1916, eight years after its inception, 472,000 were sold. By 1918 one family in thirteen owned a car; eleven years later, four out of every five families possessed one. Ford also broke with other manufacturers by offering the unheard-of wage of five dollars a day (so that his workers could buy one of his cars). The interplay between mass production and mass consumption was later called Fordism.

The invention of the car was transformative for American culture. It greatly increased personal mobility, thereby destabilizing patterns of living that were based on the biological family. More important, it gave people access to private space away from home. The 1912 song "Bump, Bump, Bump in Your Automobile," in which Willie Green and Molly May go driving, ends suggestively with the lyric, "Molly May said she loved Willie Green. Best of all, she loved Willie's machine." By the 1920s the automobile was fully established as a site of sexual freedom, especially for young people, who now had access to "lover's lanes." This new innovation in romantic and sexual privacy was also a boon to those engaged in same-sex relationships.

At the same time, the new wave of mass consumption worked with the cultural need to define and reinforce traditional gender roles. The gender of consumption could never start too early. By 1902 department stores had inaugurated "children's day," and by 1926 the United States was the largest toy producer in the world.[2] While there had always been some differentiation between girls' and boys' toys, the mass production and consumption of toys during this time became increasingly gendered. In 1916 *American Boy* magazine offered boys incentives for selling subscriptions, including "erector sets, a Daisy Air Rifle, a rotary press, and even a Big Dick machine gun."[3] After World War I and through the 1940s, boys' toys were often military, while girls' toys taught them about motherhood. Dolls, in particular, were instrumental in teaching girls how to be mothers. In 1919 as much money was spent manufacturing doll carriages as baby carriages.[4] As the national birthrate dropped in the late 1920s and 1930s, leaving many girls without younger siblings for whom to care, sales of baby dolls increased.[5] This push toward traditional gender norms was, like the rest of the growing consumerism of the decades, an attempt to solidify the place of the heterosexual family as the cornerstone of American life.

The organization, through mass consumerism, of American culture as heterosexual, middle-class, and white rearticulated a masculine—and by extension, American—manifest destiny. The car, · as well as advances in other forms of transportation and the rise of a middle class, led to institutionalized vacations and formalized leisure time. With the rise of commercial beach resorts, mountain lodges, dude ranches, and other holiday destinations, vacations quickly became integral to American consumption and were structured around either family-based activities or heterosexual flirting and coupling.[6] This gendered image intersected politics, society, and popular culture; it encompassed individual achievement, economic opportunity, nationalism, and imperial expansion as the American way. Finally, it aligned with ideas from the social purity movement, sexology, and the new science of eugenics.

PRODUCING MANLINESS

Teddy Roosevelt—soldier, hunter, adventurer, and president of the United States in the first eight years of the century—became emblematic of American masculinity in the popular imagination. Born to wealth in 1858, he overcame a habitually unwell childhood by sheer force of will to become a star college athlete. In 1898 he became the leader of the Rough Riders, volunteers who fought in Cuba during the Spanish Civil War. Their exaggerated exploits became mythical accounts of American manhood. For Roosevelt, manhood and the strong, athletic, white male body were inseparable from America and patriotism. By the time Roosevelt was in the White House, "the entire nation knew of Roosevelt's youthful bodybuilding to overcome frailty" and "young boys began strengthening regimens, and grown men reveled in what the *New York Tribune* in 1907 called Roosevelt's 'opulent efficiency of mind and body.'" He even brought a professional boxer to the White House as a sparring partner.[7] The conflation of robust maleness, heterosexuality, and whiteness set a standard for citizenship that was the antithesis of the invert.

Roosevelt's representational power drew strength and scope from Progressive Era reform thinking. Progressivism involved fighting for shorter working hours in factories, rehabilitating dangerous tenements, starting regulatory commissions for labor and finance, and battling corruption in government, as well as social purity projects such as Prohibition and protecting women and children from nonwhite people. Charlotte Perkins Gilman, a brilliant feminist economist and theorist who supported many progressive social reforms, believed in the supremacy of the "white race." She argued that Jews had "not passed the tribal stage," that "orientals" were innately connected to crimes, and that African Americans essentially should be forced into industrial work because of their low intelligence.[8] Such thinking was a logical outcome of social purity advocates' valuing, in their language, the "white race" over others. As Beryl Satter points out:

> The white middle-class vision of Progressive-era reform could embrace censorship campaigns, Jim Crow laws, eugenics, and

even lynching, as well as sanitation and tenement reform, factory regulations, women's suffrage, and socialism. All were
potential means for safeguarding the evolutionary development of the Anglo-Saxon or human race and hence of inaugu-
rating a purified republic.[9]

Given these attitudes about race, it is not surprising that Gilman, and many other women and men involved in these movements,
believed in eugenics—a social-political theory that advocated the
improvement of the human race by deterring the reproduction of
those people deemed to have less-than-desirable traits. Eugenics was
not just a social purity movement belief but was widely taken up by
the legal and medical systems in the United States. Sixty-five thousand Americans were sterilized from the turn of the century into the
1970s, and in 1927 the Supreme Court ruled in *Buck v. Bell* that
compulsory sterilization was constitutional "for the protection and
health of the state."[10] Michael Amico notes that eugenics produced a
scientific model of "fitness" that would be used for the next century
to describe and limit the lives of LGBT people in numerous, substantial ways. Their obvious "unfitness" denied them full citizenship
and rendered them medically inferior, legally unequal, morally suspect, and socially outcast, with no right to reproduce.[11]

Roosevelt embraced eugenic thought. For Roosevelt, masculinity
and nationhood were completely tied up with worries about "racial degeneracy." In a speech to the National Congress of Mothers
on May 13, 1905, Roosevelt bemoaned the idea of family planning
and claimed that "if the average family in which there are children
contained but two children the nation as a whole would decrease in
population so rapidly that in two or three generations it would very
deservedly be on the point of extinction." He added that such "race
suicide" would not be regrettable, since a race that wants to have
fewer children does not deserve to exist.[12]

As Roosevelt was becoming the emblem of American manhood,
a group was forming in Great Britain that would soon affect American boys. In 1907 Robert Baden-Powell, a noted lieutenant general
in the British Army stationed in India and Africa, adapted a military
training manual, *Aids for Scouting*, for boys. A year later he wrote

Scouting for Boys and founded what would become an international movement, the Boy Scouts. Baden-Powell was a product of British colonial political policies, and they are reflected in his thinking. In 1896, in a book about one of his African campaigns, he wrote, "The stupid inertness of the puzzled negro is duller than that of an ox; a dog would grasp your meaning in one-half the time. Men and Brothers! They may be brothers, but they are certainly not men."[13] Like Roosevelt, Baden-Powell was deeply concerned with racial degeneration.

For Baden-Powell, Scouting was a "character factory" whose purpose "from the very beginning [was] conceived as a remedy to Britain's moral, physical, and military weakness."[14] Intrinsic to Baden-Powell's vision of the Boy Scouts was the formation of an idealized national citizen who would embody the perfect white male. Baden-Powell's emphasis on national patriotism flirted with fascism, since as late as 1937 he was arguing for links between the British Scouts and the Hitler Youth groups; he was overruled by the Boy Scouts International Committee.

The production of the perfect male citizen (not unlike Ford's mass-production factories), combined with the ideals of the social purity movement, produced a refined American national identity and bolstered a national concept of masculinity. The Scouting movement quickly moved to the United States and was formally recognized in 1910. It drew on the British movement but combined it with two earlier boys' movements that were symbolic of the American West and the new American man: the Woodcraft Indians, founded in 1902 by naturalist Ernest Thompson Seton, and the Society of the Sons of Daniel Boone, founded in 1905 by writer Daniel Carter Beard.

For Baden-Powell and Roosevelt, personal sexual immorality and racial degeneration were unarguably connected. Both men repeatedly voiced concerns that boys were being physically and morally harmed by social ills, including smoking, card playing, swearing, indecent literature, movies, public dancing, and sexual immorality. Echoing the concerns of religious guides for girls and marriage manuals, guides for boys suggested that young, impressionable boys were as susceptible to social threats as were girls. The widely read

1910 *A Young Man's Guide: Counsels, Reflections, and Prayers for Catholic Young Men* by Rev F. X. Lasance makes a point of singling out masturbation—"it is said of Onan that the 'Lord slew him because he did a detestable thing'"—as well as homosexuality: "Remember also the fate of the cities of the plain: 'The cry of Sodom and Gomorrah is multiplied, and their sin is become exceedingly grievous.'"[15]

Yet unlike religious instructional guides for girls, which focused on what *not* to do in order to remain pure, the messages for boys in these guides were about becoming a man through correct action and belief. Lasance continually equates morality with traditional manliness: "Manliness implies self-control, conscientiousness, moral courage, fearless discharge of duty in the face of obloquy and prejudice, firm determination to do what is right and pleasing to God." He routinely identifies the opposite of manliness as "effeminacy."[16]

Religious tracts such as these were popular because they were a cunning mixture of the devotional, the instructional, and the titillating. They were not, however, the only popular genre that told boys how to become real men. Mass-marketed literature with engaging, adventure-filled narratives describing idealized masculinity were also popular.

One of the most salient, and durable, manifestations—one that was to become pervasive in popular culture—began with the publication of *Tarzan of the Apes* in 1912. American writer Edgar Rice Burroughs created Tarzan, a British Lord who, abandoned in the African jungle as an infant, is raised by apes and becomes "lord of the jungle." Burroughs wrote over two dozen Tarzan novels and avidly allowed the character to appear in newspaper comics, film serializations, and a massive amount of merchandising.

The popularity of the character was striking. He represented the unspoken fantasy of the innate superiority of the white male who was feeling attacked and beleaguered in early twentieth-century culture.[17] Burroughs's novels are replete with scenes that portray Tarzan, by his very nature, triumphing over both apes and Africans, who are often equated with one another and subdued by violence. *Tarzan of the Apes*—published in a year during which African Americans were being lynched at the rate of one every 5.8 days—

was a reflection and grisly imitation of American race violence of the time. In one scene, Tarzan, in imitation of white American lynch mobs that murdered African American men to protect the purity of white women and the sanctity of motherhood and home, brutally kills the African Kulonnga, who has murdered Kala, Tarzan's ape mother: "Hand over hand Tarzan drew the struggling black until he had him hanging by his neck in midair; then Tarzan climbed to a larger branch drawing the still threshing victim well up into the sheltering verdure of the tree."[18]

Tarzan continues to lynch Africans throughout the novels. To reinforce strict ideologies of heterosexuality, Tarzan has to kill. When describing Tarzan's killing habits, Burroughs is quite clear about what makes an ideal man:

> He killed for food most often, but being a man, he sometimes killed for pleasure, a thing which no other animal does; for it has remained for man alone among all the creatures to kill senselessly and wantonly for the mere pleasures of inflicting suffering and death.[19]

This, certainly, is not what the social purity movement endorsed, but it is close to Roosevelt claiming that "work—fight—breed" were the requisites and qualities of a worthwhile race or nation.

At times the African American man and his "primitive" body were simply demonized as the "black rapist," a threat to white women, who needed to be saved by the heroic, civilized white man. This is the theme of Merian C. Cooper's incredibly popular 1933 film *King Kong*. But Tarzan is a more complicated character; his civilized, lordly heritage makes him smart, but his "primitive" jungle training (he continues to believe he is an ape until he meets other white people) makes him strong and manly.

Burroughs's Tarzan series, twenty-two books in all, was aimed at men and boys. The superior-white-male-in-the-jungle theme continued its extraordinary popularity in a series of twenty books that began in 1926 with *Bomba the Jungle Boy*. The Bomba series was written by various authors under the pseudonym "Roy Rockwood." These books define the difference between white and nonwhite people by asserting that Bomba, who is white, has a soul that is "awake" in his body, but the souls of his native companions are "sleeping." This religious rhetoric, which portrays a race-based conversion rooted in the body, is closely related to social purity thought. It also harkens to the ideology of the Boy Scouts, in which religious sentiment can truly reside only in a healthy and clean body. The Scouts, unlike the homoeroticized cowboys of the past century, were connected to nature but were not outlaws; rather, they were civilized, respectable, and admirable white, heterosexual citizens.

CONSUMING MANLINESS

Public discussion about American masculinity is, at heart, about bodies. In the first three decades of the twentieth century, moral degeneration, "race suicide," and the threat of homosexuality needed to be combated by strong, white, male bodies. These decades also saw the rise of an American physical culture movement that promoted a strong, healthy male body, available to any man who would work for it. In tandem with Roosevelt's personal story of physical transformation and the racialized fantasies of Tarzan, constructing the strong white male body was becoming a consumer industry.

This new commerce in male bodies was started by Eugen Sandow, a Prussian circus strongman who became a London music hall performer in the 1890s. In 1894 he published *Sandow on Physical Training*, a how-to guide for bodybuilding. In 1898 American physical culture and health enthusiast Bernarr Macfadden began publishing *Physical Culture*, a monthly magazine that would grow into a publishing empire. *Physical Culture* offered instructions for physical exercises and promoted good nutrition, but its main message was warning men against drinking, smoking, gambling, masturbation, and nonprocreative sexual intercourse.

Physical Culture unashamedly praised the human body. Macfadden even ran into trouble with Anthony Comstock for his posters of women in tights and men in breechcloths.[20] The motto of *Physical Culture* was "Weakness Is a Crime. Don't Be a Criminal." The magazine discussed health for both women and men, but was obsessed with masculinity. In addition to publishing books such as *Superb Virility of Manhood* (1904), Macfadden marketed devices for enlarging the penis. Throughout the first two decades of the century, he inveighed against homosexuals as well as other perceived social ills. In the 1930s he became an avid anti-Communist and penned editorials such as "Communistic Agitators in Our Schools—Hang the Traitors."[21]

This conflation of physical strength, traditional gender roles, heterosexuality, and patriotic manliness solidified a concept of manhood that increasingly seemed to be under attack. Threats included the increasing visibility of the homosexual, a more urban economy that valued masculine strength less than before, and the emergence of the independent woman. In the midst of all this, the country itself was at war. The rise of a military culture during these years—the Spanish-American War at the end of the nineteenth century, the invasion of Mexico in 1914 and 1916, the occupation of Haiti in 1915, and the United States' entrance into World War I in 1917—contributed to the cult of idealized, heterosexual manhood.

In time, the discussion of masculinity became increasingly sexualized, giving rise to an American visual culture that idolized the exposed, muscular male body as pleasurable in itself. Eroticized images of men appeared in a wide variety of venues: covers and illustrations of books aimed at boys, mainstream advertising art, popular magazines, fine art, and physical culture magazines. For the first time in American consumer culture, the male image, once equated only with toughness, was beginning to be viewed as a sexualized object. Many homosexual artists took advantage of this cultural moment.

Advertising art was one of the first to reflect the shift. The rapid class and social changes that were occurring mandated new forms of dress and deportment. For social and economic mobility, men needed to buy clothing that indicated class or business status. In advertisements and on magazine covers, J.C. Leyendecker's noted illustrations of young, attractive, middle-class businessmen overtly glorified the male body. Leyendecker, who was openly homosexual, designed the iconic "Arrow Collar Man," who represented both stalwart masculinity and urban, middle-class upward mobility. Leyendecker's slightly sleek and prettily dressed office clerk drew on homosexual traditions of the dandy and the fop. The Arrow Collar Man was so enormously popular that even Theodore Roosevelt singled out the image as "a superb example of the common man." Commentators never mentioned that Leyendecker's model for the Arrow Collar Man was his lover, Charles Beach, with whom he openly lived and socialized.

Another homosexual artist of this era was Paul Cadmus, who often worked on government commissions from the Works Progress Administration (WPA). His raucous, sexualized images of obvious homosociality, including murals such as *The Fleet's In!* (1933) and *YMCA Locker Room* (1933) and etchings such as *Two Boys on a Beach* (1938), are considered important contributions to American pictorial art. *The Fleet's In!* prompted complaints from the Navy and the public on the grounds that it gave a negative image of men in the armed forces. Ironically, even though the mural features a clearly homosexual character and interactions, critics more often complained about the female prostitutes.

Consumerism for women also became culturally sexualized. The rise of the department store, with its beautifully arranged, and often erotically enticing, displays of luxury clothing and accessories for women, signaled a shift in how the average shopper thought about the acts of looking and buying. The pervasiveness of this new consumer mentality affected the economy as well as basic structures of sexuality and gender in everyday living. Women's clothing (and even lingerie), once piled on or behind counters, was now beautifully displayed behind large picture windows for the sidewalk public. In the first two decades of the century, women's groups, reflecting the sentiments of the social purity movement, routinely protested such displays. Some cities saw disturbances caused by men gathering outside department store windows. These shockingly new displays of public sexuality were common in almost all American cities.[22] By the 1920s and 1930s, the art of window design and display was spearheaded by homosexual men who, like Leyendecker, drew on a tradition of homosexual aesthetics to promote this wave of consumerism. Vincente Minnelli, who had relationships with women and men and later became a noted Hollywood film director, got his start as a window designer in Chicago. The role of the female consumer also became more and more important as women gained more access to money, either earned or through their husbands.

In the popular imagination and advertising, consumption was continually linked to personal worth: the more money you had, the more you could consume, thus making you a better person. Consumer goods sold to women to enhance their attractiveness— lingerie, dresses, cosmetics, and luxury items such as furs, gowns, and expensive jewelry—enhanced their social status. But they also reflected on the women's status, within their heterosexual relationships, as consumer goods themselves. In a clear critique of heterosexual relationships, economist and sociologist Thorstein Veblen suggested in his 1899 *Theory of the Leisure Class* that the ownership of valuable material objects is indistinguishable from the ownership of women, especially "in a predatory society."[23]

Men during this time were faced with a consumption culture that generated mixed messages. Class mobility was easier for single men, since they did not have to support a family and thus had the disposable income and leisure time to engage in activities that were indicative of a high-class status. Conversely, as Veblen proposed, male consumption was innately tied to heterosexuality. The acquisition of a wife was an essential aspect, if not *the* essential aspect, of American manhood. Due to the rise of what Veblen called "conspicuous consumption" (the purchasing of goods to gain class status), heterosexuality, gender roles, and class status were all costumed performances, and all acquisitions, including wives, were essentially disposable.

The new commodified, ostentatious definitions of masculinity and femininity—partly designed by homosexuals—changed the appearance of American culture, including religion. Americans had embraced conspicuous consumption, spectacle, and the sexuality of the Arrow Collar Man and luxurious woman. The next step was religion sold as entertainment. These decades saw a rise in populist religious figures who preached a distinctly American, heterosexual gospel. The American public responded with enthusiasm. The new technology of radio enabled these preachers to build huge, devoted followings.

Two of the most popular evangelists—they each preached to millions of people in their careers—were Billy Sunday and Aimee Semple McPherson. Each had distinct effects on how Americans conceptualized the links between sexuality, gender, and religion. Sunday, a former baseball player, was an athletic man—yet dapper in conservative, well-made suits—who championed the United States' entry into World War I, spoke out against immigration, and presented himself as an old-fashioned married man. McPherson relied on a sexualized femininity that conveyed a compelling image of the traditional heterosexual woman. The rumors of sexual impropriety that followed McPherson—including an international scandal in which a purported four-week-long kidnapping was thought by many to be a cover-up for an adulterous affair—greatly increased her followers' support and enhanced her embodiment of normal heterosexuality. McPherson's fame and sexual appeal were so great that she was parodied in Broadway shows, as in this ironic lyric from "A Lady Must Live" by Richard Rodgers and Lorenz Hart (from their 1931 show *America's Sweetheart*):

If she is not a cold-blooded person,
What is a girl to do?
But if I looked like Aimee McPherson,
I'd be a good girl too.[24]

The lyric, by the homosexual Hart, highlights the parody inherent in McPherson's and Sunday's performances: they were, in essence, becoming "camp."

Sunday and McPherson reflected the concerns of most social purity activists. They believed in a literal reading of the Bible and preached against drinking, gambling, and the relaxing of traditional gender roles. They denounced representations of immorality in film and theater, decried public dancing, strongly emphasized traditional ideas about sexuality, and were dedicated foes of evolution. Decisively formed by the Gilded Age, both were avid believers in capitalism. Sunday's and McPherson's popular iconography—Sunday's "pitching" for the Lord in an exaggerated pose; McPherson's pearls, furs, expensive cars, and her famous catchphrase "We are passing around a collection plate, be as generous as you can, and no coins please"—was nationally recognizable. Their avid heterosexuality, exaggerated gender roles, money, and success were foregrounded as the hallmarks of American Christianity.

The availability of news broadcasts and entertainment technology turned personal salvation from a private relationship with God into an all-American spectator sport. McPherson, who eschewed Hollywood, routinely relied on sophisticated show-business spectacle in her meetings. The major break from the social purity movement was seen most clearly in Sunday's and McPherson's embrace of a new image of Jesus, one that was radically different from the sentimentalized nineteenth-century version held dear by the social reformers. This new Jesus was a forthright, manly, decisive American who was physically strong, an adventurer, political, and certainly a capitalist.

This was the new "American" Jesus popularized in Bruce Barton's 1925 best seller *A Young Man's Jesus*. Here Jesus had "a strong handshake and a good sense of humor" and "shoulders . . . as broad as his chest was deep." He was a "man's man" as well as a "woman's man."[25] Sunday's virile Jesus conflated the idea of a "real man" with a "real Christian." Sunday's plea— "Lord save us from off-handed, flabby-cheeked, brittle-boned, weak-kneed, thin-skinned, pliable, plastic, spineless, effeminate, sissified, three-carat Christianity"— was a forceful attempt to break from what he saw as the woman-centered Christianity of the nineteenth century, in which Jesus was passive and suffering, not bold and dynamic.[26]

THE FIRST RED SCARE—AND REFORM

As this new religion of stage spectacle and its image of Jesus as capitalist superpatriot were evolving, a fever-pitched theatricality animated a series of harsh crackdowns by the federal government. Called the Red Scare by historians, it brought life-changing consequences to many Americans.

The Red Scare began with the Espionage Act of 1917. The stated intention of this law was to protect the U.S. military during World

War I, but its true aim was to silence speech critical of the government. This intention became clear when the Sedition Act, passed a year later, prescribed severe punishment, including extended time in prison, for anyone who "shall willfully utter, print, write, or publish any disloyal, profane, scurrilous, or abusive language about the form of government of the United States or the Constitution of the United States."

In a new twist on the Comstock Act, the law stipulated that the postmaster general could monitor the U.S. mails for violations of the Sedition Act. The mailing of any political material that was critical of the United States government was now prohibited. The hysteria of the Red Scare was "an orgy of superpatriotism" and a "ferocious burst of supernationalism." But more important, following Mary Douglas's theories, "it was a purification rite—a reaffirmation of American values." These "American" values were primarily the values of the social purity movement, now articulated through a different lens.[27]

The Espionage and Sedition Acts provoked a series of raids between 1919 and 1921, organized by U.S. attorney general Alexander Mitchell Palmer. Known as the Palmer Raids, they were aimed at known and suspected radicals, including aliens, U.S. citizens, and groups. J. Edgar Hoover, newly in charge of the Federal Bureau of Investigation's General Intelligence Division, in less than a year had collected 150,000 names of potential suspects. In the next two years, over 20,000 people were arrested and 556 people, including Emma Goldman and Alexander Berkman, were deported to Russia. Palmer and Hoover cast a wide prosecutorial net. After W. E. B. Du Bois mocked their notion that African American unrest was being caused "by the Russian Bolsheviki," they began investigating the NAACP magazine, the *Crisis*. In 1919, Hoover wrote "Radicalism and Sedition among Negro Publications," a lengthy report that labeled the *Crisis* and similar publications as dangerous to the American way of life.

Though often conceptualized as motivated solely by anti-anarchist or anti-Bolshevik sentiment, these government actions were a response to the social and political changes that had occurred since the later nineteenth century. They included the struggles of immigrants to "become American," the push for racial equality for African Americans, the rise of organized labor, and enormous changes in gender roles and sexuality. The anti-immigrant sentiment—aimed at recently arrived European Catholics and Jews—dovetailed with the white supremacist and eugenicist thinking of the social purity movement.

Most anti-Red propaganda included pro-marriage and pro-family sentiments. In his 1920 *Americanism versus Bolshevism*, Ole Hanson noted that "Americanism is founded on family love and family life; Bolshevism is against family life" and that "Americanism stands for one wife and one country; Bolshevism stands for free love and no country."[28] Royal Baker's 1919 *The Menace of Bolshevism* used language that was directly resonant with the social purity movement:

> This free love idea is undoubtedly the greatest attack against the female sex that has ever been devised. Even the lowest form of savages who indulge in the wildest spirit of cannibalism is far superior to such barbarism as this indecent, hellish state license. . . . What has free love done for Russia? Every woman can be a legalized prostitute.[29]

Although rarely stated in anti-Red material, clearly the new visibility of the invert, the mannish lesbian, and the pansy were instrumental in fueling panic over the sexual threat to the American family and domesticity. Cities were the prime location of suspected Bolshevik activity and presented many other threats as well. Large numbers of newly arrived immigrants lived in cities, as did many African Americans fleeing the South. Cities were also the place where homosexuals were present, evident, and establishing communities that struck at the heart of traditional gender and sexual norms.

The Red Scare began in April 1919 and was essentially over by the late summer of 1920. The great Bolshevik threat never materialized, public opinion turned against Palmer, big business began seeing the value of immigrants as workers, and more traditional ideas about sexuality and gender began to change. Nevertheless, the impact of the Red Scare was tremendous. The formation and growth of conservative, patriotic groups was startling. The American Legion, for example, was founded in May 1919; it had one million members by December and would be a core of conservatism activism for the next century. After the Red Scare, membership in the Ku Klux Klan increased, union membership decreased, antistrike legislation flourished, and forms of racism and anti-immigrant sentiment became institutionalized.[30]

The hysteria of the Red Scare was a successful attempt to "freeze and preserve nineteenth-century economic liberalism and eighteenth-century political institutions." In doing so it shaped a contemporary political philosophy that promoted whiteness as central to an American identity, Gilded Age capitalism over more equitable forms of economic structures, and traditional gender roles and sexual arrangements. Each of these characteristics would have a strong effect of the formation of an LGBT movement in the following decades.

Nevertheless, the progressive spirit continued. In 1918 union leader and presidential candidate Eugene V. Debs, after being found guilty under the Espionage Act, gave this reply to the court:

> Your honor, years ago I recognized my kinship with all living beings, and I made up my mind that I was not one bit better than the meanest on earth. I said then, and I say now, that while there is a lower class, I am in it; while there is a criminal element, I am of it; while there is a soul in prison I am not free.[31]

Many politically active women began to understand that the people most vulnerable to social and physical abuse were ultimately hurt by benevolent protectionism, which at its worst eagerly fed Red Scare paranoia. These social justice activists argued that what America's disenfranchised needed was the economic security and independence to protect themselves and the political skills and social tools to maintain this independence. Many of these women were emotionally involved with other women and worked on projects that affected the everyday lives of women in the workplace and in the home. Their political identifications were often radical, and in their lives and work are the origins of what we now think of as the lesbian feminist social justice movement.

These women came from a variety of backgrounds and approached their work, and lives, though a variety of political approaches. Marie Equi was born to Irish and Italian immigrant parents in New Bedford, Massachusetts, in 1872. At the age of twenty-one she moved to Portland, Oregon, with her partner, Bess Holcomb, who had a job offer there. Several years later they moved to San Francisco, where Equi studied medicine. Her disaster relief work after the 1906 San Francisco earthquake earned her a commendation from the United States Army. In Portland, she performed abortions and worked with Margaret Sanger, with whom she may have had a sexual relationship. A member of the Wobblies, Equi was known for her suffrage and labor organizing. She later became an anarchist. In 1915, with her partner Harriet Speckart, she adopted a child named Mary, who referred to her mothers as "ma" and "da." In 1920, convicted under the Sedition Act, Equi began serving a three-year sentence in San Quentin State Prison. Her crime was protesting against the United States' entry into World War I; during a rally in Portland supporting preparedness for war, she had unfurled a banner that read "PREPARE TO DIE, WORKINGMEN, J. P. MORGAN & CO. WANT PREPAREDNESS FOR PROFIT."

Equi's openly lesbian life contrasts with the life of Elizabeth Gurley Flynn, a noted socialist and Wobblie member who was to become her partner in 1928. Flynn was born in 1890 to working-class parents who identified themselves as socialist and were deeply connected to the Irish independence movement. At an early age, Flynn began seriously study socialism. By age sixteen she was an acclaimed pubic speaker on political issues. After meeting Emma Goldman, Flynn flirted with anarchism, but eventually joined the Wobblies.

Flynn's work as a labor organizer often focused on the problems of women workers. In 1912 she helped run the highly successful factory strike in Lawrence, Massachusetts, in which ten thousand women won safer working conditions and higher wages after a three-month walkout. Flynn, with the help of Margaret Sanger, made temporary foster care arrangements in New York for the children of the striking workers. When police prevented the children from boarding the train in Lawrence, Flynn alerted the press; after national headlines, Congress threatened to investigate.

Flynn was also active in the birth control movement, and she was a founding member of the American Civil Liberties Union in 1920. Although Flynn was married for twelve years to a fellow organizer, and later seriously involved with anarchist Carlo Tresca, she lived from 1928 to 1936 in a relationship with Marie Equi, who had nursed her through a serious heart condition. After they separated, Flynn joined the Communist Party, which did its best to cover up her relationship with Equi.[32] Flynn continued to work with the Communist Party and focused a great deal on the lives of women. In 1945 she was a delegate to the Women's Congress in Paris, which led to the formation of the Women's International Democratic Federation and the U.S.-based Congress for American Women.

Female camaraderie and relationships often had political implications. Trade union organizing, for example, was often split on gender lines. As a result, women union members, because they were not competing with men for attention or social status, often had both the training and the personal confidence to advance into local politics. Single-gender union organizing launched many women into electoral politics. Annie Malloy, for example, an Irish working-class woman and the head of the Telephone Operators' Union, ran for Boston City Council in 1922. Margaret Foley, a pivotal member of the Hat Trimmers' Union in Boston, became a major figure in the powerful Women's Trade Union League as well as the suffrage movement. She continued her political work until the 1940s. Foley lived most of her life with her companion, Helen Elizabeth Goodnow, a suffrage worker from a well-to-do Boston family.[33] For women like Annie Malloy and Margaret Foley, all-women spaces provided an intensive network of friends and political support, allowing them to interact with a larger political world and form long-term relationships across class lines.

The commitment to women's rights and labor issues that was woven into these personal relationships was often connected to a third issue: antimilitarism. Equi and Flynn, like Jane Addams, were outspoken opponents of World War I. In 1915 Addams was elected the first head of the Woman's Peace Party at that organization's founding meeting; later that year she presided over the International Congress of Women, a peace conference held at The Hague. At the congress, the Women's International League for Peace and Freedom was formed, with Addams as its first president.

World War I was opposed by some mainstream women as well. Jeannette Rankin, a Republican congresswoman from Montana, was the only person to vote against the United States' entry into World War I and World War II. Rankin spent years—first as a congresswoman after she was elected in 1916, and then as a lobbyist after she unsuccessfully ran in 1919—fighting for legislation that would promote women's and children's health, including federal money for midwife education and visiting nurse programs for pregnant women. In 1921 her lobbying helped pass the Sheppard-Towner Maternity and Infancy Protection Act, the first federal act that addressed maternal and child health concerns. (It was repealed eight years later due to lobbying by the American Medical Association, which argued that it was government interference with their professional authority.) Along with Flynn, Rankin was a founding member of the American Civil Liberties Union. While she had no apparent intimate relationship with a woman or a man, she did have a network of women confidants. These most notably included Katherine Anthony, whose biographies of Margaret Fuller, Louisa May Alcott, and Susan B. Anthony (no relation) won her acclaim, and Elisabeth Irwin, Katherine's lover, a progressive educator who founded the Little Red School House in Greenwich Village.

The federally funded programs in the 1930s and 1940s that were designed to care for children, workers, and the poor and disenfranchised have their metaphoric, as well as structural, roots in the work done by women such as Jane Addams and Lillian Wald. In addition to promoting the arts, these programs brought about reforms in labor practices, regulation of banks and financial markets, economic support for retirees and those unable to work, and child welfare laws. These reforms ensured a level of economic and personal security for many citizens who would otherwise have been severely disadvantaged.

This shift from the private philanthropic sector to the federal government also engendered roles for women. Many of the women who became prominent in shaping the New Deal were lesbians. Esther Lape, a journalist, and her partner, lawyer Elizabeth Reed, were Eleanor Roosevelt's political mentors. Nancy Cook occupied a high position in the Democratic Party's Women's Division; her partner, Marion Dickerman, ran for public office and was involved in education reform. Molly Dewson was influential as the director of the Women's Division of the Democratic National Committee; her partner, Polly Porter, had a long history working in the suffrage movement. All of these women were deeply committed to women's rights, progressive education, labor reform, racial justice, international human rights, and antimilitarism. The person who helped their ideas influence government policy—they were unofficially called the "ladies' brain trust"—was Eleanor Roosevelt, the wife of the president, a close friend to all of them, and in many ways the center of their circle.

FDR's appointments, on Eleanor's advice, of Frances Perkins as the first female secretary of the treasury and of Mary McLeod Bethune as director of the Division of Negro Affairs in the National Youth Administration—making her the first African American woman appointed to a position in the federal government—were groundbreaking. Eleanor Roosevelt's "ladies' brain trust" was the logical outgrowth of earlier female support networks. These networks were ongoing and complicated. Political change originates in a multiplicity of intersections of the personal and organizational that are always the result of many years of social and political evolution. The historic moment in which Eleanor Roosevelt and her trusted friends were able to help shape national policy was the result of a wide variety of mainstream and radical groups that fought for social justice, as well as the complicated lives of all the women and men involved in these struggles.

Eleanor Roosevelt had a deeply committed relationship with her husband that involved working together closely and raising five children. They also both had lovers and committed relationships outside of the marriage. For several years Eleanor Roosevelt was romantically and sexually involved with journalist Lorena Hickok; later this relationship was replaced by a profound, if complicated, friendship. Hickok reported on Roosevelt's political work and, in 1959, authored a book for young adults, *The Story of Eleanor Roosevelt*, that detailed her former lover's life and work. Their letters give a profound sense of their involvement. On February 4, 1934, Roosevelt wrote to Hickok from the White House:

> Hick darling, I just talked to you, darling, it was so good to hear your voice. If I just could take you in my arms. Dear, I often feel rebellious too & yet I know we get more joy when we are to-gether than we would have if we lived apart in the same city & could only meet for short periods now & then. Someday perhaps fate will be kind & let us arrange a life more to our liking [but] for the time being we are lucky to have what we have. Dearest, we are happy to-gether & strong relationships have to grow deep roots.[34]

Roosevelt remained intensely involved with her "ladies' brain trust" for decades. Later in life, working with the United Nations, she was deeply committed to international human rights.

By the 1930s, after the advent of sexology, female romantic friendships were widely, and suspiciously, viewed as sexual and unhealthy. In addition, freer discussion of lesbianism and sex allowed female social justice activists, and all Americans, to understand gender and sexuality in a new light. Although her letters do give us a portrait of an intensely passionate woman, we can never know exactly what Eleanor Roosevelt felt—it is widely believed that, in addition to her affair with Hickok, she also had an affair with her bodyguard, Earl Miller, who was ten years her junior—but we know that her close female friendships sustained her life and her progressive political vision. As her life, loves, political interests, and passions demonstrate, Roosevelt, unlike the women in the social purity movement, valued personal and social freedoms over the idea of restricting human behavior. Eleanor Roosevelt and her female friends believed in creating a world in which people were helped to find and make their own lives and happiness, not simply be protected from social evils. In this way, their work was a rejoinder to the divisive strictures of the persecuting society, which had retained its hold on much of American social and political culture over the previous two centuries.

As the United States moved into World War II and the second half of the twentieth century, it was evident that, at least for the moment, the persecuting society was losing ground to progressive reform and that women and men who loved those of their own sex were finding more freedom then ever before. The ideals that led to the New Deal would resurface in more radical form, resembling the political thinking of Victoria Woodhull, Emma Goldman, and Alexander Berkman, among others, in the late 1950s and early 1960s, as a wave of personal, political, and cultural liberation movements began to revolutionize the basic fabric of society in the United States.

EIGHT

SEX IN THE TRENCHES

It is impossible to overestimate the effect of World War II on American culture, and in particular on lesbians and gay men. The United States entered World War II, which had been ongoing since September 1939, after the Japanese attacked Pearl Harbor in December 1941. This decisive turning point in U.S. history reordered American social life and mores, public and private space, and virtually all social interactions having to do with gender and sexual behavior.

The country's entrance into the war radically transformed the domestic economy into a booming war economy, ending the Depression. The war economy not only provided much-needed jobs for Americans—the unemployment rate dropped from 17.2 percent in 1939 to 4.7 percent in 1942 and 1.2 percent in 1944—but also stimulated production of manufactured goods and increased farm production. As military-related industries such as shipyards, munitions plants, and aircraft manufacturing factories thrived, they provided employment for millions of women and men and drew workers to move from their towns and cities of birth. Between 1941 and the late 1960s, more than five million African Americans moved to urban areas, a shift that greatly helped facilitate the work of the civil rights movement of the 1960s.

These changes posed fundamental questions of citizenship. Throughout American history, full citizenship—the ability to fully partake in the obligations of governance, including voting and defending the nation, as well as to receive entitlements, such as equal protection under the law and access to state-sponsored programs—was influenced by a variety of factors. These included race, ethnicity, and religious affiliation as well as gender, gender expression, and sexual behavior. The enormous challenges that the United States had faced since the turn of the century, including waves of immigration, the rise of cities, the Great Depression, and World War I, had redefined citizenship. It was now a society more tolerant of racial, ethnic, and religious differences and one that was striving, however imperfectly, to embrace social and personal freedoms.

WAR, GENDER, SEX

Although new freedoms in the early twentieth century centered increasingly on gender and sexual behavior, social anxiety about homosexuality remained. In some cases, it became more prevalent. Margot Canaday documents how a fear of the single man, the non-family man, was conflated with male homosexual behavior by the Federal Transient Program (FTP) and the Civilian Conservation Corps (CCC). Both of these single-gender New Deal programs gave work to displaced adult men. Men living together generated anxiety, as did the imagined possibility of younger men being sexually exploited. This anxiety eventually caused the federal government to focus less on programs aimed at unattached people, and ultimately to avoid implementing policies that might be seen as enabling "sexual perversion."[1]

Ironically, the first major change that occurred after Pearl Harbor was the massive relocation of men into the armed forces, where they would be living together. After the war began and conscription started, most Americans supported the war effort. By the end of the war in 1945, more than sixteen million United States citizens and residents had joined the armed forces. Ten million of those had been drafted. Although the armed forces accepted men up to the age of thirty-eight, the majority in all branches were in their twenties; 35 percent of navy personnel during the war years were teenagers.

The majority of men in the armed forces were white, but other racial groups were also represented. Seven hundred thousand, or 4 percent of the military, were African Americans; they were joined by 350,000 Mexican Americans, Chinese Americans, Native Americans, and Puerto Ricans. Throughout the war—until President Truman issued Executive Order 9981 in 1948—the American armed forces were segregated. This meant that, with rare exceptions, only white men could become officers or fight in combat. African Americans and other racial groups worked as cooks, truck drivers, stevedores, or warehouse workers. (There were some attempts at integration, and at the instigation of Eleanor Roosevelt, the USS *Mason* was manned with an African American crew trained to fill all of the ship's positions, not just cooks and mess hall workers. The *Mason* was nicknamed "Eleanor's Folly.")

As men entered the armed forces, a major shift in gender roles occurred. With men at war, women were hired in occupations and positions that traditionally had been held by men, including office work and factory jobs. Previously, women's employment was often predicated on class and race. Many working-class women, including minority women, already worked because they had families to support. Now middle-class women were expected to work. When the war began, married women and mothers of young children were urged to stay at home. As the war continued, they too began entering the workforce. Before 1941, women made up less than 25 percent of the U.S. workforce—about twelve million workers. By 1945, that number had reached over eighteen million, a full third of the workforce. (Simultaneously, the number of women employed as domestic workers fell from 17.7 to 9.5 percent.) Over a million women—"government girls"—worked clerical jobs in Washington, D.C.; three million worked nationally in war plants. There was a 462 percent increase of women in defense industry jobs. After initial industry skepticism, women ultimately performed as well as men, and in jobs that demanded manual dexterity, even better. These women were seen as vital to the war effort as the fighting man.

These workplace shifts substantially altered gender roles. Home-front women workers were regarded as independent and strong. Ubiquitous government propaganda posters featured Rosie the Riveter in bright colors, with her masculine factory uniform and a kitchen head scarf, flexing her biceps, with the slogan "We

Can Do It!" Images of women working heavy machinery and driving trucks routinely appeared in *Life* magazine and other publications.

In a decisive break from the past, large numbers of women experienced independence, economic security, and psychological satisfaction. Women were paid less than men for the same jobs, but they were paid better than before and for jobs not previously open to them. In 1940 Los Angeles, 55 percent of nonwhite women worked as help in white homes. By 1950 this number had dropped to less than 40 percent. Fanny Christina Hill, an African American who went to work at a munitions factory, claimed, "The war made me live better, it really did. My sister always said that Hitler was the one who got us out of the white folks' kitchen."[2]

Once they entered the workforce, most women liked being able to support themselves or their families, find new communities, and acquire useful skills. Most gained a stronger sense of self. Many lived on their own or with roommates, away from their families, and conducted their social and romantic lives as they pleased. For single women who did not rely on a man to support them, and for lesbians who had never expected a man to support them, this was a major step in economic and social independence.

Conscription into the armed forces was limited to male citizens, but many women enlisted. This was a major change in United States culture since, aside from nurses, women had never before been admitted into the military. Military women were granted a social status and respect not offered them in civilian life. Over 250,000 women served in the war: 140,000 in the Women's Army Corps (WAC) and over 100,000 in the U.S. Navy as WAVES (Women Accepted for Volunteer Emergency Service). By 1945, 43,000 women had joined the Marine Corps Women's Reserve and 10,000 had enlisted in the Coast Guard Women's Reserve, known as SPARs. Women in the military performed numerous jobs, including nursing, clerical duties, weather forecasting, photography, and air traffic control; most vital was the work of radio and telephone operators and communication directors. Now able to work in jobs from which they were excluded before, women could be viewed as strong, competent, and skilled professionals.

Widespread public support of the war was indicative of a cohesive mid-century American identity. The growing threat of Germany, Japan, and Italy was great enough that Americans, including members of traditionally disenfranchised groups, felt obligated to defend their country. That is not to say the patriotism of minority groups was without critique. Large numbers of African Americans who had moved north for war-related work faced discrimination there, just as they did in the South. In 1942 the *Pittsburgh Courier,* the oldest African American newspaper in the country, started the Double V campaign, arguing that victory over fascism overseas must be accompanied by victory over racism at home.

The war drastically accelerated the massive movement of people that had begun with the rise of cities. Men moved from their hometowns to join the armed forces. With fathers, sons, and brothers overseas, and mothers, daughters, and sisters often working in distant defense plants, members of the extended biological family did not necessarily live close to one another. Increased contact with new people and ideas often challenged the religious and moral upbringing of these women and men.

In response to all of this, many aspects of marriage changed. During the war, "the proportion of persons never married and the median age at first marriage declined by as much as they had during the preceding half century"; one commentator called the skyrocketing rate of marriage "the war disease."[3] Between 1940 and 1943, over a million more couples than expected got married.[4] Many of these marriages occurred hurriedly, as couples publicly declared their love for one another before the men left for war.

World War II changed ideas about private and public, broadening the parameters of social permissibility. It was now permissible to show deeply felt personal emotions in public. Crying as a loved one shipped out, weeping over a death, and other displays of emotional pain and distress were acceptable public behaviors. This was also true of sexual passion and desire, as illustrated by Alfred Eisenstaedt's famous photograph *V-J Day in Times Square,* in which a sailor is passionately kissing a nurse in broad daylight. Such behavior, unthinkable before the war, was now acceptable. Servicemen on leave, even if intoxicated, were respected by civilians. The emotional urgency of the war changed social and sexual expectations. Women could now socialize, even flirt, with servicemen in public venues.

The female body, once seen as in need of protection, was now a fortified body that built ships and defended democracy. This was happening as sons, fathers, brothers, uncles, and friends were killed, wounded, paralyzed, and shell-shocked during the ferocious battles in Europe and the Pacific. The destruction of the male body was evident, even as government censorship shielded civilian from the worst images. In the national imagination, the nobility of the cause made these bodies heroic, highlighting the tragedy of their destruction. Images of fighting men in the popular press were a jarring paradox—extraordinarily valiant and extraordinarily fragile. Documentary combat photographs were often juxtaposed with pictures of shirtless men on battleships or in trenches—dirty, sweaty, and vulnerable. Images of patriotic men, many of them teenagers, dying for their country highlighted their fragility and nobility. This new standard of national masculinity, and its counterpoint image of strong women, radically altered how America viewed men and women.

AN ARMY OF LOVERS

The physically and emotionally vulnerable "new American man" was a reality for men living under the stress of battle and threat of death. For the first time in American history, large-scale, highly organized single-sex social arrangements were considered vital to national security. Men on battleships and battlefields lived together in close quarters with little privacy. The physical intimacy and stressful conditions often led to emotional and sexual intimacy. Servicemen in these all-male groups turned to their fellow troops for emotional and psychological support. The stress of leaving home, shipping out, active battle, and years of war allowed men to be vulnerable with one another in ways impossible outside of this environment.

Servicewomen were undergoing similar experiences. Without men in their everyday lives, WACs and WAVES formed emotional friendships that were, perhaps, similar to the female romantic friendships of the nineteenth century. But now a more open culture encouraged awareness of sexual possibilities. Certainly women's new social freedoms, such as access to higher education, reproductive control (albeit limited), and the vote, made these relationships markedly different than in the past.

Wartime conditions produced social systems appealing to homosexuals. Single-sex environments encouraged homosocial relationships. Lesbians who were economically and socially independent of men found the military a haven. Homosexual men could now avoid their family's heterosexual expectations.

Many men, including homosexuals, found outlets for their abilities and talents in the military. The United Service Organization (USO), a private organization founded in 1941 to boost morale by providing recreation and other services for the military, brought entertainment to the troops and offered a place for men with theatrical interests. Director and actor Tyler Carpenter writes about how he was recruited to put together a series of USO shows using professional entertainers and enlisted men. When his heterosexual commanding officer discovered the projected cost, he suggested using recruits in drag to play the female parts.[5]

The benefits of the military for homosexuals were outweighed by the reality that sodomy was prohibited by Article 125 of the Uniform Code of Military Justice. The article stated: "Any person subject to this chapter who engages in unnatural carnal copulation with another person of the same or opposite sex or with an animal is guilty of sodomy. Penetration, however slight, is sufficient to complete the offense." Anyone suspected of being homosexual, and thus presumed to be engaging in sodomy, could be discharged and punished under military regulations.

While the code regulated the behavior of homosexual service members, it did nothing to keep them out. But by mid-1941 the Selective Service had instituted a policy to screen homosexuals from joining the military (although the policy did not always succeed). This decision had a complicated history. During and after World War I, in which there was little recruit screening, many soldiers were diagnosed with severe emotional trauma. Some of it was certainly "shell shock," but the military thought preenlistment screening could have prevented the worst cases. To avoid a recurrence, in 1940 the government, in conjunction with psychiatrists—including Harry Stack Sullivan, who was quietly homosexual—set up a psychological screening process to weed out men ineligible for military service.

At first this process focused on mental and emotional disorders; little attention was paid to sexual practices, although effeminate men were suspect. As the screening process was amended by other psychiatrists and the army surgeon general over the next year, homosexuality became a disqualifying category. The armed forces now banned people with "homosexual proclivities" because they had "psychopathic personality disorders." These new categories conflated the idea of the "sexual psychopath" with stereotypes predicated on gender norm deviation. The result was a government-sponsored definition of the homosexual. The navy broadened these categories by issuing vaguely worded orders that banned people "whose sexual behavior is such that it would engender or disturb the morale of a military unit."[6] For the first time, a direct link was being made between homosexual behavior and a threat to national security.

Although Harry Stack Sullivan refused to categorize homosexuality as an emotional disorder, the army surgeon general disagreed. But both views were irrelevant after December 1941. The immediate need for women and men to join the war effort outweighed any other considerations. Homosexuals eager to join the armed forces found little to prevent them. Ample personal stories attest to how homosexuals enlisted. Historian Allan Bérubé writes of Robert Fleisher enlisting in 1943 and worrying about being rejected: "My God . . . couldn't they see my curly platinum blond hair that was partly bleached, the walk, maybe the sissy *S* in my voice—all the things that I thought would give me away?" The only question he was asked about his sexuality was "Do you like girls?" to which he answered "yes," since it was true.[7] Pat Bond describes the recruiting sergeant at her 1945 enlistment as "like all my old gym teachers in drag. Stockings, little earrings, her hair slicked back and very daintily done so you couldn't tell she was a dyke, but *I* knew!"[8]

Bond claims that many women arrived at recruitment centers "wearing argyle socks and pin-striped suits and the hair cut just like a man's with sideburns shaved over the ears—the whole bit." She remembers that when she entered the barracks for the first time, a voice loudly proclaimed "Good God, Elizabeth, here comes another one!"[9] Tyler Carpenter remembers how in 1941 his lover, Eddie Fuller, went with him to the induction center in New York, where they waited in line with heterosexual couples:

> Finally, it was time to enter. The boys and the girls kissed. Eddie and I shook hands, a convention that feel far short of the kiss we both wanted and deserved. "Tyler, you'll be fine. You can do anything that any of the other guys can do," Eddie said. I breathed deep, climbed the steps and entered into an unknown world.[10]

It is impossible to know how many homosexuals served during the war years. Lillian Faderman argues that the "'firm public impression' during the war years that a women's corps was 'the ideal breeding ground for lesbians' had considerable basis in fact."[11] Hypothetically, if Alfred Kinsey's 1948 study of male sexual behavior was correct, then somewhere between 650,000 and 1.6 million male soldiers primarily had sex with other men.[12]

Millions of young women and men, many of whom may never have heard the words "fairy," "invert," "homosexual," or "lesbian" and may not yet have discovered all aspects of their sexual desires, had enlisted. Being thrown together with so many different people of the same sex gave them an opportunity to understand their lives in new, radical ways. Bérubé weaves a broad, textured tapestry of the lives of same-sex-desiring service members during the war. Many speak of erotic, affectional, and sexual relationships with their fellow enlistees. Some of these relationships—like that of Tyler Carpenter and Eddie Fuller—began before the war and lasted for decades. Others occurred during the war, ending when the partners reentered civilian life. Many were brief sexual encounters, similar to heterosexual liaisons on the home front. Many women and men enjoyed same-sex romantic and physical relationships during the war, but for the reminder of their lives engaged in different-sex relationships.

In spite of potential harassment and prosecution, homosexual women and men began forming communities within the military. Maxwell Gordon, stationed at the San Diego Naval Training Station, remembers feeling a sense of recognition:

> Here's all these interesting people from all over the United States. . . . There were some teachers and some clerks and office workers. For the most part they were rather "sensitive" boys. . . . I thought, "Oh, these are more my kind of people. You know, we can communicate." . . . We became very chummy, quite close, very fraternal, very protective of each other.[13]

Homosexual men, especially if effeminate, were often harassed, but groups such as the one Gordon describes were frequently ignored for the sake of unit cohesiveness. David L. Leavitt, along with his homosexual shipmates stationed in Guam, claimed a secluded island beach as their own. Only a select group of men knew of the existence of this beach, which they called Purple Beach Number 2, reminiscent of a perfume brand.[14]

While on leave, homosexual men and women also found community in bars, baths, and private homes. This was particularly true for women who were stationed on bases near cities. Jean S. recalls socializing during the war after joining the Women's Army Corps:

> My commanding officer turned every head at the Boston Army base—5′6″, curly blonde hair, cute as can be and a smart cookie. She played around, but had a partner in Georgia. . . .There were women in the detachment I knew were lesbians, there was no question in my mind, but we never spoke of this. You just didn't at the time. You just wouldn't make any reference to it. We would socialize together, both straight and lesbian.[15]

"Sensitive" men often found one another while working on the extraordinarily popular "soldier shows" for which the USO provided the know-how and the materials. These shows were written, directed, and performed by men in the armed forces. Since there were no women in outlying camps, enlisted men would perform female roles in drag. Performances ranged from comic portrayals of burly men in dresses to realistic female impersonation. For actors and audiences, these performances were a needed relief from the stress of war. For men who identified as homosexual, these shows were a place where they could, in coded terms, express their sexual desires, be visible, and build a community. These lyrics for a "female" trio in a soldier show demonstrate how homosexual enlistees introduced their own humor into skits:

Here you see three lovely "girls"
With their plastic shapes and curls.
Isn't it campy? Isn't it campy?

We've got glamour and that's no lie;
Can't you tell when we swish by?
Isn't it campy? Isn't it campy?[16]

Later in the war, when WACs were available to perform with men, their involvement was limited; usually they worked backstage to help the men be made up as women. An indication of the popularity of female impersonation in soldier shows is evident in Irving Berlin's *This Is the Army*. Written for an all-soldier cast, it premiered on Broadway in 1942 and a year later became a hit Hollywood film with Ronald Reagan. Both the Broadway and film versions featured soldiers dressed as women.

Surprising images of military male bodies appeared in advertisements for popular products in the national press. The most startling of these, placed in *Life* and *Better Homes and Gardens,* was a series of six "True Towel Tales"—each based on a story from a serviceman—produced by the Cannon Towel company. Set on different battlefronts, the ads featured men in various stages of undress using Cannon towels while bathing. "True Towel Tales: No. 6" showed a group of presumably naked soldiers in a grounded canoe; the central figure is standing, covered with a palm frond, in a bathing-beauty pose. The advertisement clearly displays the men as sexual objects and highlights their vulnerability, in sharp juxtaposition to the realities of war.

Advertisements for Pullman sleeping cars (civilian train cars used to move troops) featured half-naked servicemen partying. One Pullman advertisement showed two soldiers, following tradition, removing their shoes and socks to enter an Egyptian residence during the day; the sexually suggestive caption was "I never did this in *daylight* before!"[17] An analysis of advertising in *Life* magazine demonstrates that "just before the conflict, in 1940, there had been several issues of the magazine with no adult men alone together, without women; by 1943 and 1944, only one issue had no such male-to-male interaction in advertising."[18]

Communities of homosexuals in the service and in civilian life mutually reinforced one another. Numerous venues in cities across the nation catered to homosexual clientele. African American servicemen, banned from bars in many cities, were welcomed in the Harlem jazz club Lucky's Rendezvous, where, *Ebony* reported, black and white patrons "steeped in the swish jargon of its many lavender costumers."[19] The Black Cat in San Francisco welcomed female prostitutes, lesbian civilians, and homosexual servicemen. For heterosexuals, sexual activity outside of marriage was so prevalent that special terms were coined for young women who would socialize and have sex with servicemen as a patriotic duty: "victory girls," "khaki-wackies," and "good-time Charlottes."

The enormous social shifts of this era also changed how people wrote about homosexuality. Medical professionals and popular journalists did not radically alter their views of same-sex behavior, but new ways of thinking about homosexuality were emerging. In 1941 George W. Henry, a psychiatrist and director of the Committee for the Study of Sex Variants, wrote *Society and the Sex Variant,* one of the first comprehensive scientific studies of homosexual behavior. Based on interviews with homosexual women and men starting in 1935, the study frequently reaffirms stereotypes of homosexuality as inverted behavior. For instance, it describes male homosexuals' speech as "excessive, chatty, gossipy, mincing," with "many sexual innuendoes" and "extravagant superlatives," whereas lesbian speech is "cautious, businesslike; response prompt, precise, often monosyllabic." With all of its flaws, the study gave the 1941 reader interviews with female and male homosexuals who spoke honestly about their lives. Henry's vision—he thought it unscientific to classify persons as fully male or female—was startling for the time.

A year later, Philip Wylie's enormously popular, and harsh, critique of American culture, *Generation of Vipers*, was published. Not particularly sympathetic to homosexuals, his view, like Henry's, was guardedly tolerant. Attacking sexual ignorance, Wylie stated that "America is still populated with male ignoramuses who stand ready to slug a nance on sight and often do so." He argued that homosexual activity was increasing in the United States and was "common in the navy, the army, and in colleges both for men and for women," and that "a very large portion of the upper-class and upper-middle-class citizens of the nation have made one or more experiments in that form of erotic activity." Suggesting that all people have homosexual feelings and that "inborn sluggers of nances" are repressing their own homosexual tendencies, he noted that most Americans find homosexual acts "horrible, repulsive, loathsome, and altogether beyond the pale of thinkability. . . . The fact that it goes on all the time means only that millions of people have dangerously guilty consciences."[20]

Even the government displayed its own ambivalence. In 1943 the federally funded National Research Council, Penguin Books, and the *Infantry Journal* jointly published *Psychology for the Fighting Man*. A guide for young men new to the service, it forthrightly and calmly addressed men's fears about homosexual impulses:

> A soldier can take what comfort he may in the knowledge that other men are confronted with just about the same problems as he is and that, while they may never find an escape from them, most men manage to endure them and do not allow them to impair their efficiency seriously.
> It helps to work hard.
> It helps to avoid the company of those preoccupied with sex.

It helps to get as much fun as possible. Companionship with the other men and the varied social activities of camp life keep a soldier from lonely brooding and day-dreaming. So does the intensive activity of campaign and battle. For those who enjoy them, athletic sports—boxing matches or ball games—are diverting and healthful.[21]

The guide also noted that some homosexuals in the military were not conflicted about their sexuality. It advised that if such men "readily apply their interest and energy to the tasks of army life" and "if they are content with quietly seeking the satisfaction of their sexual needs with others of their own kind, their perversion may continue to go unnoticed and they may even become excellent soldiers."[22]

At the same time that it was distributing *Psychology for the Fighting Man,* the military was beginning to purge homosexuals. In 1941 secretary of war Henry Stimson ordered all "sodomists" be court-martialed and, if found guilty, sentenced to five years of hard labor. The courts-martial quickly became too costly. In 1942 Stimson allowed Section 8 discharges—called "blue discharges," after the color of the paper on which they were printed—for homosexuals. A Section 8 discharge was not a dishonorable discharge, issued after a court-martial, but neither was it an honorable discharge. The Veterans Administration quickly determined that a Section 8 discharge precluded a former service member from entitlements. These included access to health care at a VA hospital and accessing the numerous benefits of the GI Bill, such as college tuition, occupational training, mortgage insurance, and loans to start businesses. Worse, a Section 8 discharge often meant that the former service member was unable to get a job in civilian life.

The army alone issued between forty-nine thousand and sixty-eight thousand Section 8 discharges. As the war drew to a close, Section 8 discharges were given more frequently. Homosexuals were not the only ones affected. African Americans were discharged, often for protesting civilian and military Jim Crow laws, in such disproportionate numbers—22.2 percent for a group that made up only 6.5 percent of the army—that the national black press started a campaign against the practice.

For homosexuals, receiving a Section 8—which essentially indicated mental illness—could be devastating. Women and men were often committed to hospital psychiatric units for examinations, grilled about their sexual thoughts and practices, and forced to give names of their sexual partners. Many men were physically and sexually abused, and public humiliation was commonplace. In some places, homosexual servicemen were rounded up and placed in "queer stockades" until they could be processed. More than five thousand homosexuals were released with Section 8 discharges from the army, and more than four thousand from the navy. Margot Canaday notes that the military stepped up purges of lesbians after the war, when women were supposed to go back into the home.[23]

The implicit inclusion of homosexuals in the military, juxtaposed with official discrimination, complicated the homosexuals' relationship to the ideal of American citizenship. This model was to be enacted in numerous ways over the next decades. While visibility brought benefits to homosexuals, it also brought opposition, particularly the stigma of a pathological identity. As Canaday notes, "What was an inchoate and vague sort of opposition between citizenship and perversion in the early twentieth century became a hard and clear line by midcentury."[24] The effect of these witch hunts was personally traumatic. Pat Bond states that at her base in Tokyo, over five hundred women were sent home and discharged. She vividly recalls a specific tragic incident: "They called up one of our kids— Helen. They got her up on the stand and told her that if she didn't give names of her friends they would tell her parents she was gay. She went up to her room on the sixth floor and jumped out and killed herself. She was twenty."[25]

Such events illustrate an ongoing struggle between legal principles, which categorized homosexual behavior as a crime, and the more "enlightened" principles of medicine, which viewed homosexuality as an illness. As medicine's power to define homosexuality grew, so did the implications of what it meant to be homosexual. Psychiatry, which had once defined homosexuality simply as a sexual act, now defined it as a psychological state, present with or without physical acts. Many psychiatrists believed that homosexuality should not be punished, but as a profession, they believed it could be cured.

BRINGING THE WAR HOME

When the war ended, society expected women and men to revert to traditional gender roles. As men came back from the war, women were expected to give up their jobs. However, while some women did leave the workforce to raise a family, many women wanted, or needed, to continue working. Lesbians, who were never going to have the economic support of a husband, worked to support themselves. Polls taken between 1943 and 1945 showed that 61 percent to 85 percent of women wanted to keep their jobs, including 47 percent to 68 percent of married women. This massive realignment of the workforce, economics, and gender roles played a decisive role in shaping how Americans viewed both the housewife and the working, economically independent woman.

American postwar life was marked by trauma. Virtually everyone in America had lost a family member, work colleague, friend, or neighbor. Physical trauma was most visible on the wounded or maimed male body. Emotional trauma was equally apparent. Men were now more able to be emotional, express their feelings, and even cry. The stereotypical "strong, silent type," quintessentially heterosexual, that had characterized the American Man had been replaced with a new, sensitive man who had many of the qualities of the homosexual male.

After the war, homosexual novelists began exploring the intense emotional lives of men who had fought in the war. These novels were an attempt to uncover how the severe trauma of the war affected not only fighting men but American masculinity. They detailed the complicated connections between the war, American men, and homosexual identity in society.

Some novels took place during the war and explored men's relationships with one another. John Horne Burns's 1947 *The Gallery* presented a sympathetic portrait of military patrons of a gay bar in

Naples. Another example is *The Invisible Glass*, a 1950 novel by Loren Wahl (the pen name of Lorenzo Madalena, who took the title from a quote by W. E. B. Du Bois). The novel details the tragic relationship of Steve La Cava, a white lieutenant, and Chick, an African American driver, who are stationed in Italy in 1945. In a scene in which the two men are sharing a bed, Wahl made the homosexuality clear:

> With a slight moan Chick rolled onto his left side, toward the Lieutenant. His finger sought those of the officer's as they entwined their legs. Their faces met. The breaths, smelling sweet from wine, came in heavy drawn sighs. La Cava grasped the soldier by his waist and drew him tightly to his body. His mouth pressed down until he felt Chick's lips part. For a moment they lay quietly, holding one another with strained arms.[26]

The Invisible Glass contains surprising nuances. Chick, a former UCLA student, is straight but has sex with men; Steve is just coming to terms with his sexuality, even though he has fallen in love with men. Much of the plot revolves around military racism, reflecting the complexity of men's lives in the war.

Novels such as Gore Vidal's *The City and the Pillar* (1948), Fritz Peters's *The World Next Door* (1949), and James Barr's *Quatrefoil* (1950) examined men who had come out during the war and the effect on their lives after the war. An ongoing theme in these novels is how the rising presence and acceptance of homoerotic desires in men's lives was transforming American masculinity.

Homosexual writers were not the only ones concerned with same-sex relationships in the postwar novel. Norman Mailer's 1948 *The Naked and the Dead*, on the *New York Times* best-seller list for sixty-two weeks, dealt with masculinity. One of its main characters, General Cummings, a repressed homosexual, embodied all of the contradictions of American masculinity. James Jones's 1951 *From Here to Eternity,* which won a National Book Award, contained numerous references to sex between men. One of its main characters, a heterosexual soldier, spent a great deal of time socializing and having sex with wealthy gay male civilians for money. The enormous popularity of these works demonstrates that large numbers of people were ready to consider questions about how Americans thought about sex.

Other heterosexual novelists explicitly critiqued what they saw as destructive American masculinity. Richard Brooks's 1945 *The Brick Foxhole* detailed the brutal murder of an openly gay man by a sociopathic soldier. Brooks, later a noted film director, made it clear that his antagonist's hatred of homosexuals (as well as Jews and African Americans) was directly linked to his ideas about white American masculinity. The "brick foxhole" in which these soldiers are trapped signifies, among other things, masculinity.

Social conservatives objected to the content in these books, claiming they misrepresented the wholesomeness of the American fighting man. Mailer's editor made him change the frequently used "fuck" to "fug," and Jones's editor made him remove scenes describing, or even discussing, the characters' homosexual activities. According to James Rorty, the National Organization for Decent Literature, a group founded in 1937 with support from the American Council of Catholic Bishops, was one of a myriad of censorship and reform groups at work after the war. These groups were reinvigorated in the late 1940s and early 1950s, in direct opposition to the changes brought about by World War II. The goal of the National Organization for Decent Literature was "to organize and set in motion the moral forces of the entire country" by prohibiting, through use of boycotts, the sale of "the lascivious type of literature which threatens the moral, social and national life of our country."[27] Their list of indecent books, including Hemingway's *A Farewell to Arms*, Lillian Smith's antilynching novel *Strange Fruit*, Flaubert's *Madame Bovary*, Zola's *Nana*, and Boccaccio's *Decameron*, was sent to parishes, women's clubs, drugstores, and supermarkets.[28]

Because so many Americans were now enjoying the freedoms that had emerged during the war—including the freedom to read about sexuality—the censorship groups made limited headway. Civil liberties organizations, librarians, and free speech advocates resisted these groups, although with uneven results. Compared to heterosexual themes, homosexual material was seen by free speech advocates as less defendable in the legal system or the court of public opinion. Therefore homosexual material was the most likely to be banned. This two-tiered system was instrumental in reasserting a decisive separation between heterosexuality and homosexuality in the public imagination.

The tension between the possibility of new freedom and the heightened sense of danger that it brought was instrumental in forming the postwar homosexual. As Allan Bérubé states, "The veterans of World War II were the first generation of gay men and women to experience such rapid, dramatic, and widespread changes in their lives as homosexuals."[29] The new postwar openness created a more openly sexual society that placed hostility to homosexuality in sharp relief.

After the war, marriage rates among young people rose precipitously. The age of marriage dropped—many marriages happened right after high school—and the birth rate in the United States increased tremendously. January 1946 saw 222,721 births; in October, there were 339,499. The 1940s saw 32 million births, up from 24 million during the 1930s. This trend continued into the next decade. Many heterosexual couples and their new families moved to the suburbs that were being built across the country. Their migration out of the city again radically changed the nature, texture, and population of urban areas.

Meanwhile, lesbians and gay men—terms that were beginning to be used with more frequency, first within the homosexual community and then in popular speech—were understanding their relationship to American society primarily through cities. Lesbian and gay male veterans frequently decided not to return to their towns of birth; instead they moved to large cities, where they knew they could live more openly. Homosexuals had undergone a sexual revolution during the war. This revolution contributed almost immediately to a new sense of community, first in the armed forces and then in civilian life. Large cities across the country—especially those on the East and West coasts, where women and men from overseas disembarked on their return—saw enormous growth in the number of lesbians and gay men. While these urban homosexual communities were not entirely new, their numbers were now much larger. Their formation was also aided by technological advances—inexpensive paperback books, wider access to the telephone, 78 RPM and then long-playing records, and eventually television—that precipitated the faster circulation of ideas and images.

Even fundamental ideas about space and community changed. In contrast to communities organized around the biological family, the new homosexual communities needed smaller living spaces for single people or couples, but a much larger space for community activities. These social spaces included restaurants, theaters, bars, coffeehouses, and parks. Most large cities had neighborhoods that accommodated these needs. Many of them, such as San Francisco's North Beach, the west side of Boston's Beacon Hill, or New York's Greenwich Village, were neighborhoods that had previously been occupied by newly arrived immigrants, who required vibrant public social space in which they could sustain their own culture.

These neighborhoods were often in the less prosperous sections of cities. One reason is that most veterans, even those with access to GI Bill benefits, had little money. A second is that the small-scale economy of these areas facilitated affordable retail space—a necessary building block for newly forming communities, especially since many lesbians and gay men decided to start their own businesses. Having made the decision to be more open about their sexuality, they understood they might have a difficult time finding employment; going into business for themselves allowed them to act, dress, and speak as they chose. And if they were veterans, they could take advantage of the GI Bill's business loan guaranty program. (These businesses are the source of the stereotype of a gay man running an antique shop or a lesbian running a dog-grooming service.) Third, the less affluent neighborhoods of a city were often less policed—a plus for lesbians and gay men, who were acutely aware of how social and legally marginalized they were. But lower-income urban neighborhoods also had their disadvantages; for example, city officials were less interested in providing services such as street cleaning. Furthermore, a distinctly homosexual neighborhood allowed the police to always know where homosexuals were.

The lesbian and gay bar was a central pillar of these communities. It offered space for socializing, hearing community news, and meeting new friends or sexual partners. Boston's gay bar scene in the late 1940s ranged from the upscale Napoleon Club in Bay Village, where jackets and ties were required, to the Lighthouse in the city's notorious Scollay Square, which catered to sailors and gay male civilians.[30] Not far from the Napoleon Club was Vickie's, a lesbian bar in the Hotel St. Moritz, and Cavana's, a tough bar described by the *Mid-Town Journal,* a local scandal sheet, as "the bistro where muscular amazons, who could punch as hard as Popeye after he had eaten three cans of spinach, would cuddle blonde cuties on their laps as they guzzled boilermakers."[31] Many of these neighborhoods had nightclubs featuring performers who played to homosexual audiences using lesbian- and gay-specific language, stories, and songs.

These bars and clubs promoted the crossover appeal of drag performers and gay comics, who blurred gender and sexual lines as they had earlier in the century. The Jewel Box Revue, which started in 1930, was an elaborate touring show of female impersonators, lavish spectacle, and gay-themed comedy. The revue played smaller clubs, such as the Garden of Allah, but also large theaters in cities such as New York, where the show headlined at Loews State Theater at Forty-fourth Street and Broadway and Harlem's Apollo Theater. In production numbers such as "It's an Old Mannish Custom" and "Can't Do a Show Without Girls," the performers spoofed and took seriously the conventions of gender roles.

These overtly homosexual shows were sometimes unwelcome in smaller cities. Butch lesbian singer Frances Faye, born Frances Cohen in Brooklyn, had a far easier time as a performer in small clubs. Noted enough to appear in a 1937 Bing Crosby film and on television, she was famous for singing jazz and show tunes in nightclubs. In the mid-1940s she began tossing off bawdy lines and references to homosexuality in songs, often adding, "It's not dirty, it's just how I say it." In the late 1940s she was hardly hiding her lesbianism, and in the late 1950s she was chanting at the end of her act, "Frances Faye, all the way, gay gay gay, is there any other way?"

Sometimes bars, especially in small cities, were the only site to offer community across class and gender differences. Ricardo Brown writes that "Kirmser's was the underground queer bar in St. Paul, a hidden sanctuary for homosexual men and women in the 1940s."[32]

Homosexuals new in town would hear about a bar or club in any number of ways. Sometime bars would advertise in code. Boston's College Inn Club ran advertisements that boasted the club had "Singing Waiters—New York Style."[33] Often when local newspapers ran exposés of "sex pervert" arrests, they would mention the bar name; this too would be a key—albeit an intimidating one—to finding community.

The growth of the new gay and lesbian communities can be better understood in conjunction with how other marginalized groups were treated in cities. Race, configured differently in each city, helped define the character and the political cultures of gay bars and communities. Marc Stein writes about how complicated the racial politics were in Philadelphia during the 1940s and 1950s, when the racially diverse city was becoming less segregated. While many white homosexuals were moving to or visiting Center City, the emerging "gay neighborhood," their African American counterparts were living and socializing in the neighborhoods in which they were born.[34]

Racial tension and violence were also indicative of widespread sexual anxiety. In June 1943 a small group of white sailors claimed they were jumped by Mexican Americans wearing zoot suits—long jackets with wide, padded shoulders worn over high-waisted, pegged pants. After the accusation, two hundred sailors swept through East Los Angeles and attacked all men wearing zoot suits. Many of those attacked were teenage boys, some as young as twelve or thirteen. The victims, accused of draft dodging and assaulting white women, were stripped and thrown into the gutter, their clothing burned. The riots continued for several days; the police did nothing to stop the thousands of servicemen who were displacing their sexual anxieties onto "illegal" Mexican American youths. After Eleanor Roosevelt condemned the riots as stemming from anti-Mexican discrimination, the *Los Angeles Times* attacked her for communist leanings. The zoot-suit riots were a turning point for the Mexican American community and organizing, and "the racial battles of the 1940s promoted a clear and increasingly powerful model of oppression-driven group-based political power."[35]

Seven years later, William Parker—whom many in the homosexual community dubbed "Wild Bill Parker"—became chief of police in Los Angeles. His approach to law enforcement has been characterized as "Confront and command. Control the streets at all times. Always be aggressive. Stop crimes before they happen. Seek them out. Shake them down. Make that arrest." Parker's tough stance was clearly an attack on targeted groups. Not surprisingly, the arrests of those accused of "sex perversion" crimes skyrocketed. Police misbehavior, ranging from intimidation, threats, illegal searches, and blackmail to out-and-out violence, is never aimed at only one marginalized community. The growth of the new gay and lesbian communities, shaped not only by their members by outside forces, can be understood only in conjunction with how other marginalized communities are treated in these cities.[36]

Interracial marriage was criminalized in many states—and would be until the 1967 Supreme Court ruling *Loving v. Virginia*—and interracial dating was frowned upon. Even so, there was probably more conscious discussion of interracial relationships and racism in homosexual than in heterosexual communities. Sometimes these social arrangements were complicated. In Buffalo, New York, most African American lesbians met one another through a circuit of house parties. The more upscale and nonhomosexual black nightclubs, such as Little Harlem and Club Moonglo, were open to both black and white patrons and were hospitable to lesbians, thus creating a congenial interracial space for socializing.[37] In his July 7, 1943, diary entry, Donald Vining, who was working at the front desk of the William Sloane House YMCA in Manhattan, notes that two men, one "very blond" and the other a "very black negro sailor," who were possibly a couple, came in looking for a double room, which they could not rent because the Y was full. While his fellow clerks voiced racist opinions, Vining wrote the following ambiguous, disconcerting self-reflection:

> At all of which I sigh, for nothing has made me so hopeful and happy in a long time as the sight of that blond and the inky black sailor together, asking for a double. I suppose there's a certain amount of hypocrisy in me that lauds such a relationship and shrinks from sex with the many negroes who frequent the Lyric and even the Apollo, but the fact that one

grants equality to other races doesn't seem to me to mean that you necessarily should be willing to sleep with them. But is my revulsion a kind of prejudice? I don't know but I think not.[38]

Awareness of a shared minority status across race, complicated by racial and gender tensions, led naturally to a homosexual political identity. This political identity, formed within a potentially vibrant, self-supporting social structure, took root in major American cities after the war and grew into the LGBT movement that we know today.

NINE

VISIBLE COMMUNITIES/INVISIBLE LIVES

Gay men and lesbians had been forming community over the previous century. After World War II, they began to methodically create national organizations to address injustices against them. This incorporation of political concerns with a cultural community was the beginning of today's lesbian, gay, bisexual, and transgender movement. America had long been a country of joiners, often around nationalistic or patriotic associations and especially after wars. Combining the intents of organizations such as the Benevolent and Protective Order of Elks, a social club founded in 1868; the American Legion, a veterans' organization founded in 1919; and the Knights of Columbus, a benevolent society founded in 1881 for Irish immigrant men, homosexuals slowly formed their own "homophile" groups.

In 1945 a few homosexual men in New York formed the Veterans Benevolent Association and sponsored well-attended dances and parties. In 1947, Edith Eyde, a secretary at Hollywood's RKO Pictures, wrote and typed each issue of the first American homosexual publication, *Vice Versa*—subtitled "America's Gayest Magazine"—using the pseudonym "Lisa Ben" (an anagram for "lesbian"). Her purpose was to find and befriend other lesbians; she gave copies to friends to pass around. A year later in Los Angeles, Merton L. Bird, an African American man, and his lover, W. Dorr Legg, started the Knights of the Clocks. ("Clocks" was an acronym for "Cloistered Loyal Order of the Conclaved Knights of Sophisticracy.") One of its purposes, as Legg noted in his 1956 book *Homosexuals Today:*

A Handbook of Organizations and Publications, was to "promote fellowship and understanding between homosexuals themselves, specifically between other races and the Negro, as well as to offer its members aid in securing employment and suitable housing. Special attention was given to the housing problems of interracial couples of which there were several in the group."[1] The Knights existed for three or four years, hosting dinners, socials, and (according to some) the occasional sex party.

There is a commonly held belief that the 1950s were marked by national economic prosperity, traditional family life, sexual restraint, and a well-meaning conservatism, in clear contrast to the 1960s, a decade of radicalism and violent social change. Such simplistic categorization is misleading. In 1955, tranquilizers were rarely prescribed, but their "consumption reached 462,000 pounds in 1958 and soared to 1.15 million pounds merely a year later."[2] Mid-decade, forty to fifty million people—25 percent of Americans— were poor, and 60 percent of those over age sixty-five had annual incomes of less than one thousand dollars.[3] At the 1960 Republican National Convention, J. Edgar Hoover, director of the FBI and possibly a homosexual, warned the country that "the three most dangerous groups in America are communists, beatniks, and egg-heads." The FBI, seeking to discredit Martin Luther King Jr., spent enormous amounts of time and money spying on his private life. Cold War politics gave rise to reactionary policies, and the Kennedy administration drastically increased military spending—nine billion dollars in the first fourteen months of the administration—dangerously ramping up the arms race. Throughout the 1950s and early 1960s, homosexuality was far from being "unspoken," as popular thinking has it; America was increasingly obsessed with it.

SEX AND THE BEGINNINGS OF A MOVEMENT

Key to this obsession was the publication of Alfred Kinsey's *Sexual Behavior in the Human Male* in January 1948, permanently changing how Americans discussed sexuality. The Kinsey Report, as it was commonly known, was a detailed, scientific study of American

male sexual activity. Kinsey, who had made his reputation studying the anatomy, biology, and behavior of gall wasps, recruited a
team of trained interviewers to gather data from twelve thousand
men, then used the data from 5,300 of them to produce prelim-
inary conclusions about male sexual behavior. The findings were
nuanced by age, economic class, and education level. Kinsey was
interested only in his informants' behavior, not in how they understood their identity. In the report's "Historical Introduction," he explained that his study was "an attempt to accumulate an objectively
determined body of fact about sex which strictly avoids social or
moral interpretations of the fact."[4] Kinsey's statistics and in-depth
analysis discussed multiple aspects of sexuality, including fantasy,
masturbation, premarital sex, and sexual contacts with animals. As
the United States attempted to readjust to an overtly heterosexual
paradigm after World War II, Americans found Kinsey's findings
on homosexuality the most shocking. Not only were the findings initially unbelievable, they demanded to be acknowledged as
scientific.

The Kinsey Report was a media sensation, joked about in popular
songs, Broadway plays, and television shows. The mainstream press
carefully, and accurately, extracted some remarkable statistics: 37
percent of all males had some form of homosexual contact between
their teen years and old age; 50 percent of males who remained single until the age of thirty-five had overt homosexual experiences to
orgasm; 10 percent of males were more or less exclusively homosexual for at least three years between the ages of sixteen and fifty-five;
4 percent of males were exclusively homosexual throughout their
lives.[5]

Five years later, in 1953, Kinsey released *Sexual Behavior in the
Human Female*. This study received less attention, perhaps because
Kinsey estimated that the incidence of homosexual behavior in
women was half of what he found in men. He did note, however,
that the incidence of female orgasm was far higher in homosexual
than heterosexual contacts.[6]

Americans now understood that homosexuals were everywhere,
even if you could not see them. Kinsey devised a simple scale of sexual experience, now called the Kinsey scale. The scale ranged from

o, indicating exclusively heterosexual encounters, to 6, for a person who has experienced only homosexual encounters.

Kinsey's findings were vilified by clergy, conservative journalists, and traditional psychoanalysts. Although some Americans were outraged, most were fascinated. This was why *From Here to Eternity* and *The Naked and the Dead* were best sellers. Along with this fascination came questioning. Undoubtedly "the report gave rise to a culture of suspicion surrounding male identity and sexuality."[7] This new atmosphere of doubt was hinted at, but also openly articulated. Shortly after the Kinsey Report's publication, *Life* magazine reported that "new worlds of suspicion . . . were opened to doubting wives by Kinsey's revelations on men."[8] In the old way of thinking, the "invert" was immediately identifiable by his effeminate affect; but this new, hidden homosexual could be lurking anywhere, in any male. And he was a direct threat to heterosexuality. It was in this context that the homophile groups were founded.

The emergence of political action from within a community predicated on finding sexual partners was not only logical but vital. Although elements of politicized community and sexuality are present in Edith Eyde's work and the Knights of the Clocks, it was Harry Hay, a labor organizer with ties to the Communist Party, who brought those elements together. While circulating a petition for the Stockholm Peace Pledge in the late 1940s, as well as looking for men with whom to discuss the Kinsey Report, Hay connected with like-minded thinkers. Several months later, in November 1950, the Mattachine Society was born. Hay's training in Communist Party ideology and his conceptualization of the Mattachine Society were directly linked and had lasting influences on LGBT organizing. (Hay resigned from the Communist Party in 1951 because of its antihomosexual stance.)

Using Marxist cultural theory, Hay understood homosexuals to be a distinct and oppressed class of people able to combat ignorance with education and organize against the prejudice of the dominant culture. Rather than simply shared sexual desires, this new cohesive identity was based on common political concerns as well as a distinctive history and culture. The group's "missions and purposes" stated in part: "The Mattachine Society holds it possible and desirable that a highly ethical homosexual culture emerge, as a consequence of its work, paralleling the emerging cultures of our fellow-minorities—the Negro, Mexican, and Jewish Peoples. The Society believes homosexuals can lead well-adjusted, wholesome, and socially productive lives once ignorance and prejudice against them is successfully combated, and once homosexuals feel they have a dignified and useful role to play in society."[9]

The Mattachine Society—the name was derived from a French Renaissance secret fraternity of unmarried men—was organized on a Communist Party model of individual cells and hierarchical membership. The society was made up mainly of gay men, but included lesbians. To attract new members, the organization sponsored lectures, socials, and discussion groups. A few members started a publication, and the first issue of *ONE* came out in January 1953. Sold through subscription, and eventually on newsstands in large cities, it was published until 1972. (Its highest circulation was five thousand in 1960.) One of Mattachine's first actions was to protest the arrest of Dale Jennings, a member arrested for "lewd and dissolute behavior" in 1952. This protest was indicative of the group's commitment to challenge police harassment and arrests of women and men in bars and cruising grounds. Given the institutionalized hostility homosexuals faced, Mattachine's growth was rapid. By 1953 it had over two thousand members and sponsored over a hundred discussion groups.

Mattachine's growth brought political diversity. With a membership that entertained a wide range of opinions, the organization found it difficult to maintain its radical vision, especially since Mattachine was clearly connected to the political left. This was a concern because "McCarthyism," the communist witch hunt begun by Senator Joseph McCarthy in 1947, was gripping Washington. The "red scare" of McCarthyism led directly to the "lavender scare," a conflation of communism with homosexuality. David K. Johnson notes that "over the course of the 1950s and 1960s, approximately 1,000 persons were dismissed from the Department of State for alleged homosexuality. The highest profile cases may have involved suspicion of communism, but the majority of those separated were alleged homosexuals."[10]

The Mattachine Society underwent a major ideological split in 1953, when some members disagreed with Hay's concept of a distinct homosexual culture. During the national convention, Marilyn Rieger and others argued that homosexual equality would happen only "by declaring ourselves, by integrating . . . not as homosexuals but as people, as men and women whose homosexuality is irrelevant to our ideals, our principles, and our aspirations."[11] This split also produced, in 1955, *The Mattachine Review,* which reflected Rieger's ideological stance. (It continued publication until 1966, with a circulation never larger than 2,500.) This major distinction—between claiming an outsider status and demanding acceptance as part of the "normal" majority—has remained, in various forms, the defining division in the LGBT movement.

This split did not affect the emergence of a lesbian movement in 1955, when Phyllis Lyon, Del Martin, and three other lesbian couples, two of them interracial, formed the Daughters of Bilitis (DOB). Unlike the Mattachine Society, whose founding was intentionally political, the DOB was conceptualized as a social group and a way to meet other lesbians. Lyon and Martin chose "daughters" because it sounded respectable (like Daughters of the American Revolution), adding Bilitis, a fictional lesbian in Pierre de Louys's nineteenth-century poetry cycle *Songs of Bilitis.* Like "Mattachine," the name remained obscure to the average person.

The Daughters of Bilitis quickly began social and political work. Within a year they were sponsoring lectures and discussions, working with Mattachine when it was beneficial to both groups. In 1956 the DOB began publishing *The Ladder,* similar to *ONE* and *The Mattachine Review,* but focused only on issues of interest to lesbians. (*The Ladder* ceased publication in 1972.)

The formation of a lesbian homophile organization brought gender issues to the forefront. Many lesbians had been, or still were, married; exposure would mean losing custody of their children. As single women in the workforce, lesbians also faced pressure to earn a living while having fewer job opportunities, being paid less than men, and dealing with sexual harassment. Different sexual cultures also resulted in political disagreements. Marci Gallo quotes Billye Talmadge, an early DOB member: "There was a lot of animosity and resentment over the fact that it was the gay guys who were creating such havoc with the police—the raids, indiscriminate sex, their bathroom habits . . ."[12]

Ironically, in the 1950s and into the next decade, bars and public cruising areas were serving far larger communities of homosexual women and men than any "respectable" homophile organization. Lesbian bar culture was fundamentally a working-class phenomenon, often rooted in butch/femme culture. As D'Emilio points out, "Women who went to the bars belonged to a group that was larger, more stable, and more familiar than what DOB offered."[13] For men who had no access to the privacy of a room and lived in areas where there were no bars, the sexual culture of public parks, movie theaters, and men's rooms was one of the few options available. A wide range of public venues frequented by men has been fully documented across the country. Small Southern cites and towns had them, including "Jackson, Hattiesburg, and even Vicksburg, where homosexuals, as early as the 1950s, dubbed . . . hotels with active tearooms [men's rooms] as 'silver tray' establishments."[14] There were other places homosexuals could meet. Men could often find one another at Marlene Dietrich and Judy Garland concerts; Chris Connor, a noted jazz singer widely known to be lesbian, always had a large lesbian contingent in the audience. In the late 1950s and early 1960s, avant-garde and underground films and the theaters that screened them were the building blocks of homosexual communities.[15]

Lesbians claimed community in public space. The Legion of Decency, a Catholic film censorship group, complained to Paramount Pictures that Lewis Allen's coded lesbian ghost story *The Uninvited* was a problem because "in certain theaters large audiences of questionable type attended this film at unusual hours. The impression created was that they had been previously informed of certain erotic and esoteric elements in this film."[16]

Disagreements over the political efficacy of a distinct homosexual culture, as well as the different concerns of lesbians and gay men, resulted in two distinct responses to legal issues faced by homosexuals. The first was to work toward securing sexual freedom for all women and men by repealing sodomy laws and ending police harassment associated with homosexual socializing or activity. This approach was predicated on the anarchist belief that the state had no business in citizens' personal lives. The second was to seek equality under the law and end all forms of discrimination against lesbians and gay men, including workplace discrimination and issues relating to child custody. This approach was similar to the battles being fought by African Americans and other disenfranchised groups.

BEING PUBLIC IN PRINT

Through the 1950s and 1960s, there was an unparalleled outpouring of representation and discussion about homosexuals. Mainstream publishing houses released hundreds of novels featuring homosexual characters and themes. These included respected, popular literary works such as Carson McCullers's 1946 *Member of the Wedding,* Truman Capote's 1958 *Breakfast at Tiffany's,* and James Baldwin's 1962 *Another Country.* Popular literature by James Barr, Patricia Highsmith, Jay Little, Brigid Brophy, Lance Horner, and Jane Rule sold to a mainstream audience or, like Barr's *Quatrefoil,* a mostly gay male readership. Marguerite Yourcenar's 1955 *The Memoirs of Hadrian* and Mary Renault's books, such as the 1956 *The Last of the Wine,* set in a highly homoerotic ancient Greece, allowed homosexual readers to imaginatively construct a historical past. Lakey, a lesbian character modeled on woman-loving poet Edna St. Vincent Millay, was the most prescient and emotionally balanced central figure in Mary McCarthy's 1962 best seller *The Group.* The 1950 thriller by lesbian writer Patricia Highsmith, *Strangers on a Train,* which would become a film by Alfred Hitchcock a year later, explored issues of guilt and innocence (and the fine distinction between being an outcast and a criminal) through a homoerotic relationship that included blackmail and murder.

Some of these books were overtly political. Willard Motley, a gay African American writer from Chicago who was connected to the WPA Federal Writers' Project and helped start a literary magazine at Hull House, wrote the best-selling *Knock on Any Door* in 1947.

It explores the nurturing relationship between a basically hetero-sexual hustler and his steady john, who loves and supports him to his death. The novel is a devastating exposé, in line with the ideas of earlier progressive reformers, of the effects of crime and poverty on city dwellers. *Knock on Any Door* sold fifty thousand copies in one month, earning its author a six-page spread in *Life.* A surprising number of novels, such as John Horne Burns's 1949 *Lucifer with a Book,* Fritz Peters's 1951 *Finistere,* and Gerald Tesch's 1956 *Never the Same Again,* feature young male teens who have a clearly articu-lated homosexual identity, marking the first time that portraits of gay youth were seen in literature.

Homosexuals might see themselves reflected in these novels, but other mainstream publications facilitated their meeting one another. The 1952 *Washington Confidential,* a best-selling exposé of politi-cal and sexual corruption written by journalists Jack Lait and Lee Mortimer, contains a chapter, replete with inflammatory antiho-mosexual language, titled "Garden of Pansies." The chapter lists, with addresses, over fifteen homosexual gathering places, including bars, hotel lobbies, public restrooms, and bathhouses.[17] Similarly, the June 26, 1964, issue of *Life* included photos of gay male cruising places such as New York's Washington Square, Los Angeles's Persh-ing Square, and San Francisco's leather S/M scene. A double-page photo spread of men at the Tool Box, a gay biker bar, was captioned, "These brawny young men in their leather caps, shirts, jackets and pants are practicing homosexuals, men who turn to other men for affection and sexual satisfaction. They are part of what they call the 'gay world,' which is actually a sad and often sordid world."

Such feature stories and exposés were manifestations of Ameri-cans' desire to grapple with the changes that happened after the war. Part of this process was an intellectual reevaluation of the re-lationship between the individual and society. Harry Hay's idea of a cultural minority fit neatly with liberal, contemporary trends in sociological and psychological analysis. Both of these approaches—professionalized by "experts"—had a major role in shaping how Americans thought about the homosexual. Sociological works such as the 1950 *The Lonely Crowd* by David Riesman, Nathan Glazer, and Reuel Denney and William H. Whyte's 1956 *The Organization*

Man mapped a sociological portrait of the American character and were a template for works analyzing the homosexual.

Beginning with the publication of Donald Webster Cory's *The Homosexual in America* in 1951, numerous nonfiction works— books, journal articles, and magazine pieces—examined the place of the new homosexual in American society. Jess Stern's popular, journalistic *The Sixth Man*, published in 1962, was filled with pitiable images of homosexuals, as was his 1964 *The Grapevine: A Report on the Secret World of the Lesbian*. The "sociology of the homosexual" was frequently conflicted, and when presented through the lens and language of journalism, often exploitative. The bias of these books was balanced by others. In the 1962 *Strangers in Our Midst: Problems of the Homosexual in American Society*, Alfred A. Gross stated that "it is high time to discard the view that the homosexual's conduct excludes him from the protection of the community" and compared contemporary sex laws to the Spanish Inquisition and Nazi Germany.

Psychology had risen in American culture to be an influential lens through which people understood themselves and society. In 1956 Dr. Evelyn Hooker, a psychologist at UCLA, used funding from the National Institute of Mental Health to administer three standard personality tests to thirty homosexuals and thirty heterosexuals. The anonymous responses were read by three experts, who discovered absolutely no differences between the two groups. Hooker's paper was published in 1957, but made little impact on the thinking of the professional community. Why was this?

Professional psychological thought in the 1950s and early 1960s was in direct reaction to the social and sexual freedoms claimed by women and homosexuals. Because those freedoms were seen as fundamentally threatening to how society was organized, it was virtually impossible to treat homosexuality with any neutrality. (Kinsey did, which is why his critics were so vehement in their attacks on him.) The country was in a period of cultural panic and turned to psychologists for solutions to the "problem" of the homosexual.

Psychoanalysts such as Edmund Bergler, Irving Bieber, and Frank S. Caprio were conservative traditionalists who viewed homosexuality as a serious problem. In his 1956 *Homosexuality: Disease or a Way of Life,* Bergler wrote that "homosexuality is a neurotic condition. . . . Specific neurotic defenses and personality traits that are partly or entirely psychopathic are specifically and exclusively characteristic of homosexuals, and . . . these defenses and traits put the homosexual into a special psychiatric category."[18] Caprio was equally dismissive in his analysis: "Lesbianism is a symptom, and not a disease entity. It is the result of a deep-seated neurosis which involves narcissistic gratifications and sexual immaturity. It also represents a neurotic defense mechanism for feelings of insecurity."[19]

Psychoanalysts believed that homosexuality, like most diseases, could be cured—a template that reinforced legal codes as well as everyday social bias. These psychoanalytic theories were predicated on deeply conservative ideas about sexuality. Bergler was also against divorce, premarital sex, and all forms of sexual experimentation; he supported traditional notions of sex, gender roles, and family arrangements and believed that women's sexuality was inseparable from reproduction and motherhood.

Bergler and Beiber received great public attention, but so did more liberal theorists. Albert Ellis, whose voluminous, popular writings on sex were published for a half century starting in the early 1950s, spent his career fighting what he called "sex guilt." His radical ideas were shocking. In the 1958 *Sex Without Guilt* he stated: "Some of us are able to benefit from adultery and some of us are not. Had we dare, then, make an invariant rule for all?"[20] He also claimed that "female frigidity" did not exist; it was a male invention to control women. And in complete repudiation of a century of conservative medical advice, he argued that it is "difficult to conceive of a more beneficial, harmless, tension-releasing act than masturbation."[21] Ellis's high popularity was undoubtedly due to the fact that he gave people professional permission to do what they were already doing. It is telling that when he wrote his 1965 *Homosexuality: Its Causes and Cures,* Ellis, not unlike Bergler and other conservatives, understood homosexual desire as a serious pathology: "Most fixed homosexuals, I am now convinced, are borderline psychotic or outrightly psychotic."[22] (By the early 1970s, Ellis had changed his views and become an active supporter of the gay rights movement.)

Bergler and Ellis were philosophically antithetical to one another on many issues, but agreed on the differentiations between female and male homosexuality. Both argued that male and female homosexuals were pathological, but that it was easier for the lesbian to be "cured" if she only accepted marriage and motherhood. The male homosexual was viewed as a predatory, hypersexual loner with few friends and no connection to a "civilizing" heterosexual family. These widely disseminated archetypes—the lesbian waiting to be fulfilled as a woman, the sexually rapacious homosexual male—were fantasies that emerged after World War II. Each served a specific cultural function that was to play out in mass-market publications.

The large number of lesbian pulps written by heterosexuals confirmed the prejudices of the psychologists. Pulps—mass-market, inexpensive paperback books—had a visibility, and an audience, far wider than the mainstream titles with lesbian or homosexual themes. Pulps were sold on newsstands, not in bookstores. With their lurid, eye-catching cover art, they were a major venue through which heterosexuals and homosexuals discovered homosexual subculture. In the 1950s, many of the gay male pulps were reprints of previously published literary novels. Almost all of the many hundreds of lesbian pulps were paperback originals, edited and published by mainstream paperback houses run by heterosexual men. Some pulps, written by lesbians such as Marijane Meaker (under the pen name Vin Packer), Ann Bannon, and Valerie Taylor, presented a sympathetic view of lesbian life, although their exploitative packaging emphasized sordidness and loneliness. Valerie Taylor's 1960 *Stranger on Lesbos* was billed as "the searching novel of a lonely young wife faced with the temptations of unnatural love"; this was a complete misrepresentation. In contrast, the majority of lesbian pulps, written by heterosexual men, were exploitative and unsympathetic.

For many lesbian readers, these novels performed the same function as the *Life* magazine article did for gay men: they were guidebooks to lesbian life. Many of the pulps described Greenwich Village bar life and how women dressed to be recognizably lesbian. For heterosexuals, the books were titillating; although they reinforced stereotypes, they made lesbianism, and by extension homosexuality, visible. In her introduction to the anthology *Lesbian Pulp Fiction,* Katherine Forrest describes finding Ann Bannon's *Odd Girl Out* in Detroit, Michigan, in 1957:

> I did not need to look at the title for clues; the cover leaped out at me from the drugstore rack: a young woman with sensuous intent on her face seated on a bed, leaning over a prone woman, her hands on the other woman's shoulders.
>
> . . . I found it when I was eighteen years old. It opened the door to my soul and told me who I was. It led me to other books that told me who some of us were, and how some of us lived.[23]

Ann Bannon's novels, as did others, sold hundreds of thousands of copies. It is safe to say that millions of these books were sold, reaching an audience far beyond the homophile publications.

The psychologist's view of homosexual men was not reflected in the gay male novels, but in a new genre: the physical culture magazine for homosexual men. In 1945 Bob Mizer, a Los Angeles photographer, took "beefcake" photos of men at Venice's Muscle Beach and started a small business catering to bodybuilders who needed photographs for competitions. In 1951 he published *Physique Pictorial,* the first physique magazine aimed at the male homosexual interested in appreciating, rather than becoming (as in Bernarr Macfadden's *Physical Culture),* the idealized male form. Mizer's photographs drew on the images of von Gloeden, Day, and Eakins as well as the photographs of the male body that were prevalent during the war. There was no frontal nudity (until censorship laws changed in the late 1960s), but the eroticized male body was now more prevalent then ever in popular culture.

Physique Pictorial's circulation increased dramatically with each issue. It was sold on newsstands next to the pulp novels, heterosexual physique magazines, and heterosexual pinup magazines like *Playboy,* which started in 1955. Similar publications, such as *Vim, Tomorrow's Man, Adonis,* and *Grecian Guild Quarterly,* quickly emerged. *Tomorrow's Man,* one of the more conservative of the muscle magazines, may have had a circulation of up to one hundred thousand. Circulation estimates for other publications are lower, but there were over a hundred such titles in English-speaking countries between 1950 and 1970.[24] Clearly the lesbian pulps and the physique magazines were integral in building a national homosexual community.

Physique Pictorial printed letters from readers attesting to its importance to them: "I know that I am not alone in my beliefs." "You are doing a truly wonderful job in uniting young men from all over the world who share a common interest." "Without the *Pictorial*, those of us who share these common ideals, wherever we might be, would be isolated."[25]

The physique magazines also featured advertisements for films, paintings, photos of specific models, life-drawing instruction, and erotic clothing. David K. Johnson argues that such advertising was integral to the creation of a national homosexual consumer culture. The "mail order catalogues like Vagabond out of Minneapolis or Guild Press out of Washington . . . [offered a] host of gay consumer goods . . . including greeting cards, musical LPs, pulp novels, bar guides, lingerie, cologne, and jewelry."[26]

Over the next five decades, the rise of an LGBT consumer culture increasingly defined the community, with complicated results. The LGBT community became more acceptable, since its identity predicated on consumption, not sexual behavior. But more progressive political action was frequently impeded as acceptability in the marketplace became valued over core political values of justice and fairness.

The power of the physique magazines were in their reclamation of the sexualized male body as fundamental to homosexual community. Although they were novels, the potency of the pulps resided in the beautifully designed, emotionally vivid, sexually lurid covers. Certainly the readership for the homophile magazines and for the pulp and physique publications differed by hundreds of thousands. Many contemporary lesbians look to the pulps as prime examples of butch/femme identities that have been central to the organization of lesbian culture in the United States for much of this century.

The images in *Physique Pictorial* had an enormous influence on American culture. A preponderance of images presented young white men in a variety of hypermasculine outsider or rebel roles: cowboys, motorcycle gang members, Native Americans, gladiators, soldiers, frontiersmen, and rakish sailors on leave. These images resonated on multiple levels. Reminiscent of homoeroticized males in the works of Cooper, Melville, and Whitman, they also evoked the homoerotic images that emerged from World War II. (Leslie Fiedler's 1948 essay "Come Back to the Raft Ag'in, Huck Honey!" was as much about the homoeroticism of the war as about nineteenth-century American literature.) And the *Physique Pictorial* images were an embodiment of the dangerous, rebellious homosexual man pathologized in the writings of psychologists.

The hyperheterosexuality of 1950s American culture contained a deep distrust of the single man. This perspective was reinforced by the professional psychologists. Hendrik Ruitenbeek, a respected psychoanalyst, noted in 1966 that "contemporary America seems to have no room for the mature bachelor. . . . A single man over thirty is now regarded as a pervert, a person with severe emotional problems, or a poor creature fettered to mother."[27]

This fear of the single man is seen most viscerally in Hollywood films, with their images of dangerous, potentially violent men. The most famous of these were stars such as James Dean, Montgomery Clift, Marlon Brando, and Anthony Perkins, each embodying a different type of moody, sensitive rebel. The murderous juvenile delinquents in *The Blackboard Jungle* (1955) and the gangs of motorcyclists who invade and take over a town in *The Wild Ones* (1953) were scarier versions of the leather-jacketed men with chains and leather caps in *Physique Pictorial*.

Novels such as Irving Shulman's 1947 best seller *The Amboy Dukes* and the 1955 paperback original *The Thrill Kids* by Vin Packer (the pen name of Marijane Meaker) hinted at homosexual longings in gang members. Women and girls connected to gangs were always portrayed as sexually promiscuous, sometimes engaging in sex with both men and women.

The connection between the juvenile delinquent and the homosexual was strong in the social sciences as well. Writing in 1947, psychoanalyst Kate Friedlander connected the similar "antisocial character formation" of the homosexual and the juvenile delinquent.[28] In 1959, the national notoriety surrounding the gang-related "Capeman" murders in Manhattan increased when the press reported that the sixteen-year-old, mentally unstable, mostly homeless, illiterate killer had sex with men and that the Vampires gang with whom he was associated "was made up of individuals who were actively and passively homosexual."[29] Americans were so concerned about the juvenile delinquent—and the homosexuality implicit in the stereotype—that Congress formed two committees, the Children's Bureau and the Continuing Committee on the Prevention and Control of Delinquency, to combat it.

Rebel Without a Cause, the most famous of hundreds of delinquent films, made the teen rebel into a national hero. Nicholas Ray directed the 1955 film and also wrote the story, which was originally adapted for the screen by Irving Shulman. James Dean was iconic as misunderstood teen Jim Stark. Jim's two relationships in the film are with Judy, an unhappy young woman played by Natalie Wood, and Plato, a troubled gay teen played by Sal Mineo. Ray was clear in establishing Plato's sexuality: the teen keeps a photograph of actor Alan Ladd in his school locker and is obviously in love with Jim. In one unfilmed version of the script, Jim and Plato kiss. Mineo would later claim that he was "proud to play the first gay teenager in films."[30] Ray consciously used sexually ambiguous images—all of the young men in the film look like Hollywood versions of the *Physique* models—to enhance the film's sexual and emotional appeal. *Rebel* and other films were successfully mainstreaming an iconic homosexual type, barely concealed, to a huge audience who remained unaware of its origins.

Rebel Without a Cause resonated with audiences then, and still does today, because it addresses questions of conformity. Historically, when faced with a cultural mandate of conformity, Americans have found escape by becoming enthralled with rebels such as Jesse James, Billy the Kid, Bonnie and Clyde, and John Dillinger. The concerns of *Rebel Without a Cause* emerged from cultural tensions over conformity and rebellion that can be seen in some of the professional psychological and sociological literature. Psychoanalyst Robert J. Lindner wrote several best-selling books arguing that conformity, which he called "adjustment," is "a mendacious idea, biologically false, philosophically untenable, and psychologically harmful."[31] He claimed that rebellion against conformity is the only salvation for the human race. He also made the radical case, in a forty-five-page argument, that homosexuality is a form of sexual and cultural resistance to society's mandate to conform. Lindner admired the homophile groups and agreed that laws biased against homosexuals had to be changed, but maintained that homosexuality was a misguided and pathological response to America's culture of profound sexual repression. Lindner's work is emblematic of how conflicted progressive ideas about conformity and rebellion in relationship to homosexuality were at this time.[32]

In addition to the juvenile delinquent, *Physique Pictorial* promoted another nonconformist homosexual image that became a prototype for American men. This was the image of the muscled, handsome, sexually active man who—although not the effeminate homosexual—was softer-looking and less aggressively masculine than the traditional male image. Postwar American men—vulnerable, and comfortable with being sexual objects—appreciated the rebel image, but could relate more to this softer, sexy masculine image. Actors such as Rock Hudson, Tab Hunter, Troy Donahue, Guy Madison, George Nader, Tom Tryon, and Rory Calhoun embodied this new image: sexy but romantic, masculine but approachable.

This new prototype evolved into the sexually active "wolf" or lady-killer who, in a new plot twist for the Hollywood marriage comedy, has to be tricked into getting married against his better judgment. Films such as *The Tender Trap* (1955), starring Frank Sinatra, and *Pillow Talk* (1959), with Rock Hudson and Doris Day, revel in this conflict. These male characters are fully—even compulsively—heterosexual. However, they resist the traditional male traits demanded by gender norms and consumer capitalism. Rather than being emotionally dependable, professionally secure, and socially important, the men in these films are lying, vain, emotionally irresponsible pleasure seekers. They not only refuse to accept the responsibilities of mature heterosexual relationships, but often invent false personas to fool people and society. (In *Pillow Talk*, Rock Hudson's character even invents an overtly homosexual persona to court Doris Day and highlight his own manliness.)

This prototype and its more dangerous twin, the rebel, were part of a larger shift in American culture. Barbara Ehrenreich explores the myriad ways in which men rebelled against postwar culture's strict male gender roles. Men retired into their basement workshop on a Saturday afternoon to avoid their wife and kids, or they retreated into the sexual and consumer fantasies of *Playboy*. Homosexuality played an enormous role in shaping the lives of heterosexual men in the 1950s and early 1960s. Ehrenreich notes that "the ultimate reason a man would not just 'walk out the door' was the taint of homosexuality which was likely to follow him. Homosexuality, as the psychiatrists saw it, was the ultimate escapism."[33]

The relationship of these images to American culture was complicated. The man featured in *Physique Pictorial* was the dangerous single man who was never burdened by the expectations of marriage, family, and children. He was the object of social scorn, yet he was the sheer embodiment of male pleasure-seeking without consequences. As such, he was both a threat and an object of envy. Homosexual males—and in a slightly different way, lesbians—were culturally trapped in these years between the image of the perverted, psychopathic outcast and a beacon of possibility of some other way to live.

The new ideas about masculinity that emerged from homosexual culture were reinforced by the homosexual influence in the film industry. Actors such as Hudson, Nader, and Hunter "helped set the style and tone of masculinity for a generation," even as their homosexuality and relationships were open knowledge within the industry.[34] Not coincidentally, *Rebel*, a film with tremendous impact on American culture, had roots in nontraditional sexual cultures. Nicholas Ray, who was married four times, was sexually involved with both women and men for most of his life. James Dean and Sal Mineo were both primarily homosexual. Jack Simmons, allegedly Dean's boyfriend at the time, played one of the gang members. The film industry was tolerant of nonheterosexual behaviors as long as they were not publicized, and most actors were able to be successfully closeted while having great influence on the popular, heterosexual imagination. This was true of Tryon, Perkins, Dean, and

Clift. Teen heartthrobs Guy Madison and Rory Calhoun had a long-term affair.[35] Many homosexuals had marriages of convenience. Hudson was married to Phyllis Gates, who was his agent's secretary and a lesbian, for a short period of time to please his fan base and the studio executives.

It would have been career suicide for a Hollywood star to be openly homosexual, yet personal lives often become public. As early as 1948, movie magazines were hinting at Clift's private life with headlines such as "Is It True What They Say about Monty?" and "He's Travelin' Light" (a veiled reference to the phrase "light in the loafers," indicating male homosexuality).[36] James Dean's sexuality was an open enough secret that in Walter Ross's 1958 best-selling novel *The Immortal*, the main character, who was clearly modeled on Dean, was a homosexual who also slept with women. Published just over two years after Dean's untimely death, the book, with cover art by the young Andy Warhol, was advertised with a forty-foot by twenty-foot billboard in midtown Manhattan.

As much as bias against homosexuals existed, the cultural obsession with homosexuality increasingly blurred the line between heterosexual and homosexual. The buff, approachable, sexually vulnerable young Hollywood male actor often appeared shirtless and in revealing positions in publicity shots and fan magazines. Often the only difference between these photographs and those in *Physique Pictorial* was the context. The December 1953 issue of *Tomorrow's Man* included an eight-page feature on Tab Hunter at home on his ranch, where "he leads an athletic life to keep in shape for the rigors of theatrical life." Illustrated with twelve posed beefcake photos, ten of them shirtless, the article claimed that Hunter's "single greatest asset is his resemblance to the down-to-earth, wholesome, 'red blooded American boy.'" With no mention of dating or girlfriends, Hunter's image as an emerging big star was shockingly ambiguous.

As the 1950s evolved into the 1960s, the two types of American masculinity appeared in different artistic forms and guises. The emotional power of rock and roll was in its sexual exuberance. Early white rock-and-roll performers, such as Elvis Presley, Bill Haley, and Buddy Holly, displayed a juvenile delinquent image that was overtly sexual, exhibitionistic, and flamboyant. They chose this image in part because they were drawing on the highly emotive African American roots of rhythm and blues in the music of Fats Domino, Chuck Berry, and Bo Diddley. Social reformers, clergy, and conservative civic groups claimed that rock and roll caused juvenile delinquency and called for a boycott of record companies and radio stations. In California, legislators banned certain records from public play; in Memphis, Tennessee, local police confiscated jukeboxes that contained "offensive" records. Linda Martin and Kerry Segrave note that in 1954, the industry was so worried about the backlash against risqué lyrics that *Billboard*, the industry trade magazine, urged radio stations not to play some songs that were listed on the magazine's Top Ten charts.[37]

To the moralist, the threat of rock's sexual content was often linked to homosexuality. Little Richard, whose flamboyant stage presence and appearance was seen by most audiences as an indicator of homosexuality, changed the lyrics of "Tutti Frutti" when he cut the record in 1955. His original version included the lines "Tutti Frutti, good booty / If it don't fit, don't force it / You can grease it, make it easy." W. T. Lhamon argues persuasively that Little Richard's "Long Tall Sally" is about the singer's Uncle John's involvement with a transvestite, the "bald-headed Sally," who is "built for speed" and with whom he is sneaking into alleys.[38]

If Elvis and Little Richard were the bad boys—the delinquents—of rock, the new wave of pretty, teen-boy crooners such as Frankie Avalon, Fabian, Pat Boone, and Ricky Nelson were the musical analogues of the new, more gently masculine male stars. These young men, almost all in their mid to late teens with crew cuts or pompadours, resembled the young, preening, less muscled physique models. Teen culture at times overtly acknowledged the influence of male homosexual culture. In the 1964 film *Muscle Beach Party* with Frankie Avalon and Annette Funicello, the wholesome teens' beach fun is threatened by professional musclemen wearing hot pink and lavender trunks and capes. The film is filled with coded jokes about homosexual bodybuilders; for example, the men are being managed by a promoter named Jack Fanny.

In the postwar era, style and dress for heterosexual women and men evolved quickly as they began reacting to changes in gender roles and gender presentation. Gay men and lesbians had created cultures that produced specific physical markers—clothing, speech, imagery, affect, and deportment—crucial to identifying one another and creating group identity. Ironically, many of these styles and new ways of displaying gender, which often made gay and lesbian people more vulnerable, were ultimately adopted by mainstream culture. The changes for men were perhaps the most striking. Robert Wood argues that mainstream male fashion trends in the 1950s and early 1960s were primarily influenced by trends that first surfaced in the male homosexual community. Popular styles such as patterned and brightly colored shirts, strapped undershirts, black sports shirts, tighter-fitting pants, chinos, loafers, and low-cut boots all began as homosexual fashions. The same was true of flashy watchbands, ornate rings, pinky rings, wrist jewelry, and neck chains. All of these fashions were worn to eroticize the male body or to make it more sexually attractive through ornamentation.[39]

Styles for women had already begun to change during the war, and women's dress and grooming were becoming increasingly more casual. Women "bobbed" their hair in the 1920s, shedding the Victorian style of long tresses, but short hair became far more common in the 1940s and 1950s. The idea of women wearing pants and men's shirts was popularized during the 1930s by actors such as Greta Garbo, Katharine Hepburn, and Marlene Dietrich. The war made these once-bold fashion statements into everyday wear. By the 1950s, heterosexual women took many presentational cues from lesbian's wardrobes, partly because they were in essence a rejection of older fashion that sexually highlighted the female body for the male gaze. Even with fewer women having full-time jobs than during the war, the level of social engagement—caring for children, driving to stores, running parent-teacher associations, participating in community groups—was higher than before and demanded far more casual clothing. These changes gave women the social permission to wear slacks at home or at informal events and to choose simpler blouses, blazers, and outerwear, such as car coats, that were practical and not necessarily glamorous.

"HIDING" IN PLAIN VIEW

The emerging gay culture was beginning to be acknowledged by heterosexuals as a major influence on mainstream culture. This was especially true of the influence of gay males on the mainstream arts. Censorship on the Broadway stage had loosened up enough so that homosexuality could be discussed—even if it occurred offstage—in plays such as *A Streetcar Named Desire,* Tennessee Williams's 1948 Pulitzer Prize winner. John Van Druten's 1950 *Bell, Book and Candle,* a comedy about witches who live in Greenwich Village and have their own hidden clubs and code words, was understood by New York theatergoers as an obvious allegory about a homosexual community. Two years later, Christopher Isherwood's *Berlin Stories*—whose main character, based on its author, is clearly gay—was adapted for the stage by Van Druten as *I Am a Camera.* Robert Anderson's 1953 *Tea and Sympathy* was a hard-hitting look at suspected homosexuality in a New England boys' school. That same year, Calder Willingham adapted his novel *End as a Man,* which examined homosexuality in a military school, for Broadway. Tennessee Williams won a second Pulitzer in 1955 for *Cat on a Hot Tin Roof,* about a married man haunted by his love for his late best friend. In 1956, Patrick Dennis's best-selling novel *Auntie Mame* became a stage hit by Jerome Lawrence and Robert E. Lee. Although the play had no overt homosexual content, its sensibility, as in the novel, drew enormously from homosexual culture, and the main character changed her elaborate outfits as often as a drag performer. The popular revue *New Faces of 1956* featured T. C. Jones, a noted female impersonator who had already toured extensively with the Jewel Box Revue. The following year Jones appeared in his own show, *Mask and Gown,* to great acclaim. Clearly, Broadway audiences were more than accepting of male homosexual themes and culture.

Hollywood was eager to film these plays; all of them, with the exception of the two Jones vehicles, were made into movies, with adjustments to the homosexual content. Film censorship was finally breaking down as producers and directors dodged the Production Code. *Some Like It Hot,* predicated on men dressed as women, and

Suddenly Last Summer, clearly about homosexuality, were released in 1959. A film of Lillian Hellman's 1934 play *The Children's Hour* grappled with a lesbian scandal, and the 1961 British film *A Taste of Honey* portrayed a gentle homosexual man. At least three movies in 1962 featured gay themes: *Advise and Consent,* centered on a Washington, D.C., political scandal; the British film *Victim,* which took a sympathetic look at homosexuals who were being blackmailed; and *That Touch of Mink,* a sex comedy. Lesbian characters offhandedly appeared in *All Fall Down* and *Walk on the Wild Side* in 1962, and in *The Balcony* and *The Haunting* in 1963. The next year, Gore Vidal's *The Best Man* combined politics and sex; *Goodbye Charlie* tossed lesbian jokes into a sex comedy; and *Black Like Me* grappled with homosexuality and race. Open homosexuality was clearly now a staple of mass entertainment.

During this time, openly gay artists were writing and presenting their work without the interference of mainstream producers, managers, or curators. This new wave of theater, film, and art emerged in urban areas with thriving lesbian and gay communities. Caffe Cino, a Greenwich Village coffee house founded by Joe Cino, was the first off-off-Broadway theater. Joe Cino began by producing dramatic readings, but soon moved to presenting works by homosexual writers such as Oscar Wilde, Thornton Wilder, William Inge, and Terence Rattigan in ways that brought out their coded subtext. The radicalism of Caffe Cino and other companies that followed—Judson Poets' Theater, Ridiculous Theater Company in 1964, the Cockettes in San Francisco in 1968, and New York's Hot Peaches in 1969—was in presenting plays with explicit gay content in an openly gay environment. Major American playwrights such as Robert Patrick, Al Carmines, Lanford Wilson, Tom Eyen, Charles Ludlam, Jean-Claude van Itallie, and William M. Hoffman all emerged from this setting.

Most of the people involved in these companies (with a few exceptions, such as the lesbian playwright and director Maria Irene Fornes) were white gay men, reflecting the fragmentation of both communities and movements. African American companies were formed later; the New York–based New Lafayette Theater and the Negro Ensemble Company were both founded in 1967. Lesbian theater thrived later as well, with the growth of women's and feminist theater companies. The alternative arts scene in New York culture, including theater, fine arts, music, and literature, was intricately tied to the continual growth of homosexual culture. Similar cultural scenes were evolving in Los Angeles's Silver Lake and San Francisco's North Beach. The impact on national American culture was enormous.

Concurrent with theater, underground film culture was thriving during the 1950s and 1960s. As early as 1947, twenty-year-old Kenneth Anger, formerly a child actor in Hollywood films, made the homosexual-themed *Fireworks,* a masturbatory dream film starring himself. *Fireworks* became a touchstone for underground film culture. By the early 1960s, openly gay filmmakers such as James Broughton, Michael and George Kuchar, Andy Warhol, and Jack Smith—whose 1964 *Flaming Creatures* was continually banned throughout the United States for decades—were in the forefront of redefining the possibilities of American film. This was a pivotal cultural moment for homosexual artists. They now had the permission to produce openly gay work without clear traditions and antecedents.

The filmmakers began drawing on past mass-produced popular culture—1930s films, classic film stars with exaggerated gender expression, and vintage mass-produced artifacts such as lamps, jewelry, and clothing—to express their ideas. This reclaiming of past popular culture, often making fun of it while simultaneously using it to comment on the present, was called "camp." Lesbian cultural critic Susan Sontag states that "the essence of Camp is its love of the unnatural: of artifice and exaggeration. And 'Camp' is esoteric— something of a private code, a badge of identity even, among small urban cliques."[40] Sontag's "small urban cliques" were homosexuals, who had traditionally used codes as a way of identifying one another and, ostracized from the mainstream, formed their own satiric take on "normal."

This transformative use of material entered the mainstream imagination and became a predominant means of expression. Andy Warhol noted that "drag queens are ambulatory archives of ideal movie-star womanhood." Considered the primary theoretician of the pop art movement, Warhol specialized in taking the everyday and the mundane—the familiar image of a Campbell's soup can—and insisting that viewers adjust their reality to see them differently.

As Warhol stripped away artifice by calling attention to it, another artistic movement called attention to the radical potential of what was left after exposing themselves emotionally and psychologically. The Beats were members of a small literary movement that started in the homosexual and bohemian enclaves of San Francisco and New York in the early 1950s. The movement produced great works that changed American culture, such as Allen Ginsberg's poem "Howl," Jack Kerouac's novel *On the Road,* and William Burroughs's *Naked Lunch.* The word "beat," with origins in drug and jazz culture, originally meant "robbed," and came to mean, for these writers, "The world is against me."[41] Ginsberg noted that "the point of beat is that you get beaten down to a certain nakedness where you are actually able to see the world in a visionary way."[42]

The Beat movement and homosexual culture were inextricably intertwined. The Beat writers' rejection of enforced gender roles and sexual behaviors, their reliance on self-expression through the arts and resistance to censorship, their antimilitarist and antistatist stance, and their insistence on being true to their own vision were all qualities that had been manifested by homosexual communities. Not all Beat writers were openly homosexual, but many were: Allen Ginsberg, John Wieners, Robert Duncan, William Burroughs, Peter Orlovsky, Jack Spicer, Steve Jonas, Herbert Hunke, Harold Norse. Some heterosexual Beats, such as Kerouac and Neal Cassady, also had sex with men.

The Beats' disaffected position was shared by many in America, explaining why their mythos became an object of such fascination. By the mid-1950s, beatniks—a term coined by Herb Caen, a San Francisco columnist—appeared. Beatniks were "avant garde camp followers" and a "faddish commercialization" of the Beats, as well as "a slightly more adult alternative to rock and roll." But the phenomenon was indicative of how much average Americans longed for alternatives, even in their imaginations, to their lives.[43] The Beat movement and beatnik culture were a conduit of homosexual culture to a much wider audience. They were also a sign of how remarkably omnipresent homosexuality was in mid-century America. In a 1982 essay, "A Definition of the Beat Generation," Ginsberg credits the Beats with launching the radical women's liberation, Black Power, and gay liberation movements; promoting sentiment against the war in Vietnam; igniting an interest in Eastern religions and philosophy; and fostering the idea of free love—or as the 1960s hippies, the spiritual descendants of the Beats, called it, "do your own thing."[44]

The cultural valorization of the Beats coincided with the legal validation of homosexual representation in the media. In 1954, the October issue of *ONE* magazine, which contained a lesbian coming-out story and a comic poem about a British sex scandal, was seized by the U.S. Post Office as nonmailable because of obscenity. *ONE* lost two appeals at the federal level because, according to the court, "an article may be vulgar, offensive, and indecent even though not regarded as such by a particular group . . . because their own social or moral standards are far below those of the general community. . . . Social standards are fixed by and for the great majority and not by and for a hardened or weakened minority." The court left no doubt that homosexuals, as a group, were not part of the "general community." In 1958, on final appeal, the Supreme Court ruled in *ONE's* favor, simply citing their 1957 decision in *Roth v. United States* that to be considered obscene, material must be judged in its entirety and not singled out for its content alone. The same decision had previously been cited by a San Francisco court in a ruling that overturned a ban on distribution of Ginsberg's *Howl and Other Poems* because of its blatantly homoerotic imagery.

Like the gay men who made advances in theater and film, the Beats were mostly concerned about men. Ginsberg wrote empathetic poems about his mother, and, like Whitman, writes of universal sexual liberation. But as a movement, the Beats treated women as subservient to male needs and created no room for women to explore their individual potential. The Beats, who drew enormous inspiration from African American street culture and jazz, were also almost entirely white, with a few exceptions, such as LeRoi Jones (later Amiri Baraka), on the fringes of the movement.

MOVEMENTS GROWING TOGETHER AND APART

The LGBT movement grew quickly and effectively because of its mix of people of different races, classes, and genders. It did not work in coalition with other social justice movements, even though many LGBT people had personal investments in other movements. This was the case for several reasons. Except for the Gay Liberation Front and the Radicalesbians, which would emerge in a few years, most LGBT groups were not interested in other issues. In addition, many heterosexual feminists and civil rights advocates held biases against homosexuals. Some heterosexual feminists felt that open lesbians in the feminist movement would give credence to the accusation that feminists were all man-hating lesbians. The irony is that the feminist movement's fundamental critique of sexual power differences, inequalities in the workplace, and the legal inequities and problems faced by women in relationship to family, marriage, and children were all first articulated by the Daughters of Bilitis. Issue after issue of *The Ladder* contained articles and letters describing the problems faced by women. Heterosexual feminists never acknowledged their debt to lesbians.

There were, of course, people whose social analysis had its origins in multiple identities, especially the experience of being both black and homosexual. One example is playwright Lorraine Hansberry, author of *A Raisin in the Sun* (1959) and *The Sign in Sidney Brustein's Window* (1964), which included an openly homosexual character and dealt with issues of race, freedom, and responsibility. In a letter to *The Ladder* in 1957, Hansberry argued that in the homophile movement, "there may be women to emerge who will be able to formulate a new and possible concept that homosexual persecution and condemnation has at its roots not only social ignorance, but a philosophically active anti-feminist dogma."

James Baldwin's 1955 *Giovanni's Room* and 1962 *Another Country* dealt with the complicated intersections of sexuality and race through homosexual characters. As early as 1949, in his essay "The Preservation of Innocence," Baldwin directly connected heterosexual hostility toward homosexuals to white hostility toward African Americans. He saw both as a failure of the imagination to connect fully with one's own humanity. He explores this idea in his 1963 *The Fire Next Time:* "White people in this country will have quite enough to do in learning how to accept and love themselves and each other, and when they have achieved this—which will not be tomorrow and may very well be never—the Negro problem will no longer exist, for it will no longer be needed."[45] Historian John Howard charts how interracial homosexual relationships, some-times less obvious than heterosexual ones, were often the way that white men became involved in the civil rights movement.[46]

Action was needed as much as thought. Bayard Rustin, long-time advisor and mentor in nonviolence thinking to Martin Luther King Jr., was a gay black man responsible for several major successes of the civil rights movement. According to John D'Emilio, in 1953 Rustin was asked to leave the Fellowship of Reconciliation and the Quaker-based American Friends Service Committee, both of which were deeply committed to traditional Christian morality along with their peace-based work, after he was arrested on a morals charge for having sex with two men in a car.[47] Soon after, Rustin was deeply involved with the Montgomery bus boycott and then became chief organizer of the March on Washington, for which he was featured on the cover of *Life* in September 1963. Attempting to discredit him, white supremacist Senator Strom Thurmond read into the congres-sional record Rustin's morals charges and said that the march was being planned by a "communist, draft-dodger, and homosexual." Perhaps the confluence of these identities is what made Rustin so successful, but larger social changes demanded more of him. Pauli Murray—the first African American female Episcopal priest, co-founder of the National Organization of Women, and a closeted lesbian—chastised Rustin and others for their exclusion of black women from the march's speakers list.

Along with the battle for civil rights, other changes were happen-ing in America, most clearly seen in highly politicized youth coun-terculture. The teen culture of the 1950s had by the early 1960s transformed itself into a new, vibrant national youth culture that was politically aware, responsive to social issues, and understanding of personal experience in a larger context. It also promoted experi-mentation with sex, gender, and drugs. Beginning with the Beatles'

U.S. television debut in February 1964 and continuing through the introduction of the Rolling Stones, Jefferson Airplane, the Doors, David Bowie (whose even more outrageous alter ego, Ziggy Stardust, would emerge a few years later), and others, American teens were faced with rock stars that radically broke from traditional masculine affect and hinted at their own homoerotic longings. Performers such as Janis Joplin, Grace Slick, Aretha Franklin, and Dusty Springfield gave voice to women's sexual desires, although in a context of traditional heterosexuality.

The hippie ethos espoused free love, antimilitarism, communal living, anticapitalism, and a soft version of anarchistic antiestablishment sentiment. It brought together many of the ideas of the Beats, homophile groups, feminism, and civil rights. It was also resonant with the nineteenth-century anarchists, free lovers, transcendentalists, commune advocates, and some radical labor activists. Gender roles were quickly changing. Women were beginning to think of themselves as independent from men and place value on being able to form friendships with other women. Men—many of whom grew their hair long, sported earrings, and wore colorful clothing that would have been condemned as too feminine five years earlier—were no longer immediately chastised for expressing their feelings. The cultural terror of men wearing their hair long is a vivid example of how change in gender affect was deeply threatening. For years, mainstream media posted the panicked response: "You can't tell whether it's a boy or a girl."

The flourishing of 1960s youth culture, with its integration of sexuality and sexual freedom into everyday life, was the result of a slow, incremental, yet constant homosexualization of America. It was also the beginning of a new kind of homosexuality that was, first and foremost, a form of political resistance.

TEN

REVOLT/BACKLASH/RESISTANCE

COUNTRY IN REVOLT

Throughout the 1960s and until peace was declared in 1975, the Vietnam War was the continual backdrop—dramatic, violent, appalling, and tragic—that defined everything that was happening in the United States. The Eisenhower administration had sent close to nine hundred advisors to South Vietnam to prevent what the U.S. saw as a potential communist takeover by the North Vietnamese. By 1963, President Kennedy had dispatched sixteen thousand American military personnel. Howard Zinn, in *A People's History of the United States*, notes:

> From 1964 to 1972, the wealthiest and most powerful nation in the history of the world made a maximum military effort, with everything short of atomic bombs, to defeat a nationalist revolutionary movement in a tiny, peasant country—and failed. . . .
>
> In the course of that war, there developed in the United States the greatest antiwar movement the nation had ever experienced.[1]

By the end of the war, the losses on all sides were tremendous. The United States suffered the least, with 58,159 men dead, 303,635 wounded, and 1,719 reported missing. The South Vietnamese government reported 220,357 dead and 1,170,000 wounded. The National Liberation Front in North Vietnam reported 1,176,000 dead or missing and a minimum of 600,000 wounded. The civilian casualties were staggering: two million in North Vietnam and over a million and a half in South Vietnam. United States citizens were constantly divided over the war, often along generational, race, and gender lines.

The popular movement against the war started in the early 1960s with national faith-based peace groups, such as the Fellowship of Reconciliation (of which Jane Addams was a founding member), the American Friends Service Committee, and the Catholic Worker Movement. It then quickly spread to youth-based political groups such as the Students for a Democratic Society (SDS), one of the founding groups of the New Left. SDS was organized in 1960 with the writing of its manifesto, the Port Huron Statement. Maurice Isserman points out that "in 1961 SDS had roughly 300 dues-paying *members;* by 1968 it had roughly those many *chapters.*"[2]

The United States saw the worst outbreaks of sustained public violence since the labor riots and strikes of the 1920s. The most shocking events were the assassinations of Medgar Evers, John Kennedy, Malcolm X, Martin Luther King Jr., and Robert Kennedy. Between 1964 and 1969, close to seventy-five major urban race-related riots broke out across the country, in cities as large as Los Angeles and New York and as small as York, Pennsylvania, and Plainfield, New Jersey. After the King assassination, there were riots in sixty cities. In total there were close to one hundred and twenty deaths; over three thousand injured (by a conservative count); over fifty thousand women, men and children arrested; and billions in damage.

Almost all of the people killed, injured, or arrested were African Americans. In 1966, the Black Panther Party formed in order to further the Black Power movement using more militant and aggressive tactics than mainstream African American civil rights groups. Private and police assassinations of civil rights workers, both black and white, and of members of Black Power groups were not infrequent.

Along with the Vietnam War and racial tensions, the rise of feminism was dividing the country. After women won suffrage, the organized feminist movement had little public presence. Beginning in the 1960s—with the approval of the birth control pill by the U.S.

Food and Drug Administration—the second wave of the feminist movement began. For nearly half a century, feminists had identified lack of reproductive control as a central impediment to women's personal, sexual, and economic independence and freedom. The Pill suddenly, and simply, separated sex from reproduction, marriage, and the family. In 1961 doctors wrote prescriptions for four hundred thousand women. A year later, 1.2 million women were taking it. Three years later that number had jumped to 3.6 million women.

The introduction of the birth control pill, interestingly enough, helped the cause of homosexual liberation and struck against anti-homosexual prejudice. The major moral, scientific, and legal argument against homosexual activity had always been that it does not lead to reproduction and is thus unnatural. The birth control pill made the separation between sex and reproduction socially acceptable.

By the end of the 1960s, radical feminism added an analysis of heterosexuality—an analysis often implicit in the writings of the homophile groups—to the understanding of women's oppression. Groups such as the Redstockings and Cell 16 often drew on a Marxist analysis of women as a distinct cultural group and an oppressed class of people. Like the anarchists and radical labor activists in the early part of the century, and the more recent Black Power advocates, radical feminists were interested not in reforming a system they considered essentially corrupt, but in replacing it with one that was more just and equitable. Under the umbrella of the Women's Liberation Front, radical feminist groups began staging high-profile demonstrations, including the September 1968 "No More Miss America!" protest in Atlantic City, New Jersey.

The progressive politics of the late 1960s were predicated on the principle that a person had complete autonomy and control over her or his body. This included freedom from violence, control of reproduction, the ability to engage in any consensual sexual behavior, and the freedom to take drugs. The massive numbers of men killed in Vietnam or returning wounded or mutilated was a constant reminder—increasingly broadcast on television—of the fragility of the body as well as the importance of making your own choices about it.

This new wave of activism was constituted mainly of younger people, because of the strong antiauthoritarian views emanating from anger over U.S. policy in Southeast Asia.

Like much of the counterculture, political messages were framed in sexual contexts. To promote draft resistance, folk singer Joan Baez and her sister Mimi Farina posed for a poster that read "Girls Say Yes to Boys Who Say No."

At the August 1968 Democratic National Convention in Chicago, conservative Democratic mayor Richard Daley deployed twenty-three thousand police officers to manage ten thousand antiwar demonstrators. Violent chaos ensued as police tear-gassed and beat the mostly peaceful demonstrators. The official government investigation of the convention violence called it a "police riot." Captured on film, the violence was so extreme that it received worldwide condemnation, even as U.S. polls showed widespread support for the police. In October 1968, SDS passed a resolution titled "The Elections Don't Mean Shit—Vote Where the Power Is—Our Power Is in the Street."

Following these models, homosexual liberation became predominantly a political question. In early 1969, Carl Wittman, the son of Communist Party members and a drafter of the Port Huron Statement, wrote "A Gay Manifesto" while living in the midst of the political and gay scenes in San Francisco. It became the defining document for a new movement. The conclusion lists "An Outline of Imperatives for Gay Liberation":

1. Free ourselves: come out everywhere; initiate self defense and political activity; initiate counter community institutions.
2. Turn other gay people on: talk all the time; understand, forgive, accept.
3. Free the homosexual in everyone: we'll be getting a good bit of shit from threatened latents: be gentle, and keep talking & acting free.
4. We've been playing an act for a long time, so we're consummate actors. Now we can begin to be, and it'll be a good show![3]

Wittman's combination of community building, constructive dialogue, goodwill, trust, and fun was a mixture of New Left organizing, homosexual playfulness, and the single most important directive of gay liberation: to come out. (The term "coming out" had not been in common use before; previously the metaphor had been about *coming into* the homosexual world.) For gay liberationists, coming out was not simply a matter of self-identification. It was a radical, public act that would impact every aspect of a person's life. The publicness of coming out was a decisive break from the past. Whereas homophile groups argued that homosexuals could find safety by promoting privacy, gay liberation argued that safety and liberation were found only by living in, challenging, and changing the public sphere.

Physical resistance was the logical course of action in this context. For over two days in August 1968, transvestites and street people in San Francisco's Tenderloin District fought with police at the Compton Cafeteria after management called in the officers to eject some rowdy customers. Undoubtedly there were numerous similar, but unrecorded, incidents in which gay individuals and groups resisted arrest and police violence. But the most famous incident took place a year later.

In the early hours of Saturday, June 28, 1969, police conducted a routine raid on the Stonewall Inn at 53 Christopher Street in the heart of Greenwich Village. They evicted patrons and arrested some of the staff. A crowd gathered outside and refused to leave. Clashes with the police ensued. Even though the bar had been closed, crowds gathered again and the scene was repeated, with less violence, late Saturday evening. After a few days of calm, more protests and some violence occurred the following Wednesday night. The events at Stonewall were not riots, but sustained street altercations of raucous, sometimes violent, resistance. The larger culture of political militance was evident in the slogans that emerged immediately after Stonewall, such as GAY POWER and, as someone chalked on the front of the now closed Stonewall Inn, THEY WANT US TO FIGHT FOR OUR COUNTRY [BUT] THEY INVADE OUR RIGHTS.[4]

The only viable gay political organization that existed in New

York at the time was Mattachine. Its members viewed the Stonewall incident and the highly public political activities that ensued as a disruptive departure from their political process. On June 28, Mattachine members were already working with the police to stop further protests. They even posted a sign on the closed bar:

> WE HOMOSEXUALS PLEAD WITH
> OUR PEOPLE TO PLEASE HELP
> MAINTAIN PEACEFUL AND QUIET
> CONDUCT ON THE STREETS OF
> THE VILLAGE—MATTACHINE

At one of the last Mattachine meetings before the police attack on the Stonewall Inn, Jim Fouratt, a younger member, insisted: "All the oppressed have to unite! The system keeps us all weak by keeping us separate."[5]

Stonewall was less a turning point than a final stimulus in a series of public altercations. A coalition of disgruntled Mattachine members, along with lesbians and gay men who identified with the pro–Black Power, antiwar New Left, called for a meeting on July 24, 1969. The flyer announcing the meeting was headlined, "Do you think homosexuals are revolting? You bet your sweet ass we are."

This radical change in rhetoric was indicative of fiercely antihierarchal, free-for-all, consensus-driven discussion. Out of it emerged the Gay Liberation Front (GLF). The group took its name from the Women's Liberation Front, which in turn had taken its name from the Vietcong National Liberation Front. More traditionally anarchist than leftist, the lack of structure and clash of ideas in GLF was perfectly indicative of the intellectual, social, sexual, and political excitement of the time. A GLF member stated that "GLF is more of a process than an organization."[6] But it was a powerful process that produced results. Within a year, GLF had organized Sunday night meetings, nineteen "cells" or action groups, twelve consciousness-raising groups, an ongoing radical study group, an all-men's meeting, a women's caucus, three communal living groups, and a series of successful community dances, in addition to publishing the newspaper *Come Out!* The publication became a model for numerous highly influential LGBT community newspapers, including Michigan's *Gay Liberator,* Philadelphia's *Gay Alternative,* San Francisco's *Gay Sunshine,* and Boston's *Fag Rag* and *Gay Community News.* Hundreds of independent GLF groups immediately sprang up on college campuses and in cities across the country.

GLF's open-ended process, as well as its refusal to see antigay bias or hatred as disconnected from other forms of oppression, neither resulted in hoped-for coalitions nor appealed to all members. Women's liberation, Black Power, antiwar, and labor groups were unwilling to work with GLF because of their own dislike or fear of homosexuality.

By November 1969, after a discussion of donating money to the Black Panthers, some GLF members decided to start the Gay Activists Alliance (GAA). This new organization would, according to its constitution, focus only on achieving civil rights for gay people, "disdaining all ideologies, whether political or social, and forbearing alliance with any other organization."[7] Although GAA disdained official political ideologies, it was forthright in confronting antihomosexual bias in media, legal, and social venues. Much of its power came from its "zaps"—high-profile public confrontations of people and institutions that promoted antihomosexual sentiments—which garnered enormous attention and brought LGBT issues into the media.

GLF and GAA coexisted until GLF's demise in 1972. As GAA grew and some of its leaders began to have political ambitions, their agenda became more reformist and conservative. Transgender activists Sylvia Rivera and Marsha P. Johnson had left GLF to help form GAA, but ultimately found themselves, and issues of gender identity, excluded. In 1970 they started Street Transvestite Action Revolution (STAR), which became the foundational group for contemporary transgender activism. By 1974 GAA was crumbling, and prominent members such as Bruce Voeller left to start the National Gay Task Force (now the National Gay and Lesbian Task Force). When GAA finally folded in 1980, it had, according to historian David Eisenbach, reverted to GLF's inclusive political analysis.[8]

The split between the pragmatism of GAA and the idealism of GLF echoed the earlier division within Mattachine and can be traced back to nineteenth-century political discussions of suffrage, free love, labor reform, and anarchism. GLF's comprehensive vision of social justice was mirrored in Martin Luther King Jr.'s "no one is free, until everyone is free." This approach distanced King from many civil rights activists and supporters as he began to vocally oppose the war in Vietnam, in his 1967 "Beyond Vietnam: A Time to Break Silence" speech, and to connect capitalism to black oppression. GAA's single-issue politic had a much greater impact than GLF on mainstream gay political organizing. It became the template for the contemporary gay rights movement, which works to change, not overthrow, the system.

GLF had a more lasting impact on the formation of gay and lesbian youth groups across the nation. Between 1969 and 1980 nearly fifty youth support groups—aimed at lesbians and gay men in their teens—were founded. Some of these were grassroots and came out of the gay liberation movement; others were founded by progressive social service organizations.[9] The advent of these groups made perfect sense, since gay liberation emerged, in part, from the youth counterculture, but also because young people were engaging in sex earlier. Lesbian and gay youth now had a political and social framework in which to declare and celebrate their identity. These youth groups provided them with a vital social outlet that was badly needed, since underage people could not go to bars to meet people, and coming out at school or home could be dangerous.

The men in GLF and GAA had grown up in a prefeminist world. Their actions, even after lesbians confronted them, often reflected their upbringing, which was not to take women and their concerns seriously. Nevertheless, many lesbians joined these groups because they were not welcome in the National Organization of Women (NOW) or even in some radical feminist groups. Betty Friedan's antilesbian sentiments were so present in NOW that a group of lesbians, including Karla Jay and Rita Mae Brown, formed the Lavender Menace, a guerilla action group. They confronted NOW's members at its Second Congress to Unite Women in May 1970, where they passed out their manifesto, "The Woman-Identified Woman." A year later, NOW passed a resolution affirming that lesbian rights were "a legitimate concern for feminism." But a critical break had occurred. The Lavender Menace, who now called themselves Radicalesbians and understood that their concerns were distinct from those of heterosexual women and gay men, began a distinct movement: lesbian feminism.

Lesbian feminism created a new political and social identity for lesbians that had not existed previously. Jill Johnston, a New York–based dance critic and activist nationally famous for her outspokenness and flair for publicity, stated in her 1973 book *Lesbian Nation: The Feminist Solution:*

> Historically the lesbian had two choices: being criminal or going straight. The present revolutionary project is the creation of a legitimate state defined by women. Only women can do this. Going straight is legitimizing your oppression. As was being criminal. A male society will not permit any other choice for a woman.[10]

Faderman describes lesbian feminism as being "pro-women and pro-children" and compares it to the utopian vision of reformers such as Jane Addams.[11] In the early 1970s, women started national networks of small presses, such as Daughters Inc., which published Rita Mae Brown's groundbreaking lesbian novel *Rubyfruit Jungle.* They also founded over a hundred newspapers, magazines such as *Amazon Quarterly,* and music cooperatives and festivals such as the Michigan Womyn's Music Festival. Many lesbians still worked with gay men and heterosexual feminists on shared concerns, and lesbian feminism addressed many of the concerns that women in the Daughters of Bilitis had voiced about lesbians in the workplace, lesbian health, and legal discrimination that lesbians faced in relationships. But a world centered around women brought new ideas. Lesbian feminists set up health clinics, created grassroots political organizations, and instituted a widespread national network of communal living collectives that, although unaffiliated, saw themselves as part of a movement.

In their pursuit of making the world a safer place for children and women, some lesbian feminists, in conjunction with heterosexual feminists, articulated views about sex and gender perceived as antithetical to radical feminism and gay liberation. As a group, they were often called "cultural feminists" by their detractors. They criticized nontraditional sexual activity such as S/M and bondage, and they condemned drag queens and drag shows (which they saw as a parody of women's oppression). They offered harsh critiques of transsexual and transgender people, such as Janice Raymond's 1979 *The Transsexual Empire: The Making of the She-Male*, in which she argued that sex-reassignment surgery is violence against women's bodies. In the mid to late 1970s they conducted censorship campaigns against pornography, which they saw as a cause of rape. Many of these positions generated heated, and often angry, discussion. Historian Alice Echols argues that "advocating sexual repression as a solution to violence against women [ends up] mobilizing women around their fears rather than their visions."[12] Lesbian theorist Gayle Rubin makes concrete comparisons of these policies to the ideas of the social purity movement.

The exciting, confusing, and often contradictory whirlpool of LGBT politics in the years after Stonewall helped, along with other forces, to shape the movement. It is striking, however, to realize that the numbers of people actively involved in these organizations were minuscule. As with the Mattachine, the Daughters of Bilitis, the Women's Liberation Front, and the Black Panther Party, the work of a few people in small organizations touched the lives of large numbers of people and changed the world. One way the LGBT political groups did this was through their enormous influence on mainstream culture, now that homosexuality was more openly discussed than ever before. Publishing, film, TV, and the press reached millions of Americans.

Much of the mainstream press was implicitly positive. On October 31, 1969, just four months after the Stonewall conflict, *Time* had a cover story called "The Homosexual in America." The article inside featured photos of gay liberationists on a picket line and a drag queen in a beauty contest. A discussion sponsored by the magazine among a panel of "experts," including psychiatrists, clergy, liberals, and gay activists, was clearly won by the latter two. As *Time* noted, "the love that once dared not speak its name now can't keep its mouth shut." The April 1971 issue of *Playboy* featured a long "roundtable" on homosexuality that was clearly skewed against the conservative voices. The December 31, 1971, issue of *Life* included an eleven-page spread titled "Homosexuals in Revolt." It was decidedly affirmative, featuring numerous upbeat photos of lesbian and gay activists.

The mainstream publishing industry, having discovered that positive depictions of lesbian and gay male life were a niche market, quickly published books on the subject. In *Sappho Was a Right-On Woman: A Liberated View of Lesbianism*, published in 1972, Sidney Abbott and Barbara Love argued—as Phillip Wylie had in the 1940s—that society has to be cured of its negative attitudes toward sexuality. In the same year, GAA member Peter Fisher's *The Gay Mystique: The Myth and Reality of Male Homosexuality* argued that young people over the age of sixteen have a right to act on their sexuality and that lesbian and gay teachers would be positive role models for students. Dozens of fiction and nonfiction books presenting similar material were published by mainstream and smaller publishers over the next five years. Unlike pulp novels and sociological studies, these books determinedly affirmed homosexuality.

New freedom in Hollywood now allowed complex and compelling images of LGBT people. Sidney Lumet's 1975 *Dog Day Afternoon* featured Al Pacino as a gay male bank robber who was financing his lover's sex change operation. George Schlatter's 1976 *Norman . . . Is That You?*, about an interracial gay couple dealing with one set of parents, was funny and politically incisive. Even television censorship—which had always been stricter than censorship in Hollywood, since television images entered the home—began to be relaxed. As early as February 1971, the enormously popular *All in the Family* featured a gay male character who was a former professional football player. Nine months later, the popular TV series *Room 222*, about an African American teacher in the fictional Walt Whitman High School, dealt with homosexuality and teens in the episode "What Is a Man?" In 1972 ABC presented a made-for-TV movie, *That Certain Summer*, in which a formerly married gay man comes out to his fourteen-year-old son. The only outcry was from gay liberationists claiming the movie was too timid. That same week NBC broadcast "A Very Strange Triangle," an episode on the series *The Bold Ones: The New Doctors*, about a physician still in love with a woman he dated who is now in a lesbian relationship. John J. O'Connor, the *New York Times* critic, lambasted "A Very Strange Triangle" as biased against lesbians and noted, "If taboo subjects are going to be used for little more than injecting titillation into inane plots, they should be left taboo." By 1978, in dramatizations such as the made-for-television film *A Question of Love,* legal questions of lesbian custody and parenting were being forthrightly, and sympathetically, discussed.

LIBERATION, SOCIAL PURITY, AND BACKLASH

Social, political, and cultural changes were happening on such a wide and visible range of fronts that many Americans, including the ever-expanding LGBT community, did not know what to expect next. Between 1969 and 1979, more than thirty thousand gay people, the majority of them men, moved to San Francisco. Like other great migrations, such as southern African Americans moving north, this shift—which continued into the 1980s—was vital in remaking a minority culture and formed one of the most important gay political and cultural centers in the United States. On a smaller scale, Huey Newton, chairman of the Black Panther Party, gave a speech in which he surprisingly acknowledged that the party should "try to form a working coalition with the gay liberation and women's liberation groups" and that "homosexuals are not given freedom and liberty by anyone in the society. They might be the most oppressed people in the society." This was the first, and maybe the only, time that a 1970s political group called for a coalition with gay liberation groups.

Other changes simply fell into the category of gossip, such as celebrities, both living and dead, coming out or being outed. Rock stars David Bowie, Elton John, and Janis Joplin claimed that they slept with both sexes. New biographies proclaimed that some of Hollywood's biggest stars—such as Rudolph Valentino, Cary Grant, Greta Garbo, Katharine Hepburn, Charles Laughton, Agnes Moorehead, Marlene Dietrich, and Errol Flynn—were lesbian, gay, or bisexual.

The hyped sexualization of the glitterati was indicative of widespread media coverage of a suddenly sexualized urban life. Nightlife in major American cities—especially New York, San Francisco, and Miami—was becoming identified with gay male venues. Newspapers gleefully reported on the Continental Baths, a plush gay male bathhouse located in a once-fashionable New York hotel that also housed a popular cabaret room open to heterosexuals. The Continental gained national prominence in when 1971 Bette Midler announced on the Johnny Carson show that she got her start there, playing mostly to men clad only in towels. Later that decade, *New York* magazine and other publications lavishly detailed the drug-fueled nightlife of high-profile discos such as New York's Studio 54, popular with prominent politicians, sports figures, and rock stars. This copious public discussion about sexuality continually created the impression across America that traditional norms and moralities were outmoded. The frivolous, but commonplace, tone of these articles made them even scarier to women and men who were fearful that American culture was quickly losing its moral grounding. And their fears were not without reason: The huge success of anticensorship fights, the ongoing battle for reproductive rights (including abortion rights), the wider acceptance of recreational drug use, and increasing media glorification of nonreproductive heterosexual acts in films such as 1972's *Deep Throat* all made the situation more ominous.

For conservatives, the issue was no longer simply about homosexuals. If homosexuality was a disease, as the psychoanalysts argued, it was infecting the entire body politic. To the conservative mind, this infection was seen in a number of alarming ways. Heterosexuals, for instance, were beginning to act like homosexuals. Gay people, who had never had the ability to marry, had long demonstrated that couples could maintain relationships without state or religious sanction. Heterosexuals, consciously or not, learned from their example. Census figures show that the rate of heterosexual cohabitation rose 1,150 percent from the 1960s to 2000, from one out of ten couples to seven out of ten. As more and more heterosexuals began to cohabit, the widespread cultural acceptance of the practice made it easier for homosexuals to be open about their own relationships.

As if all this was not bad enough, homosexuality was literally spreading. In May 1974, *Time* magazine reported on "The New Bisexuals," claiming that "bisexuals, like homosexuals before them, are boldly coming out of their closets, forming clubs, having parties and staking out discotheques." The article attributed the rise of bisexual women to Kinsey, feminism, and "the emphasis by [sex therapists] Masters and Johnson, among others, on the clitoral orgasm that has led to more sexual experimentation." It ended, however, with a warning about families and children. Such warnings were becoming increasingly prevalent in writing about nonstraight sexualities. In the same *Time* article, Manhattan psychoanalyst Natalie Shainess noted that "the constant ricocheting from one sex to the other . . . can create unstable friendships as well as a chaotic home life. If there are children involved, this may confuse their sense of sexual identity."[13]

By this time, however, conservative psychoanalysts had lost their battle. In December 1973—six months before the *Time* article—the American Psychiatric Association, after being lobbied by lesbian and gay activists and professionals within the organization, voted to formally drop homosexuality from the Diagnostic and Statistical Manual of Mental Disorders (DSM). The twenty thousand members were deeply divided, but the board voted 13–0. The *New York Times* headline stated, "Doctors Rule Homosexuality Not Abnormal." A highly public discussion ensued. In a December 23, 1973, *New York Times* roundtable, psychoanalyst Irving Bieber, who disagreed with the APA vote, stated that he was "interested in the implications this has for children. . . . I can pick out the entire population at risk in male homosexuality at the age of five, six, seven, and eight. If these children are treated, and their parents are treated, they will not become homosexual."

It was in this ambivalent social context, in which homosexuality was being simultaneously depathologized and viewed as the source of newly articulated threats to the family, that legal change began to happen. Mattachine members had picketed the White House and other federal buildings from 1965 to 1969, no doubt inspired by the African American civil rights marches. (Mattachine leader Frank Kameny's use of the phrase "Gay Is Good" in a 1968 speech was clearly resonant of "Black Is Beautiful.") But after Stonewall, gay rights activists—gay liberationists had little interest in specific legal issues—began to lobby to repeal sodomy laws and pass statutes outlawing discrimination against gays. By 1979, twenty states had repealed their sodomy laws, some willingly and others after legal battles. Arkansas did away with its sodomy law during a general revision of the state's penal code, but outcry from clergy and conservatives was so great that it was reinstated. State senator Milt Earnheardt, arguing to reinstate the sodomy law, told the senate, "This bill is aimed at weirdos and queers who live in a fairyland world and are trying to wreck family life." The new law criminalizing sodomy was passed unanimously.[14]

In 1975, voters in Massachusetts elected Elaine Noble to the state's House of Representatives, making her the first openly lesbian or gay state legislator in U.S. history. Around the same time, activists were introducing nondiscrimination bills, misnamed by the press as "gay rights bills," in towns, cities, and counties around the country. These laws—modeled on the Civil Rights Act of 1964, which forbids discrimination based on "race, color, religion, sex, [or] national origin"—targeted discrimination based on actual or perceived sexual orientation. Liberal university cities passed the first such laws, starting with East Lansing, Michigan, in March 1972 and Ann Arbor, Michigan, in August. Larger cities, such as Seattle, Minneapolis, and Washington, D.C., followed. By 1976, twenty-nine such laws had been passed in the United States.

The fight over the "gay rights" bill in Dade County, Florida, which includes Miami, became a pivotal turning point. On January 18, 1977, the county commission passed, by a 5 to 3 vote, an ordinance that would make it illegal to discriminate on the basis of sexual orientation in employment, housing, or public services, including both public and private schools. Local Catholics, Protestants, and Orthodox Jews, along with other conservative groups, immediately rallied a movement to fight for repeal. Included in this coalition was Save Our Children, a newly formed Christian group founded by Anita Bryant. Bryant was a minor celebrity—a singer, entertainer, and former Miss America runner-up—and deeply religious. At Save Our Children's first press conference on February

11, Bryant, backed by clergy from all of Miami's major churches, announced she had proof that gays were "trying to recruit our children to homosexuality."[15] Because this was the first time that an ordinance prohibiting discrimination against gays was under appeal, and because Bryant was a colorful figure whose statements became increasingly outrageous, the fight in Dade County gained national attention. On June 7, in a special referendum with record-breaking voter turnout, the ordinance was repealed, 69.3 percent to 39.6 percent.[16]

After the win, Bryant announced she was going to start a national campaign against "gay rights laws." But the energy generated by the Bryant campaign had already begun to spread. In April and May 1978, laws protecting gays from discrimination were repealed in St. Paul, Minnesota; Wichita, Kansas; and Eugene, Oregon, even though Bryant did not personally campaign for their repeal.

The tide turned a bit, back to favoring the rights of lesbian and gay people, when in November 1978 California's Proposition 6—also known as the Briggs initiative, after its author, state senator John Briggs—was defeated. While the referendums to repeal non-discrimination laws were reactive, Proposition 6 was proactive. It sought to prohibit lesbians and gay men, as well as any teacher who was found "advocating, imposing, encouraging or promoting" homosexuality, from teaching in public schools. Lesbian and gay activists—including Harvey Milk—spent months organizing the "No on 6" campaign, which successfully defeated the proposition by a 58.4 percent to 41.6 percent margin.

The Dade County vote and Proposition 6 vote presented different challenges, but the main reason gay and lesbian activists were victorious in the latter was a striking difference in organizing styles. Pro-gay activists in Dade County brought in outside spokespersons, used a rhetoric of human rights, and countered religious arguments with secular ones. In California, the "No on 6" campaign, using the gay liberation–influenced slogan "Come Out! Come Out! Wherever You Are," urged lesbians and gay men to explain to their families, neighbors, and fellow citizens how Proposition 6 would affect their lives. Citizens in California responded to a personal appeal that allowed them insight into the lives of lesbians and gay men, whereas the Florida vote was lost when people failed to be persuaded by intellectual or political arguments. The contrast between these two approaches is even more striking given that in both cases, the opposition focused on the threat of homosexuals to children.

These battles were a crucial moment in LGBT history for several reasons. They marked the beginning of a conservative political and religious backlash that is still happening today. This was also the point at which the gay and lesbian movement of the 1960s and 1970s, which was still in the process of defining itself, had to come to grips with two crucial, and connected, issues: its relationship to the new—and often overtly sexual—visibility of lesbians and gay men in political and popular culture, and its relationship to children and young people.

The social changes that had been unfolding since World War II were speeding up, and many Americans were frightened. The success of Save Our Children is viewed by many social historians as the beginning of the rise of the religious right; Jerry Falwell, Pat Robertson, and Jim and Tammy Bakker supported Bryant in her campaigns. Some religious historians have even described America in the late 1970s as undergoing a Fourth Great Awakening. The outpouring of religious rhetorical fervor and conservative political activity was largely, as in past awakenings, a direct response to progressive social changes. These changes included not only the new visibility and acceptance of the gay movement, but also the push for equality for African Americans, the rise of feminism (and the bitter fight over the Equal Rights Amendment throughout the 1970s), the increasingly vocal demonstrations against the Vietnam war, the decline of America's social and political status around the world, and the sexualization of popular culture.

By the mid to late 1970s, the LGBT movement had not only made progress but had radically changed how some Americans thought about homosexuality, heterosexuality, gender, gender roles, sexual activity, children's sexuality, privacy, and most profoundly, sexuality itself. Other political movements had also made vital strides; although there were still serious problems in the United States, the lives of women and African Americans were better then before. But these changes were often about civil equality and the dignity of the individual. The gay liberation movement, lesbian feminism, and even the gay rights movement (which clearly articulated a politic of equality) were far more threatening to American society because they brought into question the underpinnings of sexual identity and sexual orientation. The idea that there could be "hidden homosexuals," that a perceived sexual identity might be a mask, or that a person—child, parent, brother, friend—could suddenly "come out" was profoundly upsetting. The concept that heterosexuality and homosexuality might not be stable personal or social categories was even more disturbing. And on some level, homosexuality offered alternatives to heterosexuals that they found intriguing. That was why heterosexuals, caught between fascination and fear, experienced such ambivalence. A poster held by a lesbian at New York's Gay Pride March in 1971 summed up this irony. It read: WE ARE YOUR WORST FEAR. WE ARE YOUR BEST FANTASY.

This ambivalence, starting during World War II and growing quickly, brought the persecuting society—and its most active and effective enforcers, the social purity groups—to the forefront. Bryant's stated moral superiority was predicated on her being a woman and a mother, and in that context, her defense of the family and children made sense. This paradigm reinforced the stereotype that homosexuality—particularly male homosexuality—was extremely dangerous and threatening to morality and the country. During her Florida campaign, Bryant conjured society's primal fear of the homosexual: "As a mother, I know that homosexuals cannot biologically reproduce children; therefore, they must recruit our children."[17] The enormous success of Bryant's campaign and its resonance in American culture were due to her translation of the social purity movement's rhetoric about protecting women from male lust—which no longer made sense now that women had more freedom and sexuality was viewed more positively—into a new moral imperative of protecting children from a more vehement expression of predatory male lust: homosexuality.

There was a reality in this situation that went unacknowledged by everyone involved. The spokespeople for Save Our Children could not mention it, and the lesbian and gay community, under the worst political attack they had ever experienced, did not want to talk about it. The reality was that there were young people, teens and even younger, who saw themselves as being lesbian, gay, bisexual, or transgender. Their existence had been obvious in many of the novels from the 1950s, in *Rebel Without a Cause,* in the vibrant youth culture of the 1960s, in the writings of radical feminists such as Kate Millett and members of the Gay Liberation Front, and in the more recent gay youth groups. These young women and young men, girls and boys, were acknowledging their own sexuality and coming out at younger and younger ages. It may have been impossible at the time, given the heated social and political climate, but the events surrounding Save Our Children would have taken quite a different turn if the voices of LGBT youth—proclaiming that they were not in danger, but part of a larger LGBT community—had been publicly avowed. Their visibility would have been an antidote to the fear and lies of Bryant and her supporters.

The repeal of the ordinance in Dade County moved the issue of gay rights into the national spotlight, with tremendous antigay effects. After the Dade referendum, the story in *Time* was headlined "A 'No' to Gays"; *U.S. News and World Report* titled their story "Miami Vote: Tide Turning Against Homosexuals."[18] The "dangerous" connection between homosexuals and children was looming large in the public imagination, and much of this sentiment was enacted into law. States began passing laws that affected a range of family issues, such as banning lesbians and gay men from adopting children or becoming foster parents. Ironically, although the charges of recruitment and sexual molestation were aimed almost entirely at gay men, legal restrictions on adoption and foster care disproportionately affected lesbians. Bryant's success with an emboldened religious right helped start a series of conservative policies—including economic, foreign, educational, military, social, and ecological policies under the Reagan administration—that had long-lasting negative effects for gay people.

Bryant and her supporters made no secret that they saw this fight as a religious battle for the Christian soul of America. In her book *The Anita Bryant Story: The Survival of Our Nation's Families and the Threat of Militant Homosexuality,* Bryant wrote: "To think we live in a country where freedom and right are supposed to reign, a country that boasts 'In God we trust' and has such a rich spiritual heritage; yet where internal decadence is all too evident, where the word of God and the voice of the majority is sometimes not heeded at all."[19] Many of the "culture wars" since that time—over guidelines for sex education, funding for the arts, decisions about military policies, judicial decisions about family law and, critically important, the federal response to the HIV/AIDS epidemic—have their roots in this basic conflict. It was a battle that pitted LGBT people's demand for legal equality against mainstream culture's religiously informed, if ever ambivalent, relationship to homosexuality.

The legal and cultural wars of the late 1970s brought LGBT communities across the nation together in powerful ways, including massive rallies and campaigns against this new wave of political repression. When the repression took a violent turn—as it did with the June 24, 1973, firebombing of a New Orleans gay bar, in which thirty-two people were burned to death, or the assassination of San Francisco mayor George Moscone and city supervisor Harvey Milk in 1978—the diverse LGBT community was able to put aside its internal differences to fight a common enemy.

AIDS: RESILIENCE AND RESISTANCE

Within three years, that common enemy would take forms that were eerily familiar, but in a context that was nearly unimaginable. On June 5, 1981, the *Morbidity and Mortality Weekly,* a newsletter from the Centers for Disease Control and Prevention (CDC), mentioned five cases of an unusual pneumonia in patients in Los Angeles. A month later, on July 3, the *New York Times* printed a short article headlined "Rare Cancer Seen in 41 Homosexuals." By December the CDC had identified nonhomosexual men with similar symptoms. As the year ended, there had been 121 deaths from what was at first called gay-related immune deficiency. Eventually it would be given another name: acquired immune deficiency syndrome (AIDS).

By 2007, AIDS would claim the lives of 583,298 women, men, and children in the United States and 2.1 million worldwide. In the early stages of the pandemic, researchers did not understand, as they would by 1983, that the disease was caused by a virus that would later be called HIV (human immunodeficiency virus). At first it was largely unclear exactly how the virus was spread, and there was no easily available diagnostic test for HIV until 1985. This lack of facts rendered AIDS particularly frightening.

HIV/AIDS is not specifically connected to homosexuality or same-sex sexual behavior. But because it was first detected in gay males and rapidly spread through the gay male community, it immediately became associated with gay men in the public imagination. This quickly lead to three dire consequences. First, gay male sexuality, now synonymous with a fatal illness, became more stigmatized then ever before. Second, this stigmatization led to numerous laws that discriminated against people with AIDS in insurance, the workplace, and housing. In some municipalities, children who were HIV-positive or diagnosed with AIDS were forbidden to attend school. Third, because people with AIDS were so demonized and because they were often associated with outsider groups—by 1983 it became clear that intravenous drug users, Haitian immigrants, and a small number of hemophiliacs were also at high risk—the media and state and federal governments provided little in the way of basic education or even news coverage.

This was true of even the most respected news sources. In October 1982 the country was in a panic because an unknown person in the Chicago area had placed cyanide in Tylenol capsules, causing seven fatalities. The *New York Times* printed thirty-one stories about the Tylenol poisonings during October and another twenty-nine throughout November and December. By October 5, 1982, 634 people in the United States had been diagnosed with AIDS, and over a third of them had died. The *New York Times* ran three stories about AIDS in 1981 and three more in 1982.[20]

Because of the deep denial of the situation's gravity—denial that clearly would not have occurred if the majority of people being affected by AIDS had been white heterosexuals—medical research, prevention education, and basic care for the women and men who were sick started far too late. This lack of response, which in retrospect can only be understood as willful negligence, helped construct a social situation that allowed an epidemic to spread unchecked.

In many ways the rapid, catastrophic growth of the HIV/AIDS epidemic is a perfect illustration of R. I. Moore's ideas in *The Formation of a Persecuting Society.* Moore argues that European medieval society created categories of "dangerous" groups—Jews, heretics, lepers, homosexuals—whose ostracization made the majority feel safer. Moore's theory conflates neatly with Mary Douglas's notions of purity and danger. Douglas points out how societies put into place edicts, laws, social proscriptions, and prejudices that maintain the preexisting conservative underpinnings of society by controlling or stopping what they understand to be cultural pollution.

These two theories are essential to the larger social picture, but they are based on personal lives. Author Sarah Schulman notes that the message of her 1990 novel *People in Trouble,* set in the early days of the epidemic in New York City's Lower East Side, was "that personal homophobia becomes societal neglect, that there is a direct relationship between the two."[21] This observation—that personal prejudice has a fundamental, devastating effect on public opinion and policy—explains to a great degree how ignorance, misunderstanding, dislike, fear, and hatred of homosexuals could escalate to such an extent that large numbers of Americans could simply not care about the deaths of their fellow citizens.

Occurring just three years after the repeal of the Dade County ordinance resulted in a wave of antigay sentiment across the nation, the HIV/AIDS epidemic was perfectly suited to the rhetoric of the religious and political right. Pat Buchanan, a conservative Catholic Republican leader, wrote in a 1990 column that "AIDS is nature's retribution for violating the laws of nature."[22] Shortly after this, popular televangelist Jerry Falwell stated that "AIDS is not just God's punishment for homosexuals. It is God's punishment for the society that tolerates homosexuals."[23] These theological sentiments easily translated into political action, as shown in a funding letter from the conservative American Family Association:

Dear Family Member,
    Since AIDS is transmitted primarily by perverse homosexuals, your name on my national petition to quarantine all homosexual establishments is crucial to your family's health

and security. . . . These disease carrying deviants wander the street unconcerned, possibly making you their next victim. What else can you expect from sex-crazed degenerates but selfishness?[24]

As Gayle Rubin posited in her essay "Thinking Sex," published in 1984, "It is precisely at times such as these, when we live with the possibility of unthinkable destruction, that people are likely to become dangerously crazy about sexuality."[25] AIDS was caused by a virus, not by homosexuality. It was, however, a "gay disease" in the important sense that because many of those affected were gay men, the moral, social, political, and legal stigma attached to homosexuality shaped the country's response. As a result, hundreds of thousands of deaths occurred in circumstances that were unjust and a direct result of the behavior of the majority.

Although a great deal of excellent work was done in medicine and in prevention and education strategies, in general the fight against AIDS was inseparable from a cultural mandate to restate, and at times legally reinforce, traditional attitudes about sexuality. By 1984, cities such as San Francisco and New York began initiatives to close down bathhouses and sex clubs, claiming they were public health hazards. Certainly the transmission of HIV could happen in these sites, as well as in private homes. It is clear, from selective enforcement and the use of coded language, that these efforts were actually attempts to regulate sexuality rather than promote public health.[26] The epidemic was also used as an excuse to arrest female and male prostitutes.[27] Thanks to tremendous scientific progress since the 1950s, new drugs were able to cure or treat diseases—syphilis and gonorrhea being prime examples—that were previously untreatable. The inability to treat or cure HIV/AIDS caused a panic that allowed people to keep their anxiety and anger tied to the idea of unregulated sexuality.

Some of this sex negativity and discomfort came from within the gay and lesbian community. Many of the lists of "dangerous" sexual activities found in early HIV prevention guidelines included activities, such as S/M, that were socially frowned on but not able to transmit HIV. Even after routes of transmission were scientifically proven and the use of condoms was being promoted to prevent them, many guidelines also urged gay men to limit the number of their partners. Editorials in the LGBT press frequently called for gay men to move from a community adolescence of sexual promiscuity to a "more adult" world of monogamous relationships. Even as late as 1998, journalist Andrew Sullivan articulated these sentiments: "The gay liberationists have plenty to answer for. . . . Saving lives was less important than saving a culture of 'promiscuity as a collective way of life,' when, of course, it was little more than a collective way of death. . . . They constructed and defended and glorified the abattoirs of the epidemic."[28]

As much as the entire LGBT community was under attack because of the AIDS epidemic (despite the reality that lesbians were at extremely low risk of transmitting HIV to one another sexually), women and men formed health-focused community organizations from the moment that the first cases appeared. They continued to do so under increasingly severe conditions. The mortality rate from HIV/AIDS during the 1980s and 1990s was staggering: the total number of reported deaths was 1,476 in 1983, 11,932 by 1987, and 31,129 by 1990. Not all of these deaths were of gay men, but a high proportion were; in some urban areas, such as San Francisco, the vast majority were. The massive tide of illness and death —as Canadian poet Michael Lynch put it, "these waves of dying friends"—trumped the long history of divisions within the LGBT community. Organizations such as Gay Men's Health Crisis in New York, Boston's AIDS Action Committee, and the San Francisco AIDS Foundation provided counseling, health care, home visits, and education, often not only for the gay community but for anyone affected by AIDS. LGBT legal groups quickly began fighting discrimination against all people with HIV/AIDS.

This response was possible in part because of the tightly knit, cohesive, self-sustaining sexual communities that had been forming since the end of World War II. Sarah Schulman argues in *Stage Struck* that the bars, baths, and other meeting places that were blamed for the AIDS epidemic were the very structures that gave the community the knowledge and networking that allowed for efficient organizing when the epidemic began. This sentiment is echoed in

"The History of Gay Bathhouses," written by Allan Bérubé and submitted as a brief when the California Superior Court was deciding whether San Francisco could legally close bathhouses for health reasons.[29] The constant political backlash, going back to 1977, had also made gay and lesbian political organizing more effective.

The other major reason AIDS organizing was so productive had to do with the use of knowledge and models originating in other movements. The large number of lesbians and feminists aiding the effort included many women who had become politically active during the 1960s and 1970s and were highly familiar with the theory and practices of the women's health care movement. Beginning with the publication in 1973 of *Our Bodies, Ourselves*, feminists—knowing they could not trust the male-dominated medical establishment—began their own support networks, research groups, and publications. Their intent was both to inform women of their own health needs and to demand from the medical establishment the basic care and medical attention women needed. The organizational underpinnings of the women's health care movement were evident as people with AIDS began to better understand the complexity of their medical, social, and political needs. In addition, community-based AIDS services, such as a free breakfast program and free community health clinics, were started and executed with great success by the Black Panther Party, first in Oakland and then in other cities. The Black Panther Party's approach to community organizing was largely based on the Communist Party model of cells that was used by Harry Hay to form the Mattachine Society.

Despite some misinformation and early bias, the advent of what would eventually be called "safe sex" was a major innovation that occurred in response to the AIDS epidemic. The phrase was first used by Richard Berkowitz and Michael Callen in their 1983 pamphlet *How to Have Sex in an Epidemic: One Approach*. The phrase "safe sex" came to embody not only concrete strategies to avoid HIV transmission, but also a new approach to the epidemic that completely resisted the impulses of sexual regulation and repression that were being articulated in response to AIDS. The sheer necessity of having to negotiate sexual activity demanded that the parties involved talk about their desires and their actions. This was, in the midst of dealing with the immediacy of illness and death, a reclaim-ing of the sexually based community formation that had started decades before.

Along with this new way to discuss sexuality within the gay male community and the continued valuation of sex as a positive good, another discussion was taking place within the lesbian and feminist communities. At a 1982 conference at Barnard College, several women delivered papers that promoted a more open discussion of women's sexuality. These papers, which included Gayle Rubin's "Thinking Sex," contradicted the politics of feminists who were involved in antipornography campaigns and who were critical of nontraditional sexualities such as S/M, role playing, and changing gender identity. These women, many of whom came out of a radical feminist and gay liberation background, were interested in formulating a new language of discussing female pleasure and sexuality that was in direct opposition to the sexually regulatory modes of the social purity groups of the nineteenth century and their contemporary descendants. The connection to the AIDS epidemic, although not noted at the time, is clear in retrospect. As Cindy Patton wrote in 1986, "Lesbians/gay liberationists throughout the AIDS crisis have insisted that AIDS must not be viewed as proof that sexual exploration and the elaboration of sexual community were mistakes. . . . It is essential to maintain the vision of community in order to navigate the difficult waters of political backlash."[30]

The political and legal backlash engendered by the AIDS epidemic was tremendous, but the anger with which the LGBT community responded was fueled by other events as well. On June 30, 1986, the Supreme Court ruled in *Bowers v. Hardwick* that there was no constitutional protection for homosexual sodomy. The decision was an affirmation of the vast legal undermining of the LGBT community that had been happening since 1977. Inflammatory rhetoric ran so high that the moralism and bias of the past paled in comparison. In a March 18, 1986, *New York Times* opinion piece, esteemed political commentator William F. Buckley urged that "everyone detected with AIDS should be tattooed in the upper forearm, to protect common-needle users, and on the buttocks, to prevent the victimization of other homosexuals." The Reagan administration, meanwhile, had done almost nothing in the early years of the epidemic. The president himself—in what can only be seen as a conscious, and shocking, act of indifference—had mentioned AIDS publicly only twice, briefly, before giving a speech during the Third International Conference on AIDS in Washington on May 31, 1987. This was after 36,058 Americans had been diagnosed with AIDS, of whom 20,849 had died.

Two months earlier, at a meeting in New York City, playwright and activist Larry Kramer called for a new, grassroots AIDS organization that would perform direct action and demand the basic health care, civil rights, legal protections, and respect that Americans were guaranteed under the Constitution. Two days later, three hundred people turned out for a meeting to form such a group. The result was the AIDS Coalition to Unleash Power (ACT UP). In many ways, ACT UP was a return to the raucous street actions of the Gay Liberation Front and the "zaps" of the Gay Activist Alliance. But it was also a repudiation of the play-within-the-system approach of the reformist LGBT rights groups. Kramer was explicit about this in his original speech, in which he stated that the group Gay Men's Health Crisis, of which he was a cofounder, had no political clout in the legal or medical world. National and local groups, such as New York's Lambda Legal Defense and Education Foundation and Boston's AIDS Law Project of Gay and Lesbian Advocates and Defenders, were doing necessary legal work. But the instances of discrimination were so pervasive, and enforcement often so weak, that there was still much more to be done. With devastation increasingly evident in the gay male community and anger and frustration mounting, new tactics had to be tried and new energy harnessed. Like the Gay Liberation Front, ACT UP was predicated on the principle, traced back to anarchist thinking as well as labor and other social justice reform groups, that the people who are affected by injustice are the most effective in changing their own circumstances.

ACT UP took to the streets almost immediately. On March 24, three weeks after the first meeting, ACT UP members marched on Wall Street demanding an end to profiteering by drug companies and easier access to experimental HIV drugs. Seventeen people were arrested for civil disobedience. Within months, the Food and Drug

Administration announced that it would shorten the drug approval process by two years. On April 15, ACT UP marched on New York's General Post Office, where thousands were waiting in line to file tax returns. This was the first time ACT UP used the image of the upside-down pink triangle and the phrase "Silence = Death." In June ACT UP, along with other national AIDS groups, took part in civil disobedience at the White House to protest the federal government's inaction on AIDS. As with the Gay Liberation Front, within months of ACT UP's formation, local offshoots were started in cities across the country.

But ACT UP did not specifically see itself as an LGBT group. All communities were affected by AIDS, but in particular impoverished communities, communities of color, women, immigrants, and—as the epidemic spread—children. ACT UP's single-issue mandate translated into a multicommunity coalition.

During this time, many LGBT people began using the word "queer" to describe themselves and their culture. This was partly an act of reclaiming language, just as gay liberationists had used once-pejorative words such as "fag" and "dyke" in a new, positive context that could change their political meaning. Unlike those terms, "queer" could be used to describe people with a wide range of sexual identities who were working in coalition. For the constituents of ACT UP, using this word was a reflection of their political vision and actions. Just as "queer" had been angrily shouted at lesbians and gay men in past decades, ACT UP and other activists now shouted the word as a declaration of difference and strength. As members of Queer Nation, a direct action group founded by members of ACT UP in 1990, would chant at their marches, "We're Here. We're Queer. Get Used To It."

It had been less than forty years since Harry Hay met with his friends to start the Mattachine Society, but sexuality identity, political activism, and the world had changed tremendously. The Gay Liberation Front had protested with hand-lettered signs and banners made of bedsheets. ACT UP, in an age of new technologies, was able to reach a wider audience and get its message across with more sophistication and media flair. Posters and T-shirts created by the Gran Fury collective, a working project within ACT UP, were comparable to professional adverting art; some of them even included references to commercial advertisements. The messages continually hammered home the idea that social ignorance and negligence led directly to death. One sign, with an image of a bloody handprint in the center, read:

THE GOVERNMENT HAS BLOOD ON ITS HANDS

ONE AIDS DEATH EVERY HALF HOUR

The new technologies also reflected the original message of gay liberation. One poster announced:

I AM OUT

therefore

I AM.

ACT UP also branched into other media as well. After a January 1988 article in *Cosmopolitan* magazine assured women they could have no-risk vaginal intercourse with an HIV-positive man without using a condom, five hundred ACT UP demonstrators, organized by the Women's Caucus of ACT UP, picketed the publication's offices. Two women in the caucus made a documentary, *Doctors, Liars, and Women: AIDS Activists Say NO to Cosmo,* that detailed and explained the action; it went on to win awards and was used in fundraising and future organizing. In 1989 several ACT UP members started DIVA TV (DIVA was an acronym for "dammed interfering video activists") to document ACT UP activity and the AIDS epidemic. These documentary efforts were an acknowledgment that the mainstream media could not be trusted to tell the truth—a theme in many ACT UP posters—and that it was incumbent on activists to make certain that their own history would be preserved accurately.

ACT UP was the most effective political action group the LGBT movement had ever produced. Its constant demands for legal and medical accountability were often met with success. This was largely because ACT UP was, by intent, a bold, theatrical move. Throughout the history of the United States, entertainment, theater, film, television, and the fine arts have, through visceral response, connected people of different identities and allowed them to reimagine their lives. This kind of social justice is more than legal or even political. Sometimes, as with the patriotic statues of Harriet Hosmer and the photography of F. Holland Day, art has helped viewers understand, and maybe heal, the damage of war. Other times, the subversion of gender norms in art—such as the cross-dressing acts of vaudeville, the drag shows of the USO, and the lesbian pulps—has had both overt and subtle implications for everyday life. Similarly, the power of ACT UP's theatricality came from bringing issues of gender and sexual expression to the forefront in a way that continued to resonate in unlikely places, for audiences and actors alike. To echo the words of Carl Wittman, it was "a good show."

ACT UP's defiant theatricality was evident in one of its most famous political protests. On December 12, 1989, over five thousand activists, including members of ACT UP and a separate but affiliated group, Women's Health Action and Mobilization (WHAM), held a "Stop the Church" demonstration in front of New York's St. Patrick's Cathedral. Over a hundred of them entered the cathedral, lay down in the aisles, and were arrested for civil disobedience. They were protesting the influence that the archdiocese and Cardinal John O'Connor had exerted on city and state policy relating to AIDS, safe-sex education, sexuality, and reproductive rights. The archdiocese had lobbied heavily, with expensive public advertisements as well as political pressure, to stop a program that dispensed condoms in public high schools and youth homeless shelters, as well as to stop needle exchange programs, which were proven effective in preventing HIV transmission in intravenous drug users. The archdiocese also promoted the falsehood that condom use was an ineffective means of controlling HIV transmission. In addition, it lobbied against any HIV and sex education that did not promote abstinence as the only way to avoid AIDS and pregnancy. O'Connor was quoted as saying, "The truth is not in condoms or clean needles. These are lies, lies perpetrated often for political reasons on the part of public officials . . . [and] some health care professionals."[31]

The Stop the Church protest received enormous attention, because of both its size and the sheer audacity of confronting O'Connor in his own church. ACT UP's response to O'Connor was succinct and pointed to the high stakes involved: "The Catholic Church has long taught men and women to loathe their bodies and to fear their sexual natures. This particular vision of good and evil continues to bring suffering and even death."[32] The Catholic Church was no different, or worse, than any other organization in United States history that had tried to regulate and control women's and men's sexual desires, bodies, and actions.

ACT UP, like many forms of art, was known for "going too far." But the people who have had to go too far to assert their own independence and deeply held beliefs about social justice—such as Anne Hutchinson, Jemima Wilkinson, Harriet Tubman, Walt Whitman, Victoria Woodhull, Eleanor Roosevelt, Harry Hay, and Bayard Rustin—have made the most lasting changes in American social policy, political beliefs, and everyday lives. Their powerful effects on how we think about gender and sexuality happened both gradually and, under extreme suffering, more immediately, just as wars, after they are ostensibly concluded, can profoundly redefine what it means to be an American. America was a war zone during the first decade of the AIDS epidemic, but it had always been a theater of control and liberation, where bodies fall and boundaries break in the fervor of solidarity.

EPILOGUE

A Queer History of the United States stops at 1990, but LGBT communities have seen enormous changes since then. By the late 1980s, the rise of the so-called "Gaybe Boom" was beginning, as increasing numbers of children were born into two-parent same-sex households. Lesléa Newman's children's book *Heather Has Two Mommies*—which became a target in the culture wars of the 1990s—was emblematic of this sea change in the community. The rise of these new lesbian and gay families—different from earlier families, in which children were being raised by same-sex parents but had been born into heterosexual relationships—opened up a new field of family law. This included foundational struggles for LGBT people's rights concerning second-parent adoptions, raising foster children, and accessing sperm banks, as well as aspects of immigration law, such as seeking political sanctuary in the U.S. as an LGBT person from another country.

The LGBT movement, as distinct from the LGBT community, has also been involved in the fight to pass the Employment Non-Discrimination Act, the battle to repeal the U.S. military's "don't ask, don't tell" policy, and the Supreme Court's 2003 decision in *Lawrence v. Texas* that finally, after more than five hundred years, threw out the sodomy laws that had plagued lesbians and gay men. Most recently, the movement has been fighting to secure same-sex marriage on both state and federal levels.

Along with these changes, three other major cultural shifts have taken the LGBT community to places no one had ever dreamed of. The first is the growing presence of more LGBT youth coming out earlier and challenging basic perceptions—not so much perceptions of what it means to be queer in American culture, but what it means to be sexual, to have a sexual identity. Youth sexuality has often been, like homosexuality, unspeakable in our culture. This has been America's dirty little secret: teens and children think about sex. Some have sexual desires for members of their own gender. Young people coming out earlier, and often finding support in their homes and schools, is a major political advancement. For over a century, charges of "molestation," "corruption of a minor," and "recruitment" have been used—explicitly by J. Edgar Hoover, Anita Bryant, and others, and implicitly by many who are opposed to same-sex marriage—to demonize lesbians and gay men and deny them full citizenship. There may always be bias against LGBT people, but the charges of molestation will eventually fade as more youth come out.

Politically, the LGBT movement has made many strides and has faced many defeats. Culturally, there have been far more gains than losses. During the last twenty years, representations of LGBT people in film, on television, and on the Internet have proliferated so rapidly that they have become central to how Americans conceptualize popular culture. Major Hollywood films featuring central LGBT characters began to be made in the late 1960s and 1970s, starting with the taboo-breaking *The Killing of Sister George* and *Boys in the Band*. More recently, films such as *Boys Don't Cry, Brokeback Mountain,* and *The Kids Are All Right* have been nominated for, and won, major awards.

Television has replicated this trend. Queer characters began appearing on television in the early 1970s, but *Will and Grace,* in 1999, was the first time that homosexuality became integral to a show's narrative. Since then it has become common to have openly lesbian, gay, bisexual, and transgender characters on television dramas, comedies, reality series, and animated shows. The variety of representations is surprising. *The Education of Max Bickford,* in 2001, featured television's first recurring transgender character; and 2003's *Queer Eye for the Straight Guy* presented gay men as Cinderella-style fairy godmothers making heterosexual men look more attractive; in 2009 *Modern Family* presented viewers, for the first time, with a family consisting of gay male partners and an adopted daughter. The 2009 hit television show *Glee* happily uses gay male and coded lesbian stereotypes, presuming that the viewer is in on the joke. These images were unthinkable in 1990, much less in 1969 at the birth of the gay liberation movement.

Would LGBT people then have approved of such images? Certainly they would have been startled, but they may have been dismayed as well. As wonderful and groundbreaking as many of these shows and characters are, they are political only in the most narrow sense of the word. They almost always reaffirm traditional gender and sexual stereotypes, rarely show LGBT characters as central protagonists, and make the argument that mainstream culture should accept LGBT people, never questioning how gender and sexuality are viewed in normative culture. These characters and shows, important in so many ways, are also a reminder that LGBT visibility is no substitute for political thought or analysis.

NEWS AS HISTORY/HISTORY AS NEWS

Clearly, much has occurred in the lives of American LGBT people since 1990, but at this point it is news, not history. In many respects, news is easy to analyze. We see it analyzed every day on CNN, in the *New York Times,* and on blogs. We do it ourselves over coffee with friends and in our heads when we are driving or walking to work. But history calls for more than an analysis.

There are many ways to understand the LGBT movement's recent work using the interpretations I have offered in this book. Securing legal equality under U.S. law has been the major project of the LGBT movement. It is a traditional American approach to acceptance and freedom. Legal equality, often based on precedent, is a broad web that includes obscure, sometimes surprising, links to non-LGBT-related history. In her essay "What Married Same-Sex Couples Owe to Hippie Communes," Nancy Polikoff details how the 1973 Supreme Court ruling *USDA v. Moreno,* which allowed hippie communes to receive food stamps, was pivotal in the Court's 1996 *Romer v. Evans* decision, which forbade the state of Colorado from treating homosexuals as a group different from other groups. A 2010 U.S. District Court decision also used *USDA v. Moreno* to argue that same-sex couples married in Massachusetts should be married under federal law as well.

America is, of course, still striving to fully realize the constitutional ideal of equal protection under the law. What if equality under the law works against another unrealized American ideal: individual freedom and autonomy? The desire for legal equality has moved some to argue that same-sex marriage is a social good, not because it is equal to heterosexual marriage but because it is morally or ethically better than other same-sex relationships or sexual interactions. For instance, William N. Eskridge Jr. writes in *The Case for Same-Sex Marriage*, "Human history repeatedly testifies to the attractiveness of domestication born of interpersonal commitment, a signature of married life. It should not have required the AIDS epidemic to alert us to the problem of sexual promiscuity." Later, after arguing that "sexual variety has not been liberating for gay men," he notes that "a self-reflective gay community ought to embrace marriage for its potentially civilizing effect on young and old alike."[1]

These socially conservative views have clear and firm roots in the social purity movement. They are no different from the views of many women and men in the nineteenth century who viewed male lust as a problem that was infecting the entire nation. In these arguments, equality under the Constitution is conflated with pleas to the moral benefits and advantages of marriage. Ted Olson, in his June 2010 closing arguments to repeal California's Proposition 8, which limited marriage in that state to a man and a woman, said:

> Marriage is the most important relation in life. . . . It is the foundation of society. It is essential to the orderly pursuit of happiness. . . . The plaintiffs have said that marriage means to them freedom, pride. . . . Dignity. Belonging. Respect. Equality. Permanence. Acceptance. Security. Honor. Dedication. And a public commitment to the world. . . . The plaintiffs have no interest in changing marriage or deinstitutionalizing marriage. They desire to marry because they cherish the institution.[2]

Such language is antithetical to the other major historical root of the LGBT movement: the fight to eliminate or limit the state's involvement in consensual relationships. It is also not the language of equality under the law. Some same-sex marriage supporters believe that protecting the family and the institution of marriage is a convincing argument to win over more conservative heterosexuals to support same-sex marriage. Many LGBT people, like many people in America, agree with this language of protection themselves, even though half of married heterosexuals get divorced. It is language that, twenty years ago, would have been rare in the LGBT movement. Why is it being used now?

There are some tentative answers to what, historically, has caused this shift. The first is that the baby boomers, those women and men born between 1940 and 1955, may have passed through their age of rebellion. But there are plenty of LGBT people in their fifties and sixties who resist this language and the deeply conservative enshrinement of marriage as foundational to American society. There are also plenty of LGBT people in their twenties who accept this idea of marriage—and plenty of twenty-year-olds who are acting like 1970s radicals in their rejection of it.

A more nuanced explanation might point to how our current emphasis on the LGBT family and on family law could be a lingering reaction to the effects of both the Anita Bryant campaign and the AIDS epidemic. The backlash of the late 1970s was devastating to the LGBT community. Homosexuals, particularly gay males, were accused of being dangerous child molesters, recruiting children for sexual and political purposes. The presence of the new lesbian and gay family is a strong statement against the idea of the queer as child molester. It is saying, "We are not immoral monsters, we are mothers and fathers and families." Such a statement, while true and powerful, has still not prevented the heterosexual-family-oriented social purity advocates from protesting same-sex marriage and parenting.

A third factor is the effect that the devastation of the AIDS epidemic had on the LGBT community. Throughout the epidemic, gay men whose lovers were dying found themselves without any legal rights. Unable to visit their sick partners in the hospital, make medical decisions, or deal with complicated finances, they were legal strangers to their lovers and often treated horrendously by medical professionals and their lovers' families. These examples demonstrate beyond a doubt that same-sex relationships need some sort of legal protections. It is telling that this specific historical fact of the AIDS epidemic almost never surfaces in written discussions or arguments about same-sex marriage. Equally telling is that when the AIDS epidemic is mentioned in relation to same-sex marriage, particularly from within the lesbian and gay community, it is always to reinforce the myth that the promiscuity that allegedly led to the epidemic would never have happened if gay men had been allowed to marry. These deeply conservative responses to the nightmares of the late 1970s and 1980s are saying, "We are not obsessed with sex, we are good parents, we do not hurt children, we are not promiscuous, and we want to get married. We are, in fact, good Americans, just like you."

While we are all Americans—and heterosexuals may be a lot queerer than they think—being "just like you" is not what all Americans want. Historically, "just like you" is the great American lie. The overwhelming, even giddy, diversity of America precludes such simple analogies. "Just like" is often a false argument. In the past decade, the argument that same-sex marriage is "just like" interracial marriage has led to far more misunderstanding and anger than agreement and clarity.

As I noted in the introduction, the theme of sexual repression—from the social purity movement, conservative politicians, and even some LGBT people—has been a constant in my story. The tension between control and liberation, alive within every American, is present in the changes in gender and sexuality brought by wartime social adjustments and the many forms of artistic expression that passed the censors. When thinking about advancing the needs and desires of all Americans today, there is another reality that has shaped the lives of all Americans: violence.

H. Rap Brown, chairman of the Student Nonviolent Coordinating Committee and a member of the Black Panthers, famously said that "violence is as American as cherry pie." Historically, America is a violent society. Much of this violence is enacted on disenfranchised groups. If there is any historic similarity between these groups, I argue tentatively, it is being the target of individual and state violence. The violence faced by each disenfranchised group was unique in its structure and intensity. The similarity is that the full range of violence—emotional intimidation, physical threats, illegal searches, overt blackmail, and horrendous all-out attacks—is never aimed only at one minority community. When one minority is targeted by violence, some aspect of this violence will eventually, or quickly, be used on another.

This point is closely connected to the reality that in America, equality under the law is a complicated affair. Certainly it is true that while laws are for everyone, they are often enforced mainly against the disenfranchised. As Anatole France wrote in his 1894 novel *The Red Lily,* "The law, in its majestic equality, forbids the rich as well as the poor to sleep under bridges, to beg in the streets, and to steal bread." Equality under the law is one of the American ideals of freedom, but its worth depends on the fairness of the law and its intended effects. Nineteenth-century social purity advocates promoted marriage laws to regulate sexuality. Contemporary LGBT activists promote marriage laws as equality. Both groups' arguments are antithetical to the idea that an individual's relationships and sexuality should be free of state regulation and the violence or repression that may result. LGBT people were then, and are now, on both sides of this argument.

All of which goes to prove that LGBT people are simply Americans—no less and no more. The idea of America has existed, in some form, for five hundred years. LGBT people, despite enormous struggles to be accepted and to be given equality, have made America what it is today—that great, fascinating, complicated, sometimes horrible, sometimes wonderful place that it was in the beginning.

ACKNOWLEDGMENTS

No one ever writes a book alone, and that has been overwhelmingly true here. I am indebted to all of the historians who have spent decades uncovering and writing queer histories. I quote many of them and have been inspired by all. This book is literally unimaginable without their dedication, work, and vision. I must also thank all of my students over the past decade of my teaching LGBT studies. They have consistently taught me so much, and I hope I have given the same in return. My colleagues in the Women's and Gender Studies program at Dartmouth have been unfailingly supportive, as has the college, which presented me with the Distinguished Lecturer Award in 2009. I must especially thank Ivy Schweitzer and Tom Luxon for the comfort of their home and endless meals. My colleagues in the Harvard University Committee on Degrees in Studies of Women, Gender, and Sexuality have been equally wonderful in their support. David K. Johnson and Beryl Satter, historians I deeply admire, gave me detailed and insightful readings of the manuscript. Their input was invaluable and pushed me to rethink so much of this material. Linda Schlossberg, Richard Voos, and Alison Pirie all read the manuscript and provided excellent editorial advice. Nick Rule and Jay Connor, for over two years, listened patiently at weekly dinners as I explained some obscure bit of historical data I had just learned. My brother Jeffrey was incredibly helpful with all computer advice. My editor at Beacon, Gayatri Patnaik, was unfailing supportive, as were her assistants, Joanna Green and Rachael Marks. Finally, this book would not have happened without the help and support of Michael Amico—a former student who now in so many ways teaches me—who read, reread, edited, critiqued, and worked with me on every chapter. His friendship, intelligence, insights, and endless encouragement have been invaluable. Words cannot express the gratitude deserved.

NOTES

CHAPTER ONE: THE PERSECUTING SOCIETY

1. Ramon Gutierrez, *When Jesus Came, the Corn Mothers Went Away: Marriage, Sexuality, and Power in New Mexico, 1500–1846* (Stanford, CA: Stanford University Press, 1991).
2. Will Roscoe, *Changing Ones: Third and Fourth Genders in Native North America* (New York: St. Martin's Press, 1998), 3.
3. Richard C. Trexler, *Sex and Conquest: Gendered Violence, Political Order, and the European Conquest of America* (Ithaca, NY: Cornell University Press, 1995), 92.
4. Jacques Marquette, "Of the First Voyage Made by Father Marquette toward New Mexico, and How the Idea Thereof Was Conceived," in *The Jesuit Relations and Allied Documents*, vol. 59, ed. Reuben Gold Thwaites (Cleveland: Burrows, 1899), 129, quoted in Jonathan Ned Katz, *Gay American History: Lesbians and Gay Men in the U.S.A.* (New York: Crowell, 1976), 287.
5. "Memoir of Pierre Liette on the Illinois Country," in *The Western Country in the 17th Century*, ed. Milo Quaife (New York: Citadel, 1962), 112–13, quoted in Katz, *Gay American History*, 288.
6. Pedro Font, *Font's Complete Diary of the Second Anza Expedition*, trans. and ed. Hubert Eugene Bolton, vol. 4 of *Anza's California Expeditions* (Berkeley: University of California, 1930), 105, quoted in Katz, *Gay American History*, 291.
7. Nicholas Biddle, *Original Journals of the Lewis and Clark Expedition, with Related Documents, 1783–1854*, ed. Donald Jackson (Urbana: University of Illinois, 1962), 531, quoted in Katz, *Gay American History*, 293.
8. Howard Zinn, *A People's History of the United States, 1492–Present* (New York: Harper Collins, 1999), 4.
9. History Project, *Improper Bostonians: Lesbian and Gay History from the Puritans to Playland* (Boston: Beacon Press, 1998), 11.
10. Richard Godbeer, *Sexual Revolution in Early America* (Baltimore: Johns Hopkins University Press, 2002), 20.

11. R.C. Simmons, *The American Colonies: From Settlement to Independence* (New York: D. McKay, 1976), 98.

12. Thomas Foster, *Sex and the Eighteenth-Century Man: Massachusetts and the History of Sexuality in America* (Boston: Beacon Press, 2006), 14.

13. Katz, *Gay American History*, 16.

14. "Francis Higgeson's Journal," in *The Founding of Massachusetts*, ed. Stuart Mitchell (Boston: Massachusetts Historical Society, 1930), 71, quoted in Katz, *Gay American History*, 19–20.

15. History Project, *Improper*, 13.

16. Godbeer, *Sexual Revolution*, 48.

17. Robert C. Winthrop, *Life and Letters of John Winthrop* (1864–7; repr., New York: DeCapo, 1971), 2:427.

18. History Project, *Improper*, 20.

19. *Familiar Letters Written by Mrs. Sarah Osborn and Miss Susanna Anthony* (Newport, RI: Mercury Office, 1807), 27, 60, quoted in Nancy F. Cott, *The Bonds of Womanhood: Women's Sphere in New England, 1780–1835* (New Haven, CT: Yale University Press, 1977), 171.

20. Alan Bray, "The Curious Case of Michael Wigglesworth," in *A Queer World: The Center for Lesbian and Gay Studies Reader*, ed. Martin Duberman (New York University Press, 1997), 206.

21. Christopher Hill, *The World Turned Upside Down: Radical Ideas During the English Revolution* (New York: Penguin, 1975), 48.

22. Alan Bray, *Homosexuality in Renaissance England* (London: Gay Men's Press, 1982), 58.

23. Elizabeth Reis, "Hermaphrodites and 'Same-Sex' Sex in Early America," in *Long Before Stonewall: Histories of Same-Sex Sexuality in Early America*, ed. Thomas A. Foster (New York: New York University Press, 2007), 151.

24. Thomas Morton, *New English Canaan*, ed. Jack Dempsey (New York: Digital Scanning, 2000), 156.

25. R.I. Moore, *The Formation of a Persecuting Society* (London: Basil Blackwell, 1987).

26. Ibid., 101.

27. Mary Douglas, *Purity and Danger: An Analysis of the Concept of Pollution and Taboo* (New York: Routledge, 1966).

CHAPTER TWO: SEXUALLY AMBIGUOUS REVOLUTIONS

1. Christopher Tomlins, "Law, Population, Labor," in *The Cambridge History of Law in America*, eds. Michael Grossberg and Christopher Tomlins (New York: Cambridge University Press, 2008), 1:235.

2. Renee L. Bergland, *The National Uncanny: Indian Ghosts and American Subjects* (Hanover, NH: University Press of New England, 2007).

3. Louis Crompton, *Homosexuality and Civilization* (Cambridge, MA: Harvard University Press, 2003), 500–28.

4. Zinn, *People's History,* 77.

5. Royall Tyler, *The Contrast: A Comedy in Five Acts* (Irvine, CA: Reprint Services Corp., 1996), 111–12.

6. "Familial Letters of Abigail Adams," in *Feminism: The Essential Historical Writings*, ed. Miriam Schneir (New York: Vintage, 1972), 2–4.

7. Ibid., 3.

8. Alan Bray, *The Friend* (Chicago: University of Chicago Press, 2003), 213–16.

9. Diary of Sarah Ripley Stearns, Stearns Collection, Arthur and Elizabeth Schlesinger Library on the History of Women in America, Radcliffe Institute, Cambridge, MA, quoted in Cott, *Bonds,* 175.

10. Caleb Crain, *American Sympathy: Men, Friendship, and Literature in the New Nation* (New Haven, CT: Yale University Press, 2001), 33.

11. Marie Joseph Paul Yves Roch Gilbert du Motier M. de Lafayette, *Memoirs, Correspondence and Manuscripts of General Lafayette, Published by His Family, Volume 1* (New York: Saunders and Otley, 1837), 291.

12. Ibid., 310.

13. Charles Shively, "George Washington's Gay Mess: Was the Father of Our Country a Queen?" in *Gay Roots: An Anthology of Gay History, Sex, Politics and Culture,* vol. 2, ed. Winston Leyland (San Francisco: Gay Sunshine Press, 1993).

14. Susan Juster, "'Neither Male nor Female': Jemima Wilkinson and the Politics of Gender in the Post-Revolution," in *Possible Pasts: Becoming Colonial in Early America,* ed. Robert Blair St. George (Ithaca, NY: Cornell University Press, 2000), 337–79.

15. Daniel. A. Cohen, *The Female Marine and Related Works: Narratives of Cross-Dressing and Urban Vice in America's Early Republic* (Amherst: University of Massachusetts Press, 1997), 57–101.

16. Sandra M. Gustafson, "The Genders of Nationalism: Patriotic Violence, Patriotic Sentiment in the Performances of Deborah Sampson Gannett," in St. George, *Possible Pasts,* 380–99.

17. Zinn, *People's History,* 111.

18. Juster, "Neither," 337.

CHAPTER THREE: IMAGINING A QUEER AMERICA

1. Badger Clark, *Sun and Saddle Leather,* 3rd ed. (Boston: Gorham Press, 1919), 67–69, quoted in Katz, *Gay American History,* 511.

2. Chris Packard, *Queer Cowboys* (New York: Palgrave, 2006), 3.

3. Badger Clark, *Sun and Saddle Leather* (Boston: Gorham Press, 1920), 49.

4. Owen Wister, *Hank's Woman* (New York: Macmillan, 1928), 4–5.

5. John D'Emilio, "Capitalism and Gay Identity," in *Making Trouble: Essays on Gay History, Politics, and the University* (New York: Routledge, 1992), 3–16.

6. George Chauncey, *Gay New York: Gender Urban Culture and the Making of the Gay Male World, 1890–1940* (New York: Basic Books, 1994), 179–206.

7. Crain, *American Sympathy,* 5.

8. *The Journals and Miscellaneous Notebooks of Ralph Waldo Emerson,* vol. 1, eds. William H. Gilman, Alfred R. Ferguson, George P. Clark, and Merrell R. Davis (Cambridge, MA: Belknap Press of Harvard University, 1960), 39, quoted in Katz, *Gay American History,* 457.

9. Ralph Waldo Emerson, "American Scholar," in *The Essential Writings of Ralph Waldo Emerson* (New York: Modern Library, 2000), 43.

10. Ralph Waldo Emerson, quoted in Crain, *American Sympathy,* 170.

11. *The Journals of Henry David Thoreau,* eds. Bradford Torrey and Francis H. Allan (Cambridge, MA: Riverside Press, Houghton Mifflin, 1906), 1:120–21, quoted in Katz, *Gay American History,* 486.

12. Thoreau, *Journals,* 4:92–93, quoted in Katz, *Gay American History,* 490.

13. Margaret Fuller, "Ganymede to His Eagle," quoted in Crain, *American Sympathy,* 208.

14. *The Memoirs of Margaret Fuller Ossoli,* eds. Ralph Waldo Emerson, William H. Channing, and James Freeman Clark (Boston: Phillips, Sampson, 1851–52), 1:127–29, quoted in Katz, *Gay American History,* 464.

15. Emily Dickinson, *The Poems of Emily Dickinson,* ed. Thomas H. Johnson (Cambridge, MA: Harvard University Press, 1914), 2:13.

16. *The Letters of Emily Dickinson,* eds. Thomas Johnson and Theodora Ward (Cambridge, MA: Harvard University Press, 1914), letter 73, 175–76.

17. Herman Melville, "Hawthorne and His Mosses," *Literary World,* August 17 and 24, 1850, quoted in Katz, *Gay American History,* 470.

18. Samuel Howe, quoted in Gary Williams, *Hungry Heart: The Literary Emergence of Julia Ward Howe* (Amherst: University of Massachusetts Press, 1999), 54.

19. Julia Ward Howe, quoted in Williams, *Hungry Heart,* 10.

20. Leslie Fiedler, "Come Back to the Raft Ag'in, Huck Honey!" in *An End to Innocence* (Boston: Beacon Press, 1955), 142–51.

21. Mason Stokes, *The Color of Sex: Whiteness, Heterosexuality, and the Fictions of White Supremacy* (Durham, NC: Duke University Press, 2001), 132.

22. Richard Dyer, *White: Essays on Race and Culture* (New York: Routledge, 1997), 25.

23. Herman Melville, *Omoo: A Narrative of Adventures in the South Seas* (Evanston, IL: Northwestern University Press, 1968), 152.

24. Ibid., 157.

25. Herman Melville, *Moby-Dick* (New York: Harper & Brothers, 1851), 28.

26. Charles Warren Stoddard, *South-Sea Idyls* (San Francisco: Gay Sunshine Press, 1998), 26.

27. Ibid., 36.

28. Phillip C. Van Buskirk, quoted in B.R. Berg, *An American Seafarer in the Age of Sail: The Erotic Diaries of Philip C. Van Buskirk, 1851–1870* (New Haven, CT: Yale University Press, 1994), 78.

29. Fiedler, "Huck," 142–51.

CHAPTER FOUR: A DEMOCRACY OF DEATH AND ART

1. W.E.B. Du Bois, *Black Reconstruction in America*, quoted in Drew Gilpin Faust, *This Republic of Suffering: Death and the American Civil War* (New York: Knopf, 2008), 48.

2. Charley Shively, ed., *Calamus Lovers: Walt Whitman's Working Class Camerados* (San Francisco: Gay Sunshine Press, 1987), and *Drum Beats: Walt Whitman's Civil War Boy Lovers* (San Francisco: Gay Sunshine Press, 1989).

3. Walt Whitman, *Leaves of Grass* (New York: W.E. Chapin, 1867), 30.

4. Walt Whitman, quoted in Shively, *Calamus,* 58.

5. Walt Whitman, *The Complete Poems* (New York: Penguin, 2004), 67.

6. Bayard Taylor, *Joseph and His Friend*, quoted in Roger Austen, *Playing the Game: The Homosexual Novel in America* (Indianapolis: Bobbs-Merrill, 1977), 10.

7. DeAnne Blanton and Lauren M. Cook, *They Fought Like Demons: Women Soldiers in the American Civil War* (Baton Rouge: Louisiana State University Press, 2002).

8. Patricia Okker, *Our Sister Editors: Sarah J. Hale and the Tradition of Nineteenth-Century American Women Editors* (Athens: University of Georgia Press, 1995), 8–14.

9. Lillian Faderman, *To Believe in Women: What Lesbians Have Done for America—A History* (Boston: Houghton Mifflin, 1999), 178.

10. Elizabeth Barrett Browning, quoted in Lisa Merrill, *When Romeo Was a Woman: Charlotte Cushman and Her Circle of Female Spectators* (Ann Arbor: University of Michigan Press, 1999), 160.

11. Charlotte Cushman, quoted in Martha Vicinus, *Intimate Friends: Women Who Loved Women, 1778–1928* (Chicago: University of Chicago Press, 2004), 434.

12. Faye E. Dudden, *Women in the American Theater: Actresses and Audiences, 1790–1870* (New Haven, CT: Yale University Press, 1994), 99.

13. Kate Field, quoted in Joseph Leach, *Bright Particular Star: The Life and*

Times of Charlotte Cushman (New Haven, CT: Yale University Press, 1970), 283.

14. Rebecca Primus, quoted in Farah Jasmine Griffin, *Beloved Sisters and Friends: Letters from Rebecca Primus of Royal Oak, Maryland, and Addie Brown of Hartford, Connecticut, 1854–1868* (New York: Alfred A. Knopf, 1999), 24.

15. Martha Saxton, *Louisa May Alcott: A Modern Biography* (New York: Farrar, Straus and Giroux, 1977), 325.

16. Susan K. Harris, *The Cultural Work of the Late Nineteenth-Century Hostess: Annie Adams Fields and Mary Gladstone Drew* (New York: Palgrave, 2002).

17. Ruth L. Bohen, *Looking into Walt Whitman: American Art, 1850–1920* (University Park, PA: Pennsylvania State University Press, 2006), 136.

18. Whitman, *Complete Poems*, 73.

19. Estelle Jussim, *Slave to Beauty: The Eccentric Life and Controversial Career of F. Holland Day, Photographer, Publisher, Aesthete* (Boston: David R. Godine, 1981), 107.

20. Trevor Fairbrother, *John Singer Sargent: The Sensualist* (New Haven, CT: Yale University Press, 2000), 102–13.

21. Karl Heinrich Ulrichs, *Araxes: A Call to Free the Nature of the Urning from Penal Law*, quoted in Hubert Kennedy, *Ulrichs: The Life and Works of Karl Heinrich Ulrichs* (Boston: Alyson Publications, 1988), 175.

22. Whitman, *Leaves of Grass*, 125–26.

23. Edward Carpenter, *The Intermediate Sex: A Study of Some Transitional Types of Men and Women* (London: Mitchell Kennerly, 1912), 114–15.

24. Victoria Woodhull, "The Principles of Social Freedom," in *The Victoria Woodhull Reader*, ed. Madeline B. Stern (Weston, MA: M & S Press, 1974), 23–24, quoted in Terence Kissack, *Free Comrades: Anarchism and Homosexuality in the United States, 1805–1917* (Oakland, CA: AK Press, 2008), 35.

25. Sherrilyn Ifill, *On the Courthouse Lawn: Confronting the Legacy of Lynching in the Twenty-first Century* (Boston: Beacon Press, 2008), xii.

CHAPTER FIVE: A DANGEROUS PURITY

1. Beryl Satter, *Each Mind a Kingdom: American Women, Sexual Purity, and the New Thought Movement, 1875–1920* (Berkeley: University of California Press, 1999), 112.

2. Timothy J. Gilfoyle, *City of Eros: New York City, Prostitution, and the Commercialization of Sex, 1790–1920* (New York: W. W. Norton, 1992), 167.

3. Ibid.

4. Satter, *Each Mind a Kingdom*, 206.

5. Anna Rice Powell, "The American Purity Alliance and Its Work," in *The National Purity Congress: Its Papers, Addresses, Portraits,* ed. Aaron M. Powell (1896; repr., New York: Arno Press, 1976), 132.

6. Satter, *Each Mind,* 207.

7. Gilfoyle, *City of Eros,* 106.

8. Satter, *Each Mind,* 195.

9. Mary Harris Jones, *The Speeches and Writings of Mother Jones,* ed. Edward M. Steel (Pittsburgh: University of Pittsburgh Press, 1988), 290.

10. Frances Willard, interview in *New York Voice,* October 23, 1890, quoted in Edward J. Blum, *Reforging the White Republic: Race, Religion, and American Nationalism, 1865–1898* (Baton Rouge: Louisiana State University Press, 2007), 201.

11. *Selected Works of Ida B. Wells-Barnett,* ed. Trudier Harris (New York: Oxford University Press, 1991), 201.

12. James G. Kiernan, "Responsibility in Sexual Perversions," *Chicago Medical Recorder* 3:185–210, quoted in Jonathan Ned Katz, *Gay/Lesbian Almanac* (New York: Harper and Row, 1983), 231.

13. Katz, *Gay American History,* 137.

14. Benjamin R. Tucker, *State Socialism and Anarchism,* ed. James J. Martin (Colorado Springs: R. Myles, 1972), 21–22, quoted in Kissack, *Free Comrades,* 30.

15. Kissack, *Free Comrades,* 30.

16. Emma Goldman, quoted in Kissack, *Free Comrades,* 43.

17. Margaret S. Marsh, *Anarchist Women, 1870–1920* (Philadelphia: Temple University Press, 1981), 94.

18. Kissack, *Free Comrades,* 32.

19. Esther Newton, "The Mythic Mannish Lesbian: Radclyffe Hall and the New Woman," in *Hidden from History: Reclaiming the Gay and Lesbian Past,* eds. Martin Duberman, Martha Vicinus, and George Chauncey Jr. (New York: New American Library, 1989), 281–92.

20. Lillian Faderman, *Odd Girls and Twilight Lovers: A History of Lesbian Life in Twentieth-Century America* (New York: Columbia University Press, 1991), 48–54.

21. Charles Gilbert Craddock, "Sexual Crimes," in *A System of Legal Medicine,* eds. Allan McLane Hamilton and Lawrence Godkin (New York: E. B. Treat, 1894), 2:525–72, quoted in Katz, *Gay/Lesbian Almanac,* 257.

22. Edward Prime-Stevenson, *Imre: A Memorandum,* ed. James J. Gifford (New York: Broadview Literary Texts, 2003), 83.

23. Alexander Berkman, *Prison Memoirs of an Anarchist* (New York: Shocken Books, 1970), 439.

24. Earl Lind, *Autobiography of an Androgyne* (New York: Arno Press, 1975), 10.

25. Mary Casal, *The Stone Wall: An Autobiography* (Chicago: Eyncourt Press, 1930), 92–93.

26. Margaret Sanger, *What Every Girl Should Know* (Springfield, IL: United Sales Company, 1920), 39.

27. Ibid.

28. Rev. Fulgence Meyer, *Helps to Purity: A Frank, Yet Reverent Introduction on the Intimate Matters of Personal Life for Adolescent Girls* (Cincinnati, OH: St. Francis Bookshop, 1929), 32.

29. Joseph Collins, MD, *The Doctor Looks at Love and Life* (New York: George H. Doran, 1926), 67.

30. Joseph Collins, quoted in M.E. Melody and Linda M. Peterson, *Teaching America About Sex: Marriage Guides and Sex Manuals from the Late Victorians to Dr. Ruth* (New York: New York University Press, 1999), 78.

31. Ibid.

32. Ibid.

33. John D'Emilio and Estelle B. Freedman, *Intimate Matters: A History of Sexuality in America* (New York: Harper & Row, 1988), 235.

CHAPTER SIX: LIFE ON THE STAGE/LIFE IN THE CITY

1. Washington Irving, quoted in Gilfoyle, *City of Eros,* 109.

2. Renee M. Sentilles, "Identity, Speculation, and History: Adah Isaacs Menken as a Case Study," *History and Memory* 18, no. 1 (Spring/Summer 2006), 120–51.

3. Kristen Pullen, *Actresses and Whores: On Stage and in Society* (Cambridge, UK: Cambridge University Press, 2005), 95.

4. Howard P. Chudacoff, *The Age of the Bachelor: Creating an American Subculture* (Princeton, NJ: Princeton University Press, 1999), 51.

5. Ibid., 59.

6. Paul Groth, *Living Downtown: A History of Residential Hotels in the United States* (Berkeley: CA: University of California Press, 1994), 102.

7. Ibid., 62.

8. Ibid., 153.

9. Julie Abraham, *Metropolitan Lovers: The Homosexuality of Cities* (Minneapolis: University of Minnesota Press, 2009), 118.

10. Ibid.

11. Blanche Wiesen Cook, *Women and Support Networks* (New York: Out and Out Books, 1977), 13.

12. Ibid., 20.

13. Mabel Hyde Kittredge, quoted in Cook, *Women and Support Networks,* 24.

14. Alice Lewisohn, quoted in Cook, *Women and Support Networks,* 23.

15. Kathy Peiss, *Cheap Amusements: Working Women and Leisure in Turn-of-the-Century New York* (Philadelphia: Temple University Press, 1986), 88–90.

16. Chudacoff, *Age of the Bachelor,* 226.

17. Chauncey, *Gay New York,* 156.

18. John Donald Gustav-Wrathall, *Take the Young Stranger by the Hand: Same-Sex Relations and the YMCA* (Chicago: University of Chicago Press, 1998), 57.

19. Chauncey, *Gay New York,* 251.

20. Robert C. Allen, *Horrible Prettiness: Burlesque and American Culture* (Chapel Hill: University of North Carolina Press, 1991), 26.

21. Daniel Hurwitz, *Bohemian Los Angeles and the Making of Modern Politics* (Berkeley: University of California Press, 2007), 34.

22. Dorothy Parker, "A Musical Comedy Thought," *Vanity Fair,* June 1916.

23. Jeffrey Melnick, *A Right to Sing the Blues: African Americans, Jews, and American Popular Song* (Cambridge, MA: Harvard University Press, 1999), 110–11.

24. Robert Benchley, quoted in Emily Wortis Leider, *Becoming Mae West* (New York: Farrar, Straus and Giroux, 1997), 206.

25. Ethel Merman, vocal performance of "A Lady Needs a Change," by Dorothy Fields and Arthur Schwartz, on *Ethel Merman: Red, Hot and Blue!* (1939 Studio Cast) / *Stars in Your Eyes* (1939 Studio Cast), AEI, July 14, 1995, compact disc.

26. *New York Times,* quoted in Toni Bentley, *Sisters of Salome* (New Haven, CT: Yale University Press, 2002), 68.

27. *New York Morning Telegraph,* quoted in Kaier Curtin, *"We Can Always Call Them Bulgarians": The Emergence of Lesbians and Gay Men on the American Stage* (Boston: Alyson Publications, 1987), 95.

28. Lillian Faderman and Stuart Timmons, *Gay L.A.: A History of Sexual Outlaws, Power Politics, and Lipstick Lesbians* (New York: Basic Books, 2006), 39–69.

29. *Chicago Tribune,* July 18, 1926.

30. "I Don't Care" lyric, quoted in Susan A. Glenn, *Female Spectacle: The Theatrical Roots of Modern Feminism* (Cambridge, MA: Harvard University Press, 2000), 63–66.

31. Glenn, *Female Spectacle,* 59–63.

32. Betty Lee, *Marie Dressler: The Unlikeliest Star* (Lexington: The University Press of Kentucky, 1997), 152.

33. Faderman, *Odd Girls,* 71.

34. Nan Alamilla Boyd, *Wide-Open Town: A History of Queer San Francisco to 1965* (Berkeley: University of California Press, 2005), 48.

35. Chad Heap, *Slumming: Sexual and Racial Encounters in American Nightlife, 1885–1940* (Chicago: University of Chicago Press, 2009), 247.
36. "The Simple Things" lyric, quoted in Faderman and Timmons, *Gay L.A.*, 44.
37. Heap, *Slumming*, 248.
38. Richard Bruce Nugent, *Gentleman Jigger: A Novel of the Harlem Renaissance* (Philadelphia: Da Capo Press, 2008), 174.
39. Hurewitz, *Bohemian*, 133.
40. J. Edgar Hoover, quoted in Charles E. Morris III, "Pink Herring and the Fourth Persona: J. Edgar Hoover's Sex Crime Panic," *Quarterly Journal of Speech* 88, no. 2 (May 2002), 228–44.
41. Allan Bérubé, *Coming Out Under Fire: The History of Gay Men and Women in World War Two* (New York: Free Press, 1990), 258.
42. Davis Levering Lewis, *W. E. B. Du Bois: The Fight for Equality and the American Century, 1919–1963* (New York: Henry Holt, 2000), 224.
43. Carl Van Doren, quoted in Lewis, *W. E. B. Du Bois*, 158.

CHAPTER SEVEN: PRODUCTION AND MARKETING OF GENDER

1. Jonathan Ned Katz, *The Invention of Heterosexuality* (New York: Dutton, 1995).
2. William Leach, *Land of Desire: Merchants, Power, and the Rise of a New American Culture* (New York: Pantheon Books, 1993), 86, 328.
3. Gary Cross, *Kids' Stuff: Toys and the Changing World of American Childhood* (Cambridge, MA: Harvard University Press, 1997), 51.
4. Leach, *Land of Desire*, 86.
5. Cross, *Kids' Stuff*, 69.
6. Cindy S. Aron, *Working at Play: A History of Vacations in the United States* (New York: Oxford University Press, 1999), 83–85.
7. Sarah Watts, *Rough Rider in the White House: Theodore Roosevelt and the Politics of Desire* (Chicago: University of Chicago Press, 2003), 133.
8. Susan S. Lanser, "Feminist Criticism, 'The Yellow Wallpaper,' and the Politics of Color in America," *Feminist Studies* 15, no. 3 (Fall 1989), 225–50.
9. Satter, *Each Mind*, 216.
10. Harry Bruinius, *Better for All the World: The Secret History of Forced Sterilization and America's Quest for Racial Purity* (New York: Knopf, 2006), 71–72.
11. Michael Amico, "Breeding Injustice," *Boston Phoenix*, August 10, 2006.
12. Tim Jeal, *The Boy-Man: The Life of Lord Baden-Powell* (New York: William Morrow, 1990), 359.
13. Robert Baden-Powell, quoted in Jeal, *The Boy-Man*, 162.

14. Michael Rosenthal, *The Character Factory: Baden-Powell's Boy Scouts and the Imperative of Empire* (New York: Pantheon Books, 1986), 3.

15. Rev. F. X. Lasance, *Young Man's Guide: Counsels, Reflections, and Prayers for Catholic Young Men* (Chicago: Benziger Brothers, 1910), 326–27.

16. Ibid., 403.

17. John F. Kasson, *Houdini, Tarzan, and the Perfect Man: The White Male Body and the Challenge of Modernity in America* (New York: Hill and Wang, 2001), 203–5.

18. Edgar Rice Burroughs, *Tarzan of the Apes*, quoted in Kasson, *Houdini*, 204.

19. Edgar Rice Burroughs, *Tarzan of the Apes* (1912; New York: Ballantine, 1983), 73, quoted in Gail Bederman, *Manliness and Civilization: A Cultural History of Gender and Race in the United States, 1880–1917* (Chicago: University of Chicago Press, 1995), 225.

20. Robert Ernst, *Weakness Is a Crime: The Life of Bernarr Macfadden* (Syracuse, NY: Syracuse University Press, 1991), 42.

21. Ibid., 144.

22. Leach, *Land of Desire*, 66.

23. Thorstein Veblen, *The Theory of the Leisure Class* (New York: Random House, The Modern Library, 1934), 24.

24. Dorothy Hart and Robert Kimball, eds., *The Complete Lyrics of Lorenz Hart* (New York: Knopf, 1986), 168.

25. Stephen Prothero, *American Jesus: How the Son of God Became a National Icon* (New York: Farrar, Straus and Giroux, 2003), 99.

26. Ibid., 94.

27. Murray B. Levin, *Political Hysteria in America: The Democratic Capacity for Repression* (New York: Basic Books, 1971), 91.

28. Ole Hanson, *Americanism versus Bolshevism* (New York: Doubleday, 1920), 283–84, quoted in Levin, *Political Hysteria*, 16.

29. Royal A. Baker, *The Menace of Bolshevism* (Detroit: Liberty Bell Publishers, 1919), 238, quoted in Levin, *Political Hysteria*, 19.

30. Levin, *Political Hysteria*, 87.

31. Eugene V. Debs, quoted in Zinn, *People's History*, 368.

32. Faderman, *To Believe*, 162.

33. Sarah Deutsch, *Women and the City: Gender, Space, and Power in Boston, 1870–1940* (New York: Oxford University Press, 2000), 208–22.

34. Eleanor Roosevelt, quoted in Roger Streitmatter, *Empty Without You: The Intimate Letters of Eleanor Roosevelt and Lorena Hickok* (New York: Free Press, 1998), 78.

CHAPTER EIGHT: SEX IN THE TRENCHES

1. Margot Canaday, *The Straight State: Sexuality and Citizenship in Twentieth-Century America* (Princeton, NJ: Princeton University Press, 2009), 98.

2. Sherna B. Gluck, *Rosie the Riveter Revisited: Women, the War and Social Change* (New York: Plume, 1988), 23.

3. Ellen Rothman, *Hands and Hearts: A History of Courtship in America* (New York: Basic Books, 1984), 287.

4. Nancy Cott, *Public Vows: A History of Marriage and the Nation* (Cambridge, MA: Harvard University Press, 2000), 187.

5. C. Tyler Carpenter and Edward H. Yeatts, *Stars Without Garters! The Memories of Two Gay GIs in WWII* (San Francisco: Alamo Square Press, 1996), 40.

6. Bérubé, *Coming Out*, 12.

7. Ibid., 40.

8. Pat Bond, quoted in Nancy Adair and Casey Adair, *Word Is Out* (New York: Delta, 1978), 57.

9. Ibid., 58.

10. Carpenter and Yeatts, *Stars,* 9.

11. Faderman, *Odd Girls,* 120.

12. Bérubé, *Coming Out,* 3.

13. Maxwell Gordon, quoted in Bérubé, *Coming Out,* 64.

14. John Loughery, *The Other Side of Silence: Men's Lives and Gay Identities: A Twentieth-Century History* (New York: Henry Holt, 1998), 142.

15. History Project, *Improper,* 132.

16. Bérubé, *Coming Out,* 91.

17. Bruce H. Joffe, *A Hint of Homosexuality? Gay and Homoerotic Imagery in American Print Advertising* (Bloomington, IN: Xlibris, 2007), 95–96.

18. John Ibson, "Masculinity under Fire: *Life*'s Presentation of Camaraderie and Homoeroticism Before, During, and After the Second World War," in *Looking at LIFE Magazine,* ed. Erika Doss (Washington, DC: Smithsonian Institution Press, 2001), 187.

19. "Harlem's Strangest Night Club," *Ebony,* December 1953, 80–85, quoted in Bérubé, *Coming Out,* 116.

20. Philip Wylie, *Generation of Vipers* (New York: Holt, Rinehart, and Winston, 1955), 65.

21. National Research Council, *Psychology for the Fighting Man* (Washington, DC: Infantry Journal, 1943), 34.

22. Ibid., 340.

23. Canaday, *Straight State,* 174–213.

24. Ibid., 9.

25. Pat Bond, quoted in Adair and Adair, *Word Is Out,* 61.

26. Loren Wahl, *The Invisible Glass* (New York: Greenberg, 1950), 200.

27. Quoted in James Rorty, "The Harassed Pocket-Book Publishers," *Antioch Review* 15, no. 4 (Winter 1955), 413.

28. Ibid., 412–13.

29. Bérubé, *Coming Out,* 257.

30. History Project, *Improper,* 131.

31. *Mid-Town Journal,* quoted in History Project, *Improper,* 169.

32. Ricardo J. Brown, *The Evening Crowd at Kirmser's: A Gay Life in the 1940s* (Minneapolis: University of Minnesota Press, 2001), 3.

33. History Project, *Improper,* 179.

34. Marc Stein, *City of Sisterly and Brotherly Loves: Lesbian and Gay Philadelphia, 1945–1972* (Chicago: University of Chicago Press, 1999), 30–32.

35. Hurwitz, *Bohemian,* 191.

36. Faderman and Timmons, *Gay L.A.,* 75.

37. Kennedy and Davis, *Slippers,* 38.

38. Donald Vining, *A Gay Diary, 1933–1946* (New York: Pepys Press, 1979), 276.

CHAPTER NINE: VISIBLE COMMUNITIES/INVISIBLE LIVES

1. W. Dorr Legg, *Homosexuals Today: A Handbook of Organizations and Publications,* quoted in Martha E. Stone, "Unearthing the 'Knights of the Clock,'" *Gay and Lesbian Review Worldwide* 17, no. 3 (May–June 2010).

2. Stephanie Coontz, *The Way We Never Were: American Families and the Nostalgia Trip* (New York: Basic Books, 1992), 36.

3. Ibid., 29.

4. Alfred C. Kinsey, Wardell B. Pomeroy, and Clyde E. Martin, *Sexual Behavior in the Human Male* (Philadelphia: W. B. Saunders, 1948), 5.

5. Ibid., 650.

6. Alfred C. Kinsey, Wardell B. Pomeroy, and Clyde E. Martin, *Sexual Behavior in the Human Female* (Philadelphia: W. B. Saunders, 1953), 457.

7. Gavin Butt, *Between You and Me: Queer Disclosures in the New York Art World, 1948–1963* (Durham: NC: Duke University Press, 2003), 33.

8. *Life* magazine, quoted in Butt, *Between You and Me,* 33.

9. Harry Hay, *Radically Gay: Gay Liberation in the Words of Its Founder,* ed. Will Roscoe (Boston: Beacon Press, 1995), 131.

10. David K. Johnson, *The Lavender Scare* (Chicago: University of Chicago Press, 2004), 76.

11. John D'Emilio, *Sexual Politics, Sexual Communities: The Making of a Homosexual Minority in the United States, 1940–1970* (Chicago: University of Chicago Press, 1983), 79.

12. Billye Talmadge, quoted in Marcia M. Gallo, *Different Daughters: A History of the Daughters of Bilitis and the Rise of the Lesbian Rights Movement* (New York: Carroll and Graf, 2006), 16.

13. D'Emilio, *Sexual Politics*, 107.

14. John Howard, *Men Like That: A Southern Queer History* (Chicago: University of Chicago Press, 1999), 86.

15. Janet Staiger, "Finding Community in the Early 1960s: Underground Cinema and Sexual Politics," in *Queer Cinema: The Film Reader*, eds. Harry Benshoff and Sean Griffin (New York: Routledge, 2004), 167–88.

16. Rhonda Bernstein, "Adaptation, Censorship, and Audiences of Questionable Type: Lesbian Sightings in *Rebecca* (1940) and *The Uninvited* (1944)," *Cinema Journal* 37, no. 3 (Spring 1998), 26.

17. Jack Lait and Lee Mortimer, *Washington Confidential* (New York: Crown Publishers, 1951), 90–95.

18. Edmund Bergler, *Homosexuality: Disease or a Way of Life?* (New York: Hill and Wang, 1956), 13.

19. Frank S. Caprio, *Female Homosexuality: A Psychodynamic Study of Lesbianism* (New York: Citadel Press, 1954), 120.

20. Albert Ellis, *Sex Without Guilt* (New York: Lyle Stuart, 1958), 65.

21. Ibid., 25.

22. Albert Ellis, *Homosexuality: Its Causes and Cures* (New York: Lyle Stuart, 1965), 81.

23. Katherine V. Forrest, introduction to *Lesbian Pulp Fiction* (San Francisco: Cleis, 2005), ix.

24. Thomas Waugh, *Hard to Imagine: Gay Male Eroticism in Photography and Film from Their Beginnings to Stonewall* (New York: Columbia University Press, 1996), 217.

25. Ibid., 219.

26. David K. Johnson, "Physique Pioneers: The Politics of 1960s Gay Consumer Culture," *Journal of Social History* (Summer 2010), 869.

27. Hendrik M. Ruitenbeek, ed., *Psychoanalysis and Male Sexuality* (New Haven, CT: College and University Press Services, 1966), 12.

28. Kate Friedlander, *The Psychoanalytic Approach to Juvenile Delinquency* (New York: International Publishers, 1947), 156.

29. Eric C. Schneider, *Vampires, Dragons, and Egyptian Kings: Youth Gangs in Postwar New York* (Princeton, NJ: Princeton University Press, 1999), 26.

30. Lawrence Frascella and Al Weisel, *Live Fast, Die Young: The Wild Ride of Making "Rebel Without a Cause"* (New York: Simon and Schuster, 2005), 87.

31. Robert Lindner, *Prescription for Rebellion* (London: Victor Gollancz, 1953), 12.

32. Robert Lindner, *Must You Conform?* (New York: Rinehart, 1956), 31–76.

33. Barbara Ehrenreich, *The Hearts of Men: American Dreams and the Flight from Commitment* (New York: Doubleday, 1983), 24.

34. William J. Mann, *Behind the Screen: How Gays and Lesbians Shaped Hollywood, 1910–1969* (New York: Viking, 2001), 317.

35. Robert Hofler, *The Man Who Invented Rock Hudson: The Pretty Boys and Dirty Deals of Henry Wilson* (New York: Carroll and Graf, 2005).

36. Amy Lawrence, *The Passion of Montgomery Clift* (Berkeley: University of California Press, 2010), 147.

37. Linda Martin and Kerry Segrave, *Anti-Rock: The Opposition to Rock and Roll* (Hampden, CT: Archon Books, 1988), 16.

38. W. T. Lhamon Jr., *Deliberate Speed: The Origins of a Cultural Style in the American 1950s* (Cambridge, MA: Harvard University Press, 2002), 94.

39. Robert W. Wood, *Christ and the Homosexual (Some Observations)* (New York: Vantage, 1960), 43–55.

40. Susan Sontag, "Notes on 'Camp,'" in *Against Interpretation and Other Essays* (New York: Delta, 1966), 247.

41. Steven Watson, *The Birth of the Beat Generation: Visionaries, Rebels, and Hipsters, 1944–1960* (New York: Pantheon Books, 1995), 3.

42. Allen Ginsberg, quoted in Watson, *Birth*, 3.

43. Watson, *Birth*, 258.

44. Allen Ginsberg, "A Definition of the Beat Generation," *Friction* 1 (Winter 1982).

45. James Baldwin, *The Fire Next Time* (New York: Dial Press, 1963), 22.

46. Howard, *Men*, 158.

47. John D'Emilo, *Lost Prophet: The Life and Times of Bayard Rustin* (New York: Free Press, 2003), 191.

CHAPTER TEN: REVOLT/BACKLASH/RESISTANCE

1. Zinn, *People's History*, 469.

2. Maurice Isserman, *If I Had a Hammer: The Death of the Old Left and the Birth of the New Left* (New York: Basic Books, 1987), 202.

3. Carl Wittman, "A Gay Manifesto," in *Out of the Closets: Voices of Gay Liberation*, eds. Karla Jay and Allen Young (New York: New York University Press, 1992), 330–41.

4. David Carter, *Stonewall: The Riots That Sparked the Gay Revolution* (New York: St. Martin's Press, 2004), 183.

5. Ibid., 35.

6. Donn Teal, *The Gay Militants* (New York: Stein and Day, 1971), 154.

7. Carter, *Stonewall*, 235.

8. David Eisenbach, *Gay Power: An American Revolution* (New York: Carroll and Graf, 2006), 266.

9. Stephen L. Cohen, *The Gay Liberation Youth Movement in New York* (New York: Routledge, 2007), 203–14.

10. Jill Johnston, *Lesbian Nation: The Feminist Solution* (New York: Simon and Schuster, 1973), 277.

11. Faderman, *Odd Girls*, 216.

12. Alice Echols, "The Taming of the Id: Feminist Sexual Practices, 1968–1983," in *Pleasure and Danger*, ed. Carole Vance (Boston: Routledge and Kegan Paul, 1984), 65.

13. Natalie Shainess, quoted in "The New Bisexuals," *Time*, May 13, 1974.

14. William N. Eskridge Jr., *Dishonorable Passions: Sodomy Laws in America, 1861–2003* (New York: Viking, 2008), 202.

15. Fred Fejes, *Gay Rights and Moral Panic: The Origins of America's Debate on Homosexuality* (New York: Palgrave Macmillan, 2008), 96.

16. Ibid., 144.

17. Anita Bryant, *The Anita Bryant Story: The Survival of Our Nation's Families and the Threat of Militant Homosexuality* (Old Tappan, NJ: Fleming H. Revell, 1977), 119.

18. Fejes, *Gay Rights*, 145.

19. Bryant, *The Anita Bryant Story*, 26.

20. Randy Shilts, *And the Band Played On: Politics, People, and the AIDS Epidemic* (New York: St. Martin's Press, 1987), 191.

21. Sarah Schulman, *Stagestruck: Theater, AIDS, and the Marketing of Gay America* (Durham, NC: Duke University Press, 1998), 23.

22. Pat Buchanan, syndicated column, *Seattle Times,* July 31, 1993.

23. Jerry Falwell, quoted in Bill Press, "The Sad Legacy of Jerry Falwell," *Milford* (Mass.) *Daily News*, May 18, 2007.

24. Letter from American Family Association, quoted in Cindy Patton, *Sex and Germs* (Boston: South End Press, 1986), 85.

25. Gayle Rubin, "Thinking Sex: Notes for a Radical Theory of the Politics of Sexuality," in Vance, *Pleasure and Danger*, 267.

26. Marc E. Elovitz and P. J. Edwards, "The D.O.H. Papers: Regulating Public Sex in New York City," in *Policing Public Sex*, ed. Dangerous Bedfellows (Boston: South End Press, 1996), 295.

27. Priscilla Alexander, "Bathhouses and Brothels: Symbolic Sites in Discourse and Practice," in *Policing Public Sex*, 221.

28. Andrew Sullivan, *Love Undetectable: Notes on Friendship, Sex, and Survival* (New York: Knopf, 1998), 52.

29. Allan Bérubé, "The History of Gay Bathhouses," in *Policing Public Sex*, 185.

30. Patton, *Sex*, 142.

31. John J. Cardinal O'Connor, quoted in "Pope Condemns Bias against Victims of AIDS," *Washington Post*, November 16, 1989.

32. Quoted in Malcolm Miles, *Art, Space and the City: Public Art and Urban Futures* (New York: Routledge, 1997), 174.

EPILOGUE

1. William N. Eskridge Jr., *The Case for Same-Sex Marriage* (New York: Free Press, 1996), 9–10.

2. Transcript of closing arguments in *Perry v. Schwarzenegger,* U.S. District Court, Northern District of California, June 16, 2010, http://www .bilerico.com/2010/06/23/Transcipt of Closing Arguments.pdf.

CREDITS

In chapter 3, "Poem 518" by Emily Dickinson is reprinted by permission of the publishers and the Trustees of Amherst College from *The Poems of Emily Dickinson,* Ralph W. Franklin, ed., Cambridge, Mass.: The Belknap Press of Harvard University Press, Copyright © 1998, 1999 by the President and Fellows of Harvard College. Copyright © 1951, 1955, 1979, 1983 by President and Fellows of Harvard College.

In chapter 3, the letter to Sue Gilbert by Emily Dickinson is reprinted by permission of the publishers from *The Letters of Emily Dickinson,* Thomas H. Johnson, ed. Cambridge, Mass.: The Belknap Press of Harvard University Press, Copyright © 1958, 1986, The President and Fellows of Harvard College; 1914, 1924, 1923, 1942 by Martha Dickinson Bianchi; 1952 by Alfred Leete Hampson; 1960 by Mary L. Hampson.

In chapter 6, the Kittredge and Lewisohn letters are reprinted courtesy of the Lillian Wald Papers, Rare Book and Manuscript Library, Columbia University.

In chapter 8, the Jean S. quote from *Improper Bostonians* (Boston: Beacon, 1998) is reprinted courtesy of The History Project: Documenting GLBT Boston, www.historyproject.org.

INDEX

and, 108, 171, 172, 173; foundation of, 6; population of, 19, 106–7

Boston Gay History Project, 10–11

The Bostonians (James), 72

Boston marriages, 72–74

Bowers v. Hardwick, 230

Bowery, 122–23

Bowie, David, 204, 216

Boy Scouts, 133–34, 137

Boys in the Band, 237

Bradford, William, 14, 16, 25

Brando, Marlon, 190

Bray, Alan, 11, 12, 16, 32

Brewer, Lucy, 37–39

The Brick Foxhole (Brooks), 169

Briggs, John, 220

Brokeback Mountain, 237

Brooks, Richard, 169

Brophy, Brigid, 183

brothels, 42, 84, 85–86. *See also* prostitution

Brown, Foreman, 126

Brown, Rita Mae, 212, 213

Browning, Elizabeth Barrett, 71–72

Brown v. Board of Education, 93

Bryant, Anita, 219–20, 221, 222, 223–24, 237, 240

Buck v. Bell, 133

Burke, Cannary, xii, 42

burlesque, 113–14, 118

Burns, John Horne, 167–68, 184

Burroughs, Edgar Rice, 135–36

Burroughs, William, 200

Butterfly Man (Levenson), 126

Cadmus, Paul, 139

Caffe Cino, 198

Calamity Jane, xii, 42

Calhoun, Rory, 192, 194

California, 46–48, 220–21, 239. *See also* Los Angeles; San Francisco

camp, 199

Cannon Towel company, 162–63

capitalism: civil rights and, 212; in colonial era, 2, 5, 17, 19, 22; identity and, xvi, 83, 130; immigration and, 83; Industrial Revolution and, 83; race and, 83, 212; Red Scare and, 145; slavery and, 22. *See also* economy

capital punishment, 9, 14–15, 20

Caprio, Frank S., 185–86

The Captive (Hornblow), 117

Carpenter, Edward, 77–78, 80–81, 109, 126

Carpenter, Tyler, 158, 160

Casal, Mary, 99

Cashier, Albert, 69–70

Cat on a Hot Tin Roof (Williams), 197

Cecil Dreeme (Winthrop), 67

censorship: in 1950s, 182, 197, 200, 201; in 1960s, 195, 199; in 1970s, 214; community and, 182; of entertainment, 104, 116, 117–18, 119, 182, 195, 197, 199; of film, 87; government and, 117–18, 142–43, 145, 146, 157; LGBT movements and, 182; of literature, 125–26, 169–70, 200, 201; of obscenity, 86, 201; of pornography, 214; religion and, 117–18, 119; social purity movements and, 86, 87, 95; World War II and, 157, 169–70

Chaddock, Charles Gilbert, 96–97, 103

Charles I, 6, 7

Chauncey, George, xiv, 47, 111–12, 112–13, 122–23

children: in 1950s, 190–91; in 1970s, 218, 219–20, 221, 222–23; in 1980s, 236; gender and, 131; government and, 148; identity and, 236–37; laws and, 236; LGBT movements and, 181, 218, 219–20, 221, 222–23, 236–37

214–15, 223; public sphere and,
124; social purity movements and,
87; urbanization and, 124; World
War II and, 156, 176. *See also
individual publications*
Judaism, 16, 89, 219–20
June, Jennie. *See* Lind, Earl

Katz, Jonathan Ned, xiv, 9, 43, 90
Kellogg, John Harvey, 85
Kennedy, John F., 177, 205, 206
Kerouac, Jack, 200
Kertbeny, Karl-Maria, xv–xvi, xvii,
78, 79, 80
The Kids Are All Right, 237
Kiernan, James G., 90
The Killing of Sister George, 237
King, Martin Luther, Jr., 177, 203,
206, 212
King Kong (Cooper), 136
Kinsey, Alfred, 160, 177–79, 185, 218
Knights of the Clocks, 176–77, 179
Knock on Any Door (Motley),
183–84
Kramer, Larry, 231
Kuchar, George, 199
Kuchar, Michael, 199
Ku Klux Klan, 145

labor: in 1990s, 236; capitalism and,
83; community and, 107, 109, 171;
economy and, 83; gender and, 88,
145–47, 148–49, 154–55, 167;
housing and, 107, 109; identity
and, 155; immigration and, 83;
Industrial Revolution and, 83;
LGBT movements and, 181, 236;
livelihood, 72, 148–49, 154–55,
181; movements for, 88–89, 91–93,
109, 146–47; police and, 146–47;
race and, 83, 88–95, 155, 156; Red
Scare and, 144, 145–47; same-sex
relationships and, 91–95; social

class and, 83, 88, 154; social purity
movements and, 88–91; suffrage
and, 88; urbanization and, 107,
109; violence and, 92–93; World
War II and, 154–55, 156, 167, 171
The Ladder, 181, 202
Lafayette, Marquis de, 34–35, 45
Lahr, Bert, 115
language: in 1960s, 209; in 1980s,
232; in American Civil War era,
1, 77, 78, 80; in colonial era, 11;
historical overview of, xiv–xviii;
for LGBT movements, 95, 209,
232; social purity movements and,
90–91, 95–99; urbanization and,
114
Lape, Esther, 149
Last of the Mohicans (Cooper), 58
The Last of the Wine (Renault), 183
Lawrence v. Texas, 236
laws: in 1970s, 218–24; in 1980s,
225–26, 227, 230–31, 240–41; in
1990s, 236; in American Civil War
era, 78–82; in American Revolutionary War era, 27–28, 30; capital
punishment and, 8, 9; children
and, 236; in colonial era, 8–11,
13, 14–16, 17, 18, 20, 23, 27–28;
community and, 123–25; crime
and, xv, xvi, 123–25; cross-dressing
and, 13; Enlightenment and, 27; in
Europe, 78–79; expansion and, 47;
family and, 236, 240; immigration
and, 47; language and, xvi; LGBT
movements and, 93–95, 218–24,
238–42; marriage and, 57–58, 236,
238–41; privacy and, 125; property
and, 23; prostitution and, 86; public sphere and, 123–25; race and,
57–58; religion and, 8–11, 14–16,
22–23; reproduction and, 13,
57–58; in San Francisco, 47; sexual
psychopath laws, 123–25, 159;

ABOUT THE AUTHOR

Michael Bronski is an independent scholar and the author of *Culture Clash: The Making of Gay Sensibility* (1984); *The Pleasure Principle: Sex, Backlash, and the Struggle for Gay Freedom* (1998); and *Pulp Friction: Uncovering the Golden Age of Gay Male Pulps* (2003). He was presented with the prestigious Stonewall Award in 2000 and is the recipient of two Lammy awards. He is a senior lecturer in women's and gender studies at Dartmouth College.